The Most Wonderful Books

The Most Wonderful Books

Writers on Discovering the Pleasures of Reading

Edited by
MICHAEL DORRIS & EMILIE BUCHWALD

PUBLISHED IN ASSOCIATION WITH THE
CENTER FOR THE BOOK IN THE LIBRARY OF CONGRESS

Distributed by Publishers Group West

Published 1997 by Milkweed Editions
Printed in the United States of America
Cover design by Don Leeper
Cover and interior illustrations by Randy Scholes
Interior design by Will Powers
The text of this book is set in Galliard.
97 98 99 00 01 5 4 3 2 1
First Edition

Rachel Hadas's piece is excerpted, with minor revisions, from "The Cradle and the Bookcase," first published in *Southwest Review.* Also published in Rachel Hadas, *Living in Time* (New Brunswick, N.J.: Rutgers University Press, 1990).

Ted Kooser's piece was previously printed in the *North Dakota Quarterly* 62, no. 4, (fall 1994–1995). Reprinted by permission.

Elinor Lipman's piece was previously printed in the *Detroit News,* 23 November 1993. Reprinted by permission.

David Mura's piece is excerpted and adapted from "The Situation of the Japanese-American Writer," first published in the Association for Asian American Studies conference anthology, *Asian Americans: Comparative and Global Perspectives* (Pullman, Wash.: Washington State University Press, 1991).

Greg Sarris's piece was previously published by the *Boston Globe.*

Milkweed Editions is a not-for-profit publisher. We gratefully acknowledge support from the Elmer L. and Eleanor J. Andersen Foundation; James Ford Bell Foundation; Target Stores, Dayton's, and Mervyn's by the Dayton Hudson Foundation; Doherty, Rumble, and Butler; Ecolab Foundation; General Mills Foundation; Honeywell Foundation; Jerome Foundation; The McKnight Foundation; Andrew W. Mellon Foundation; Minnesota State Arts Board through an appropriation by the Minnesota State Legislature; Challenge and Literature Programs of the National Endowment for the Arts; Lawrence and Elizabeth Ann O'Shaughnessy Charitable Income Trust in honor of Lawrence M. O'Shaughnessy; Piper Jaffray Companies, Inc.; Ritz Foundation; John and Beverly Rollwagen Fund of the Minneapolis Foundation; The St. Paul Companies, Inc.; Star Tribune/Cowles Media Foundation; James R. Thorpe Foundation; Lila Wallace-Reader's Digest Literary Publishers Marketing Development Program, funded through a grant to the Council of Literary Magazines and Presses; and generous individuals.

Library of Congress Cataloging-in-Publication Data

The most wonderful books : writers on discovering the pleasures of reading / edited by Michael Dorris and Emilie Buchwald. — 1st ed.
p. cm.
ISBN 1-57131-216-1
1. Authors, American—Books and reading. I. Dorris, Michael. II. Buchwald, Emilie.
Z1039.A88M67 1997
028'.9—dc21 96-29624
CIP

This book is printed on acid-free paper.

"Reading anything that moves you, disturbs you, thrills you is a path into the great swirl of humanity, past, present, and future."

MICHAEL DORRIS (1945–1997)

– introduction, *The Most Wonderful Books*

This book about the love of reading
is dedicated to
MICHAEL DORRIS,
whose own "most wonderful books"
are a lasting legacy to readers.

The Most Wonderful Books

Introduction

IT'S NINE IN THE MORNING and my twelve-year-old daughter and I are at a state park in Kentucky, a place renowned for its boating, swimming, and water skiing. It's not only pouring rain, but there's lightning and thunder—forecast to remain this way till evening. You'd think she'd be sulking, disappointed, but it turns out to be her ideal day: no distractions, nothing to do but read.

She's curled under the covers halfway through the very copy of Leon Uris's *Exodus* that, at slightly older than her age, made me want to change religions and move to Israel. She is full of shock at the cruelty, awe at the bravery, lost and found in the epic sweep of the story. I know from experience that once she finishes this novel she will never be quite the same, and it both saddens me that she must lose her innocence and makes me proud of her for having the courage to grow of her own free will.

My daughter is square in the midst of the experience described in this series of essays by a diverse and thoughtful group of writers from many genres. Every one of them—whether poets, journalists or novelists, authors of children's books or romances or short stories—would understand and honor her impulse. Welcome to the club, their very personal and individual reminiscences exhort. You're not alone in your aloneness.

When Emilie Buchwald, publisher of Milkweed Editions, and I conceived of this project a year or so ago, we imagined an anthology that would inspire readers by providing a variety of examples of how well-known and successful writers first encountered the magic of the printed word. We intentionally cast a wide net in our invitations to contribute, assuming that the routes to creating literature were as varied and interesting as these writers' works themselves.

In many ways, this proved to be the case, but in other respects there emerged from this collection some significant common denominators. Our contributors remember very distinctly the precise circumstances in which they discovered the power of reading, whether it was on their mothers' laps, snuggled next to their father, having the precisely right book put into their hands by a never-to-be-forgotten teacher or librarian. They recall the color of that initial volume, its smell, its weight, its illustrations and cover. They share a sense of its ability to transport: how, like a flying carpet, it lifted them out of their particular circumstances—mundane or painful—and into worlds previously unknown. They speak of the power reading gave them—of checking out from the local library as many books as they could carry, some about "adult" or forbidden subjects. They celebrate the sense of independence they found between the covers of those early volumes—and at the same time the shock of connection these theretofore isolated budding intellectuals or adventurers experienced in meeting their fictional counterparts or role models.

This book, in its many and various answers to the same question, is an unabashed invitation to children and adults alike: open yourself up to imagination, give in to fantasy, don't protect yourself from vicarious emotion, whether joyful or tragic. Reading anything that moves you, disturbs you, thrills you is a path into the great swirl of humanity, past, present, and future.

It is also a love letter and thank-you note to every librarian, English teacher, friend, relative, and parent who handed one of the marvelous writers, outstanding in their respective fields, the, as Jane Resh Thomas so aptly puts it, "keys to the kingdom." Curiosity, empathy, bravery, compassion, sympathy, loyalty, the complexity of love—those complicated issues with which we each struggle throughout our lives—are often first exhibited if not completely comprehended in small, rectangular packages, gifts that once opened never again close.

Right on cue, as I finish this introduction, my daughter bursts through the door, her eyes shining. "They let the *Exodus* sail," she exults.

May it rain all week.

Michael Dorris
November 1996

The Most Wonderful Books

SHERMAN ALEXIE

Superman and Me

I LEARNED TO READ with a *Superman* comic book. Simple enough, I suppose. I cannot recall which particular *Superman* comic book I read, nor can I remember which villain he fought in that issue. I cannot remember the plot, nor the means by which I obtained the comic book. What I can remember is this: I was three years old, a Spokane Indian boy living with his family on the Spokane Indian Reservation in eastern Washington state. We were poor by most standards, but one of my parents usually managed to find some minimum-wage job or another, which made us middle class by reservation standards. I had a brother and three sisters. We lived on a combination of irregular paychecks, hope, fear, and government-surplus food.

My father, who is one of the few Indians who went to Catholic school on purpose, was an avid reader of westerns, spy thrillers, murder mysteries, gangster epics, basketball-player biographies, and anything else he could find. He bought his books by the pound at Dutch's Pawn Shop, Goodwill, Salvation Army, and Value Village. When he had extra money, he bought new novels at supermarkets, convenience stores, and hospital gift shops. Our house was filled with books. They were stacked in crazy piles in the bathroom, bedrooms, and living room. In a fit of unemployment-inspired creative energy, my father built a set of bookshelves and soon filled them with a random assortment of books about the Kennedy assassination, Watergate, the Vietnam War, and the entire twenty-three-book series of the Apache westerns. My father loved books, and since I loved my father with an aching devotion, I decided to love books as well.

I can remember picking up my father's books before I could read. The words themselves were mostly foreign, but I still remember the exact moment when I first understood, with a sudden clarity, the purpose of a paragraph. I didn't have the vocabulary to say "paragraph," but I realized that a paragraph was a fence that held words. The words inside a paragraph worked together for a common purpose. They had some specific reason for being inside the same fence. This knowledge delighted me. I began to think of everything in terms of paragraphs. Our reservation was a small paragraph within the United States. My family's house was a paragraph, distinct from the other paragraphs of the LeBrets to the north, the Fords to our south, and the Tribal School to the west. Inside our house, each family member existed as a separate paragraph, but still had genetics and common experiences to link us. Now, using this logic, I can see my changed family as an essay of seven paragraphs: mother, father, older brother, the deceased sister, my younger twin sisters, and our adopted little brother.

At the same time I was seeing the world in paragraphs, I also picked up that *Superman* comic book. Each panel, complete with picture, dialogue, and narrative, was a three-dimensional paragraph. In one panel, Superman breaks through a door. His suit is red, blue, and yellow. The brown door shatters into many pieces. I look at the narrative above the picture. I cannot read the words, but I assume it tells me that Superman is breaking down the door. Aloud, I pretend to read the words and say "Superman is breaking down the door." Words, dialogue, also float out of Superman's mouth. Because he is breaking down the door, I assume he says, "I am breaking down the door." Once again, I pretend to read the words and say aloud, "I am breaking down the door." In this way, I learned to read.

This might be an interesting story all by itself. A little Indian boy teaches himself to read at an early age and advances quickly. He reads *Grapes of Wrath* in kindergarten when other children are struggling through Dick and Jane. If he'd been anything but an Indian boy living on the reservation, he might have been called a prodigy. But he is an Indian boy living on the reservation, and is simply an oddity. He grows into a man who often speaks of his childhood in the third-person, as if it will somehow dull the pain and make him sound more modest about his talents.

A smart Indian is a dangerous person, widely feared and ridiculed by Indians and non-Indians alike. I fought with my classmates on a daily basis. They wanted me to stay quiet when the non-Indian teacher asked for answers, for volunteers, for help. We were Indian children who were expected to be stupid. Most lived up to those expectations inside the classroom, but subverted them on the outside. They struggled with basic reading in school, but could remember how to sing a few dozen powwow songs. They were monosyllabic in front of their non-Indian teachers, but could tell complicated stories and jokes at the dinner table. They submissively ducked their heads when confronted by a non-Indian adult, but would slug it out with the Indian bully who was ten years older. As Indian children, we were expected to fail in the non-Indian world. Those who failed were ceremonially accepted by other Indians and appropriately pitied by non-Indians.

I refused to fail. I was smart. I was arrogant. I was lucky. I read books late into the night, until I could barely keep my eyes open. I read books at recess, then during lunch, and in the few minutes left after I had finished my classroom assignments. I read books in the car when my family traveled to powwows or basketball games. In shopping malls, I ran to the bookstores and read bits and pieces of as many books as I could. I read the books my father brought home from the pawnshops and secondhand stores. I read the books I borrowed from the library. I read the backs of cereal boxes. I read the newspaper. I read the bulletins posted on the walls of the school, the clinic, the tribal offices, the post office. I read junk mail. I read auto-repair manuals. I read magazines. I read anything that had words and paragraphs. I read with equal parts joy and desperation. I loved those books, but I also knew that love had only one purpose. I was trying to save my life.

Despite all the books I read, I am still surprised I became a writer. I was going to be a pediatrician. These days, I write novels, short stories, and poems. I visit schools and teach creative writing to Indian kids. In all my years in the reservation school system, I was never taught how to write poetry, short stories, or novels. I was certainly never taught that Indians wrote poetry, short stories, and novels. Writing was something beyond Indians. I cannot recall a single time that a guest teacher visited the reservation. There must have been visiting teachers. Who were they? Where are they now? Do they exist? I visit the schools as often as possible. The Indian kids crowd the classroom. Many are writing their own poems, short stories, and novels. They have read my books. They have read many other books. They look at me with bright eyes and arrogant wonder. They are trying to save their lives. Then there are the sullen and already defeated Indian kids who sit in the back rows and ignore me with theatrical precision. The pages of their notebooks are empty. They carry neither pencil nor pen. They stare out the window. They refuse and resist. "Books," I say to them. "Books," I say. I throw my weight against their locked doors. The door holds. I am smart. I am arrogant. I am lucky. I am trying to save our lives.

 Nicholson Baker

We Think So Then, and We Thought So Still

I LEARNED HOW TO READ, in the sense of knowing how to follow a story with pleasure as it accumulates over many chapters, by being read to. My mother read us (my sister and me) the things she had liked as a child, with several additions—she took us through *The Hobbit, Mistress Masham's Repose,* Tove Jansson's Moominland books, Lear's "Pelican Chorus," *The Wind in the Willows, Winnie-the-Pooh,* the Dr. Doolittle series, some Kipling, several Tintin books, and Hawthorne's *Wonder Book.* She was an expert at the seamless substitution of a comprehensible phrase for the more involuted elegancies of Hawthornian diction, a fact I discovered only after I knew how to read by eye and could compare her version with the text. Her shoulder had a bone in it that was comfortable against my temple; I was under the impression that I was hearing some of each book through that shoulder bone. And I was interested in how much she liked certain scenes—for example, Toad sitting entranced by the side of the road near his overturned canary yellow traveling wagon, murmuring "Poop-poop!" at the dwindling sight of the motorcar that had just zoomed past. It only became funny after she laughed.

But the most emotional early reading experience I had was the devastating death of Thorin Oakenshield in *The Hobbit.* I had no practice then with the conventions of character flaws and the plot signals that such flaws provide, and thus Thorin's greed and his brusque treatment of Bilbo didn't tip me off that he, Thorin, son of Thrain, King under the Mountain, wasn't going to recover from the wounds of battle, even though my mother had gently tried to prepare me. I wept hard until I fell asleep. My mother wanted to abandon the book because it upset me so much, but the next night I convinced her that I could cry quietly, and she kept going until the end. It became one of my favorite books.

Two Tintin books—*The Secret of the Unicorn* and *Red Rackham's Treasure*—were the first things I truly liked reading by myself. Golden Books was the publisher of a few Tintin titles then, and they had Americanized the text slightly: Haddock's ancestral home was called Hudson Manor rather than Marlinspike Hall of the other Tintins that we ordered later on from England like jars of marmalade. I loved the shark-shaped one-man submarine, and Tintin's shameless habit of talking to himself in his diving helmet while he was being stalked by the real shark, and the scene in which the two Thompsons, tired out, forget to keep cranking the air pump that leads below. Following a brief post-Tintin apprenticeship with some *Freddy the Pig* volumes, the first small-type reading I did was of *The Wonderful Adventures of Nils:* attractive because it was an ostentatiously thick edition and had a promising high-altitude goose-riding scene and concerned a person with a name similar to my own. After a chapter or two I could hardly follow what was going on, though, and I finished *Nils* joylessly, out of brute pride. The second thick book was *20,000 Leagues Under the Sea,* which we owned in an old translation with fancy marbled boards. Since the only other use of *leagues* that I knew of was in the story of the cat with the seven league boots, the notion of descending a full 20,000 leagues was appealingly grown-up. And the phosphorescent undersea glow of the *Nautilus* as it approached or fled from a ship at night was a glow that I have been on the lookout for in reading ever since.

Marion Dane Bauer

A More Certain Alliance

As a writer of stories, I am always reaching toward that moment when a reader will say, "But I thought I was the only one who ever felt that, thought that, wanted that." As a reader of stories, I search for that same experience, the moment when I will discover, yet again, the universal in the personal, the core of shared humanity beneath my isolation.

I remember the first book I ever loved. It was the story of a little lamb who lost his mother—and then, happily, found her again. From the book's blue jacket onward, the lamb was covered with pettable pink fuzz . . . until one terrible turn of the page. That was when the lamb knew, beyond any doubt, that he was alone. Like Lear, he wailed into a battering storm. As it was for Lear, the storm gave no reply. Even the pages grew suddenly dark, the lamb and the storm depicted in shades of smooth gray as cold and comfortless as his terror . . . and mine. It was only after he found his mother again that the pages—and the lamb's pink fuzz—became colorful and warm once more.

Before I had yet unlocked the mystery of reading, on each visit to the children's shelves in our small-town library, I chose that same book. My mother, my constant mother, who had never once abandoned me to any kind of storm, patiently read me the lamb's story, time after time. Even after I had memorized every word, I kept returning to it.

Why? For catharsis, of course. For the purging of "pity and fear" Aristotle had spoken of so many centuries before. For keeping at bay the unnamed and the unnameable in my mostly placid existence. Because I knew instinctively, as every child knows, that chaos and loss and death lay just around the next corner, and I was preparing myself to face it.

I refer to my childhood existence as placid, and for the most part, it was. People in my family rarely raised their voices. If there was anger it was more likely to be expressed in silence than in heated words. Love was expressed the same way. And approval. And joy. And longing of any kind. My parents had both come from reserved British stock, and feelings, for us, were not quite "nice." So I turned to books in order to feel in a context of safety, to discover, wonder of wonders, that others felt too, to break through the isolation implicit in my family's placid silence. I turned to books to laugh, to weep, to burn with indignation, to revel in melancholy or silliness, to shiver with fear, and to share all those feelings with another being who felt them, too. I turned to books to know that I was alive and connected with the rest of the universe.

That search for connection has taken different forms at different times in my life. During my twenties and early thirties I read in search of God. Sacred literature and theological writings, of course, but even more especially, I read fiction. I climbed into characters'—and consequently authors'—minds in search of the most glancing reference, the most unlikely experience of the divine. I still remember acutely a comment by a character—I think he lived in a Saul Bellow novel, though I'm not sure—who said "God isn't sex, but. . . ," and left the sentence dangling as though to contradict itself. *Maybe God is sex.* I have carried that half-formed thought with me since, that in that most profoundly vulnerable experience of our humanity lies the possibility for discovering the divine. (From the perspective of a religious culture that celebrates God in a newborn child, the idea makes perfect—and rather startling—sense.)

At the awkward age of forty-seven, when I was daring to examine my sexuality for the first time, I read ravenously for any suggestion that there existed in the world other women who loved women . . . and found myself acceptable again.

Ten years later, approaching age in a culture that ignores or denies its elders, I read longing for mature characters who are potent, alive, neither foolish nor saintly. They are few and far between. Even writers of my age depict fifty-five-year-olds as doddering. I keep searching.

Will I prepare for my own death by reading books? Probably. Will they help? They will, I have no doubt, teach me what I will need to know. That others have gone before me. That it is, inevitably and ironically, death that gives meaning to life.

Still, when the final moment comes, it is a hand I will want to be holding, not a book. Yet all the books I have journeyed though in all the years before, beginning with that lost lamb made of pettable pink fuzz, will make my connection with that hand more sure.

I read in order to live, more deeply, more fully, and with a more certain alliance with this human world.

Charles Baxter

Infectious Reading

The Minneapolis Public Library in the 1950s stood on Hennepin Avenue near Tenth, just across from Gmitro's Ham 'n' Eggs and within sight of the Orpheum Theater. The place *looked* like a monument: pleasingly solemn, venerable, five stories high, a pristine imperturbable eyesore. Constructed of Minnesota red sandstone, it gave an impression of thick-walled permanence—an atomic blast couldn't have blown it away, I used to think. (The wrecker's ball finally got it.)

The first time I stepped inside, I went with my brother Tom, whose idea it had been to show me the place. He parked his Olds, valued at $120, two blocks away, and left it there unlocked. At the library's main entrance, you had to step down into a sort of well just below the sidewalk level to get in. I loved the place immediately. It was overheated, as if for people who never exercised. The old books with their aging paper made the interior smell like a bakery. After I stomped my snowy shoes in the foyer, my brother and I ambled past the checkout desks with their clicking Recordak machines making microfilm records of all the transactions, into a large room filled with blond-wood drawers. I had never seen a card catalogue that large before, and I found it hard to believe that each card represented a book in the library.

In the next room over, I carefully removed from the shelves a book about superheterodyne radios—my plans for adulthood included becoming a television and radio repairman who made house calls—and then we trudged up the circular stairs to the fourth floor, where there was a large and somewhat disorganized science exhibit on permanent display that included a stuffed lamprey, a rather cut-rate looking mummy, and a model of the solar system. You'd go into a darkened room and gaze at the plaster-and-paste planets illuminated with ultraviolet light, and the starch in your shirt would start to glow, and you'd feel, standing there clutching your book about radio repair, just like an alien, weird and purple and stylish.

By the time I was thirteen I had perfected my reading posture: I had developed a method of slouching down in a chair so radically that my book, that fort of paper and glue and cloth, guarded my face. No one could see me when I was reading. They still can't. In those days I sat in chairs with my back down on the cushion, so that my torso was parallel to the floor. Only my head was propped up, and of course it was hidden behind the book. In the chair, I was a low rider. My mother thought that this method of reading would ruin my posture. She worried that I was becoming antisocial, that I would become one of those sad-looking run-down boys whom healthy girls would shun.

As it turned out, I had a large and eager appetite for trash. Hemingway once claimed that his favorite book as a child was Jeffery Farnol's *The Broad Highway.* Myself, I liked books about hot air balloons and animals, but I wasn't really bookish until puberty arrived, and then I read art and garbage as consolation and stimulant, soaking it all up. In those days almost every novel seemed quite adequate. I liked them better, though, if they were voluptuously gloomy, or voluptuous *and* gloomy. *The Return of the Native* seemed like a perfect book to me, full of wounded stricken characters with all their eerie clumsiness and fatal calamities on display. In that novel, people are painted over with a red dye of sorrow. To quote a phrase used by the Quakers, the book spoke to my condition. You could also buy good novels in the paperback rack at the drugstore, and that's where I obtained Davis Grubb's *The Night of the Hunter* and J. R. Salamanca's *Lilith,* two books that made me want to be a writer. The first was about losing one's father and ending up in the hands of crazy people (my story exactly), and the second was about misplaced and probably crazy love, and both of them were written in a carefully wrought baroque-hypnotic style. They dazed me, those books.

I didn't want to become bookish and owlish, so I lifted weights and joined the wrestling team and pretended that the world as given to us was satisfactory, which, because the world *isn't* satisfactory, made me a hypocrite and unpredictably moody and a sort of manic-depressive athlete. All my efforts in the direction of the physical and material dimensions of my life seemed to fall short, but, armed with these other, more fugitive, psychic qualifications, I managed to become bookish anyway. I slouched in my chair and glowered and read all the time. I really don't know much about Davis Grubb (he died several years ago, and the only person I've ever met who knew him said that he looked rather like a large human frog), but I want to honor his memory here. Others can claim the truly great—Tolstoy and Shakespeare and Dante—as their childhood and adolescent inspirations. I claim Grubb. I can't read his books anymore, but they were the first ones that successfully spellbound me.

A ridiculous picture: a boy, lifting weights in the basement, takes breaks between sets of bench presses and biceps curls to read an American gothic-lyric novel by a man who looks like a frog. *The Night of the Hunter,* the novel he is reading, has at its center a luckless boy and the sister whom he must take care of and watch out for. My first novel, *First Light,* has at its center a brother and his sister, whom he thinks he must take care of and watch out for. Funny coincidence. You take your inspirations where you find them. About a year after *First Light* was published, I realized that

I had embedded *The Night of the Hunter* inside it. That book infected me; it was infectious. These days, the sight of a kid, any kid, nose stuck in a book, is a reminder of that moody and solemn time of my life when I stepped out of one world—this one—into another, the parallel universe of literature, and felt that it welcomed me.

ETHAN CANIN

How I Was Saved

I'D ALWAYS BEEN A GREAT READER in childhood but went through a period, starting in the middle of high school and lasting several years, in which science was far more important to me than literature. I came to college as a mechanical engineering major, and it was a single book that saved me from what no doubt would have been a dreadful career. I was a junior, I believe, and on vacation that year I stumbled on a thick, red hardback called *The Stories of John Cheever.*

From the first one, "Goodbye, My Brother," I felt Cheever's sad and elegant optimism in the center of my own heart. I read story after story, not particularly liking the ones I later discovered were most famous—"The Swimmer," "The Enormous Radio"—but finding in a half-dozen others—"The Ocean," "The Fourth Alarm," "A Vision of the World," "Goodbye, My Brother"—a rueful sweetness that made me more than anything else want to imitate him. I'd never before been struck by the beauty of prose, but Cheever's rhythmic elongation of epiphany in the midst of quiet suburban life brought me over and over again to a sense of longing. At first it was a longing to read. Later it became a longing to write. I still look at those stories now and then, trying to see what it is in the words he uses, the run of his sentences, the pattern of small detail and epiphanic flight, that makes his work so gorgeous and sad. Almost twenty years have passed, yet those stories remain to me as inexplicable and powerful as music.

Alan Cheuse

An Appetite As Great As Any Other

IT BEGAN FOR ME in mystery, like the mystery of sex, and in the same place. Once upon a time a young boy—he must have been about three years old—crawled into bed with his mother and father. It was a Sunday morning, in spring, probably, because even though it was light outside the window, his father still lay there beneath the blanket rather than having gone to work. His mother made a space between them where the boy might burrow under the covers. His father shifted his large body and reached over to the night table and switched on the small light. He then picked up a rectangular object about six inches by nine—it had an orange and sepia covering, with an abstract design embossed upon it that suggested not-quite-formed stars and crescents. He told the boy that he had just found the object in an old trunk that came from a place called *Roo-sha*. The boy loved the sound of that word and asked his father to say it again. All right: *Roo-sha*. . . .

The object, this thing made of paper and bound in stiff cloth, had a wonderfully intriguing smell to it, the odor of dust and oranges that had been lying for a long time in the hot sun. When his father opened the front of it, the boy noticed strange designs stretched out in rows. One thing seemed familiar—a drawing of a golden rooster-like bird.

The tale of the golden cockerel, his father announced in his oddly syncopated voice that sounded so unlike all the other voices in the family. He fixed his eye on the designs on the page and began to speak in a strange and incomprehensible fashion, making a series of glob-like and skidding sounds, with a number of phushes and ticks and bubble-like slurs and pauses in which his breath sounded as though it had sledded up to the top of a snowy hill and then rushed down again on the other side.

The boy was me, of course, and the man was my father, reading to me in Russian, a language I've never learned, from a book of fairy tales that has long ago been lost in the flood of years that washes through a family's life. And he is gone now, too, along with that first book that I never read. But that was where it began, this lifelong appetite for reading, directly from the mouth of my old man.

In school I learned to sound English—I recall remembering that process when I taught my own children the glories of phonics—and to read the ubiquitous Dick and Jane series of elemental textbooks. "See Dick run. See Jane run." I saw the sentences, but I didn't see *through* them into the lively visual world in which these proper nouns supposedly stood in for living, breathing characters. So I wanted something more than the flat adventures of these stick figures. My parents offered little help. My mother, to the best of my knowledge, sweet and loving woman though she was, read nothing but the newspaper. My father, lumbering home from his early shift as an engineering troubleshooter on the assembly line at the nearby General Motors automobile assembly plant, kept his eyes open just long enough to see what food my mother put on his plate, and then took to the sofa, listened to the radio news, and went to sleep. No more reading for me, not from his lips anyway.

That's how comic books became my passion—from *Archie* comics on through the great line of superheroes, beginning with Superman himself and then Batman, Plastic Man, Wonder Woman, and to the horror comics such as *EC Stories* and *The Heap*—and I built a collection that rivalled just about any in the neighborhood. That wasn't difficult for me since my mother's parents owned a local candy store and sold these magazines by the dozens. Along with the gifts of candy—my favorite was Hershey Bars, milk chocolate so delicious that I even chewed the paper wrapper—that would eventually rot my teeth, they gave me free choice of comics each time I visited the store. But these had a different effect on my imagination than the chocolate had on my teeth.

Appetites become more refined after a while. Within a few years I developed an urge for something better than Archie and slobbering monsters. I moved to a new higher level of comic book appreciation and began to read and collect the Classics Illustrated series, being the western world's greatest poems and novels, from *The Iliad* and *The Odyssey* on through the work of Poe and Cooper, turned into comic books. Maybe kids who had parents who read to them regularly and took them on trips to the bookstore and bought novels and poetry for them—in other words, kids who were raised the way I raised my own children—could begin at a higher level than me. No such luck in Jersey! But on Saturday afternoons in our neighborhood you could see us comic hounds pushing baby carriages leftover from the infancy of our siblings, laden high with our comic book collections, on the way to trading sessions at the houses of friends.

It wasn't until my eighth grade year that I walked through the door of a bookstore and also spent afternoons after school at the local library where I turned to actual novels for my reading pleasure. I plunged whole hog into C. S. Forester's multivolume Captain Horatio Hornblower series, and read my way through the novels of Howard Fast, beginning with a book about a young boy who survives during the Nazi advance into western Russia which I recollect was called *Struggle Is My Brother.* I suppose the Russian setting has something to do with its staying power in my mind when all that I can remember of the C. S. Forester books is a lot of salt water. Somehow after that I discovered science fiction, which became the ruling passion of my summer between eighth grade and first year of high school.

All of this was pretty predictable, I suppose. But something strange was going on in my mind, if the evidence is true. One afternoon in the local bookstore at the lower end of our town's main street, while intent on buying a new science fiction novel by Richard Matheson, I noticed an oddly appealing cover on a paperback book. Something about the colorful design caught my eye and I plucked it from the shelf. It was the first Vintage edition of D. H. Lawrence's novel of mysterious Mexico, *The Plumed Serpent*. Instead of buying the Matheson I purchased the Lawrence. It sat on my shelf for years, and every once in a while I would pick it up and flip through its pages, which seemed to be written in sentences unlike any I had ever read before—not sentences that I understood, but sentences that enticed me and lured me on with the curious payoff of their odd rhythms. A similar thing occurred one afternoon as I passed through the main library on my way to the children's room. On a recommended reading shelf just at the entrance was a hardbound copy of a new novel called *The Invisible Man*. Under the illusion that it was science fiction, I picked the novel from the shelf and carried it with me down the long tunnel that connected the main library to the children's reading room. Finding a comfortable seat, I plucked at the lines on the opening page of Ellison's masterwork, but made no music. Over the next few years I must have taken up that book a dozen times or more, each time moving a little further into it, each time moving a little further along the route toward understanding.

And after that, I became a promiscuous reader—keeping up my true love for sea stories and science fiction while branching out ever more perilously into far-flung territories. I read and read and read. I read popular junk, and took it quite seriously—*A Stone for Danny Fisher*, by Harold

Robbins, *Marjorie Morningstar* by Herman Wouk—and I read some serious material—*The Naked and the Dead*—but prized it mainly for what I took to be the salaciousness of its frank approach to sex. In my first year of high school I found a copy of *A Portrait of the Artist as a Young Man,* which I carried around like a badge of honor, though unread, until my prissy homeroom teacher confiscated it, saying it was too difficult for a boy my age. This was in Perth Amboy High School in darkest Jersey in the late 1950s. In my sophomore year, I bought myself a Faulkner paperback, which a smug study hall monitor, a chemistry teacher, quickly confiscated, saying that it was a dirty book, filled with confusion and smut. I doubt if he had read it.

But I knew instinctually by then that it was my kind of book, having discovered my hunger for fiction on that first Sunday morning years before when, in my childish discontent with the loneliness of things, I crawled into bed to lie between my parents, inspiring my father to distract me with a plot.

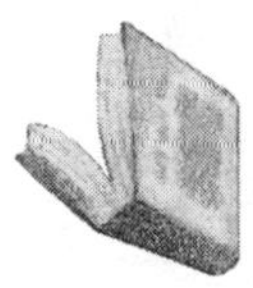

Jennifer C Cornell

A Few Thoughts on Pleasure and Meaning

When I was in primary school I kept under my bed a collection of books I planned to take with me if I ever ran away: *Old Yeller; Lad, A Dog; The Incredible Journey; Ring of Bright Water; Rascal; Sounder; Watership Down*—there were others, but those that come to mind at this distance would have been too bulky to carry on the run. As there was no urgency to the impulse, however, I never did leave home. At the time my father was writing about science for young adults, and for almost a year while he researched a book on natural disasters my family spent its Saturdays reading together on the third floor of the public library downtown. The school I attended then opened its assembly hall to Scholastic Books twice a year at a time when three crisp new paperbacks could be had for less than ten dollars. Every year the Yankee Bookstall would set up shop for charity and sell secondhand classics for five cents, hardbacks for a quarter; after hours of greedy browsing we always brought home a box-load each. My parents still live in the same apartment, and the long hall that stretches from the kitchen to the front room is still lined from floor to ceiling with shelves of books grouped roughly by subject—astronomy, opera, Italian cooking, anthropology, history, reference, literature, books in Spanish, and detective fiction. What had been my bedroom is storage space now for those books and files that can fit nowhere else.

Though such circumstances are broadly formative, certainly they are not unique, nor of course are they essential to the incubation of a passion for books. Frankly, despite the vividness of those early memories I have no idea why I was reading then. An obsession with lists, which compels me to this day, designed an ambition to read all the classics, the real objective being to place a neat tick beside each defeated title on the list I'd discovered in a publisher's catalogue of canonical books. Why I was doing this remains unclear, however. I had no sure ambition then to be a writer; if anything, all those animal stories had made veterinary medicine, steeplechasing, and marine zoology seem ideal professions. Even now my commitment to writing is incomplete. The truth is I would much rather read than write, and there has been so much of value written (amid all the worthless verbiage) that it often seems unnecessary for *me* to write at all.

Nowadays I read to discover through what moves me—in any direction—what I believe to be true about the world. Kenneth Bernard's "Preparations," Spencer Holst's "On Hope," Naguib Mahfouz's "Half a Day," Nabokov's "Signs and Symbols," whole sections of Camus's *The Rebel,* almost any of the stories in Jim McConkey's *Court of Memory*—all of these are of such depth and power that I would consider my life's work accomplished, really, to have written any one. And yet all are stories that I find almost unbearable to reread, perhaps because my response to them has been so deeply personal: a recognition of a sensibility much like my own, whose existence reassures me that I am not alone in the world.

The connection I feel to these pieces is so private and profound that any analysis appears unseemly. In the classroom I argue that our job as readers is to determine the reasons for our response to a piece, on the understanding that any reaction is legitimate as long as it's supported by the evidence (i.e., the form and content of the piece itself). This is not meant to be a proscriptive process. Its point is not to nail down THE meaning of a story, nor to impose a meaning where none is meant. What it seeks to do is to enhance the opportunity for self-discovery offered by any and every book: as centuries of scholars have discovered, through the close study of a story's particulars I have found that I can better articulate what I recognized (intuitively, subconsciously) in it as I read (i.e., my connection with the piece) and, through that experience, come close to articulating who I am myself, and why.

No doubt pleasure is always the real reason we read, whether we filter it through another purpose (escape, reassurance, self-improvement, discovery) or not. The books that have given me the most pleasure are (despite what I've said above) those that have made me want to write or, rather, have suggested a subject to write about, an idea or emotion to capture and explore; the books that have engaged me most thoroughly are those in which I've effaced the margins with my own reflections, those that I can not read straight through without stopping because so much of what they show me makes me need to stop and think. Perhaps this has always been true, even before I was conscious of it. In this sense it strikes me too that we are always reading, whether the text be film or fiction, the world around us (past and present), our own behavior or that of others. For that reason we should pledge ourselves to reading widely and fairly, and work to ensure the opportunity to do so as a universal right.

Ruth Coughlin

When a Picture Is Worth a Thousand Words

There is a photograph of me to be found in what I laughingly call the family archives, which is to say, boxes of many sizes and shapes, scattered here and there and filled with old pictures, few of them either dated or with locations noted, random snapshots of lives once led.

In this picture, I am maybe five years old and standing in a corner of my father's library, the one room in our house that was his sanctum sanctorum. A voracious and sometimes maddeningly opinionated reader, he was a man who in many ways preferred reading to real life, but nonetheless it was he who set me and my brother on a lifetime course in which books would serve as our map of the universe.

So there I am in my father's reading room, a child surrounded by books. Mostly the books are his, but there are a few shelves reserved for my treasures, the usual young girl's fare through which I was transported—*Black Beauty, Grimm's Fairy Tales, A Child's Garden of Verses, The Uncle Remus Stories* and *Sweeny's Adventure.* While I remember naming an adorable beagle I owned Sweeny and while I once memorized every word of T. S. Eliot's "Sweeney Among the Nightingales" and recall remarking that the spelling was different, to this day I cannot tell you, no matter how hard I try, what the *Sweeny's Adventure* of my youth was all about or who the writer was.

I do know, though, that my youth was spent mostly reading. Bringing a book to the dinner table was verboten, but I tried to bend the rules as frequently as possible. When I was nine my parents let me get away with it because I was reading Salinger's much-talked-about and just-published *The Catcher in the Rye,* convinced that my brother and I were wholly interchangeable with Holden and Phoebe.

Throughout high school, I was the kid the other kids made fun of because instead of being a bouncy cheerleader or a budding athlete, I was the one you'd see in the cafeteria with my nose buried in a book. Was I a social misfit? Had my father handed down to me that escape-from-reality gene? Was I truly my father's daughter? In those silent and relatively nonanalytic Fifties when Sigmund did not yet reign supreme, these were questions on which I did not dare dwell.

When I graduated from college armed with a fairly useless liberal arts degree and a major in English, it seemed natural that I would go into New York publishing. What, after all, was I trained to do except read? What other skills did I have? I couldn't type either, a small fact that didn't make me a fabulous candidate for an entry-level editorial assistant's job, but I was determined to work with writers and become an editor, which, in due course, I eventually did.

In my twenties, I lived with a writer (no, it wasn't part of the job description), and in my thirties I fell in love with a writer (neither was that), married him and moved away from New York to a city where, after having spent eighteen years in publishing, there was almost no publishing.

With no book industry in which to move in, once again I found myself in a curious position: having been an editor for my entire professional life, what other job was I prepared to do? And so began Phase Two of my life in books: I became, to some writers a most onerous thing, a book critic. Four years ago I wrote a book myself, thereby arriving, I suppose, at the full-circle point, and laying myself open to book editors and book critics alike.

The photograph of me my father so proudly took decades ago is now framed and hangs in the office where

I work at home. A lot has changed. My father is dead, and so, regrettably, is the writer I married. Sweeny, my childhood dog, is long gone. But the room in which I sit is filled with books. I am surrounded by them, as I always have been. Both my friends and my livelihood, they are a constant source of joy. Looking at that photograph, it would seem that nothing has changed in the least.

 CHARLIE D'AMBROSIO

Stray Influences

I STILL HAVE my very first book, *The Big Golden Book of Dinosaurs.* It's a great book and, like all great books, read and loved, I've made it my own. Looking at it now, I find evidence of myself everywhere in that torn, taped, chewed, cracked, stomped-on volume. I've read it hundreds of times, eaten cream cheese and jelly sandwiches off its glossy covers, and also used it to beat my sisters over the head, although not recently. In penmanship that hasn't improved one bit over time my name hops in crazy spasms across the blue inner leaf. The illustrations are lurid and the narrative encompasses the soupy advent and sad passing of an entire world. As a child I could not turn to the final chapter easily, when, on page forty-seven, the last dinosaur lies at the edge of a swamp, dead under a battering cobalt rain. Dinosaurs are gone, but they remain an excellent choice of material for a boy's first book. Fabulous creature in a world that is ours and not ours, and fabulous words, too, in a language that is ours and not ours. Tyrannosaurus Rex, the tyrant king. The eyes and the imagination stretch to take in and accept the garish illustrations of these incredible creatures, and the mouth and the tongue, only recently emerged from the wet, formless, howling world of babytalk, gasps for air and readies itself as, miraculously, these polysyllabic monsters emerge in triumph.

In Catholic grade school my prayerbook was what I loved most. With its padded leather covers, its gilt-edged pages, its tiny illustration of the Virgin on the frontispiece, its secret zippered pocket in which I stored my rosary, the book itself possessed an aura of holiness that only emphasized the importance of the material within. I never hit anybody with that book. In fact, I was a little spooked and in awe of that book because it had been blessed by a priest. And the prayers within, I think, taught me the rudiments of a relation one can have toward language itself: a prayer teaches you there are certain words, good words, that can be repeated without losing their power and efficacy; that words can invoke the world and call it to life; that you can use your voice for a higher purpose than commercial jingles; that a trust in your words will guide you in speaking aloud things you might not otherwise consider; and that words arranged in a pattern become meaningful and beautiful and lasting and belong not only to you but to all people in need of meaning and beauty and things that last. Later, of course, words lost some of their talismanic power, the world moved outside my control, but still I believe that the language I learned early on has continued to shape and influence my life.

There are certain writers whose names are holy in my mind because a smattering of their books lined the shelves in our house. Graham Greene, John Updike, Philip Roth, Saul Bellow, Joyce Carol Oates. I read them all and learned, among other things, that my parents weren't complete idiots. Over the years I swiped *Herzog; The Power and the Glory; Pigeon Feathers; Goodbye, Columbus; By the North Gate,* etc. off the shelves and I still have those pilfered books, the inexpensive pocket editions my parents bought, which then sold for seventy-five cents, or a dollar forty-five. It amazes me that my parents would read their significant contemporaries, and I never open one of their books without wondering what my mother and father were looking for in those words. Since the horizontal hold on our television went on the fritz in 1973, they were probably looking for entertainment first of all, which is no small thing. As important as they've been to me, my point is not to mention the names of writers—I was also very keen on a book on my parent's shelf called *God Goes to Murderer's Row,* whose author I've forgotten, if I ever knew his name—but rather to remember the importance of shelves and the tremendous value conferred on books by the simple act of saving them. To me, at a certain point in my life, these shelves were as crucial a validation as the priest muttering Latin over my prayer book.

And yet writers, like suicides, prepare in their secret hearts an act that will come to seem inevitable; they look back, and see fate where others might find only accidents. Dylan Thomas remembered the rhythms of the King James Bible being read to him in his baby crib, so of course he became a poet. In mild contrast, here's the way I came to Shakespeare. I was very cool in my Seafarer jeans and Cowichan sweater and lipping off in class and a priest threw a desk at my head. It was the kind of desk with a chair attached. He was a Jesuit and raised in Anaconda by a family of real hard asses—ten brothers—and he didn't have to think twice about the pedagogic efficacy of violence. He got my attention completely and if he'd been teaching entomology I'd be scooping baetis mayflies into specimen vials right now instead of writing this essay. Instead, terrified, I became a fool for *Romeo and Juliet.* I read it and learned it and loved it. Previously this priest had taught in Portland, and he knew about what was then a small Shakespeare Festival in Ashland, Oregon. He gave me a brochure, suggested I check it out, and I did. I was sixteen, newly licensed to drive, proud owner of a $350 Volkswagen with a Porsche super-90 engine and a sunroof and faded racing stripe, and initially the trip offered itself as a chance to fish the Umpqua and have sex in a hotel room. But my girlfriend and I also saw a production of *King Lear,* at a replica of the Globe, under a full white moon and stars, with an owl calling from the trees and bats circling overhead, and that night—under the influence of what? The hotel room? The gritty lithium water bubbling out of a fountain in the town square?—old blind Gloucester suicidally pratfalling on the empty stage really knocked me out.

So let's see—the desk flew at my head, the books were saved on the shelves, and the act of praying struck a secret chord. Out of the muck I emerged, a reader. It would take an Aquinas to find a prime mover in all this. At what point did that priest from Anaconda take a shine to Shakespeare? Did his big brothers think he was a pantywaist? Maybe. Maybe he had to defend his passion. Maybe he had to fight against the hostility of his brothers and the indifference of a mining town and maybe that's why he felt no compunction about pitching a desk at my head. Mysterious as it is, for me, at every juncture, the books, the words and the people who cared about them were there, and so it continues—these days I'm learning new words, currently raking them out of *The Harvard Guide to Psychiatry.* The words are foreign and monstrous like the words in my book of dinosaurs. Tardive Dyskinesia. For years I've been saying my brother's "a nut" or "insane" or "crazy" or "bonkers" or, only sometimes, "schizophrenic." Recently this demotic understanding has come to bother me for its laziness and distortion, and so I'm searching out new words, new understandings. I know there are books, and inside them will be the words, and I hope in my secret heart someone, somewhere, mysteriously influenced and moved, has written exactly what I need.

DIANNE DONOVAN

Making Friends with Nancy

SUMMERS LASTED FOREVER when I was growing up in Texas. They were hot and they were muggy and they were very still—unless I happened to be sprawled belly-down on the cool linoleum with an oscillating fan tickling my toes and a Nancy Drew mystery under my nose. To my mind, that was as close to heaven as a Houston girl could get.

I wish I could say that my love of reading—my obsession with reading—had its roots in an early chance encounter with *David Copperfield* or sprang from an epiphany after a precocious reading of *A Portrait of the Artist as a Young Man*. Alas, my guiding light into the world of literature was a slim blonde in a maroon roadster.

I don't recall reading anything before I discovered Nancy Drew. Either I hadn't been much of a reader or it all paled so by comparison as to disappear entirely from my consciousness. But once I discovered Nancy and her world—I was in the fifth grade and she was tracking down *The Secret in the Old Attic*—I never wanted to leave it. Part of the appeal, I think, was that I could race through one of those blue-bound volumes secure in the knowledge that there was a seemingly endless supply.

Surely, though, the primary appeal was that the lovely but feisty Nancy led every adolescent girl's dream life. She didn't go to school, but she didn't go to work either, except on her "adventures." She and her chums, George and Bess, talked on the phone, met for luncheon, got into scrapes, and solved crimes that stumped the cops. What could be better? It has occured to me in my middle age that from a teenager's standpoint Nancy had it all: cool car, great dad, no mom, good friends, no school, lots of money.

Of course, there was *danger.* Like the time George (a girl!) was kidnapped and her abductors stuck her with a "hypo." Or the countless times Nancy got locked up, walled in or knocked out by villains. But her pluck and wit always triumphed, usually while her ineffectual boyfriend, Ned Nickerson, wilted bouquet in hand, fretted that they would be late for the country club dance.

In sixth grade, a friend and I shunned homework entirely to furiously scour the neighborhood on our bikes for "clues." There were no crimes to be solved, but we figured there would be once we found the evidence. Julie Huggins was blonde, so she got to be Nancy; I was a tomboy, so I was George. Far too old for imaginary playmates, we found adventure in imaginary lives. I thought of those heady days ("An abandoned Coke bottle, George! What could it mean?") recently at my local library when I heard a mother bemoaning her daughter's choice of books. "Nancy Drew and R. L. Stine," she cried. "What trash!"

"Oh no, madam," I wanted to say. "Those are introductions to the transforming power of literature. Nancy Drew is a little bit Jane Austen with a dash of Tom Swift. Your daughter will learn about frocks and roadsters and tea dances and her own infinite capacity for adventure." It strikes me now that I must have learned math and history and maybe even a smattering of some foreign language in those brief preteen years, but what I most remember is madly pedaling through the dusk with my friend "Nancy," searching for clues.

 KATHLEEN EAGLE

The Outsider

I'VE BEEN AN OUTSIDER most of my life. My parents were Southerners, but I was an Air Force brat. They came from somewhere. I came from them. Everywhere we lived, I was the one who talked differently, ate differently, dressed differently, and thought differently. Although my feet fit my outsider's shoes quite comfortably now, it's taken me nearly half a century to break them in. Like most writers, I'm an observer. I've walked many a mile in a lot of other people's moccasins.

Neither of my parents was a reader. They subscribed to magazines and newspapers, and my father enjoyed *Reader's Digest,* but they were not "bookish" people. They did, however, respect reading, which I discovered when my interest in books earned their praise. I was the one who read to my little sister. It was *The Poky Little Puppy* over and over again, roly-poly, pell-mell, tumble bumble until I was blue in the face. While my brother was encouraged to develop his knack for throwing, catching, and knocking balls around, I got my "atta girls" for accumulating stars on the book report chart.

But what started as a bid for attention soon became a passion for my own piece of the world. When I outgrew books at home and those on the classroom shelves, I discovered libraries. They were quiet, comfortable places that smelled like Grandmother Pierson's attic, where marvelous treasures were stored and where a girl could lose herself in her fantasies for an hour or an afternoon. There are no outsiders in a library.

I remember Henry Huggins and Ribsy, Black Beauty and

Old Yeller. There was a waiting list for Nancy Drew, but I kept a list of every one I'd read. I started writing my own mysteries about a girl who solved mysteries with the help of her cat. (If only I'd had an agent back then!) Mythology was one of my early favorites, which sparked an interest in ancient history. I loved museums, too, and I was going to be an archaeologist some day.

When school book clubs came into my life, I set about building my own library. The family budget was always fairly tight, especially at the end of the month, and managing the cash flow was my mother's job. But I was always allowed to order from the book club flyer. Not only did the free dividend books appeal to my mother's (and therefore my own) sense of value, but so did the notion of having books, owning them. My mother imparted that idea by parting with the cash for books more readily than almost anything else, even though she was not a reader herself.

I was given a desk with a bookshelf for my birthday about the time I reached double digits, and my room became the main repository in our house for books. I developed a taste for more sophisticated stories when I started collecting Classics Illustrated comic books. About the time I hit junior high, I discovered "popular fiction." While my parents noticed what I read—my dad occasionally asked, "How's the book?"—they were not censors. I devoured Pearl Buck, Leon Uris, James Michener, and many others. Even as a child I was emotionally reserved, quiet, always the observer, but when I was involved in a story, I was *involved*. My imagination ran wild, and my emotions were readily tapped for the flowing. I was hooked for good.

I attended the college of my parent's dreams—I've never regretted it; it's an excellent school—but once again, I was an outsider. A day student, a "townie." Without a tuition grant and a work-study job I would never have been able to afford Mount Holyoke. I was a very lonely freshman, but I worked in the library. No outsiders there. Those wonderful open stacks became my home on campus. By the time I was a junior (the year I finally had the chance to move into a dorm) a couple of intended majors had been relegated to minor status, and I settled most comfortably into my English lit major. It was 1969. Our Junior Show was entitled "We Can Save the World," and I decided to dedicate a summer to the cause. I went to Standing Rock Sioux Indian Reservation in South Dakota on a volunteer project.

That summer changed the direction of my life. On the first day, I fell in love with the prairie. On the second day, I met an Indian cowboy who always carried a paperback book in the back pocket of his jeans. On the third day, a suede cloth dress and a pair of moccasins were entrusted to me for the duration of my stay, and I was taught to dance. Once again, I was hooked for good.

I went back home, finished college with an eye toward teaching, landed a job at an Indian boarding school, and eventually married that cowboy. I was still an outsider—a white teacher in an Indian school, white woman in an Indian family—but now I was an outsider in a world of outsiders. I needed to connect with the people around me. I had to find the willingness and the wherewithal. My students and my family helped me do that, but reading and writing, as always, played a big part.

The love of books has always been a connection between my husband and me. We grew up in different worlds, and we've made compromises, blended customs and philosophies, but we both brought reading into the life we share. When I started writing, he was the one who convinced me that my stories might be publishable. Only a reader would know that. And yes, he read Romance—Westerns, mostly—long before I ever deigned to "touch the stuff." He always said he was "secure in his manhood." Cowboys are like that.

Our three children are all readers. While the school

environment has at times been uncomfortable, even hostile for them—once we moved off the reservation they became outsiders, too—their love of reading pulls them through. They love Shakespeare, and they love comic books. They write poetry, and they script videos. They take all the writing and literature courses they can fit into their schedules. And here's the best part: during those terrible teen times when communication between parent and kid can get strained, we can still "talk books." And I do not censor. Recently my older son coerced me into reading a piece in a graphic novel—one of those dark comic books that gets started in someone's basement—which turned out to be a satirical bit about writers' conferences and trade shows. Hardly what I expected. He figured he was missing some of the humor, and I could help out with that. Imagine Mom—especially *this* mom, the straitlaced Scandinavian straight man in a household that thrives on Indian humor—invited to interpret the satire in a graphic comic. I felt as though I had the keys to the kingdom! And he let me know that, maybe in some ways, he thought so, too.

I decided early in my teaching career that if I could impart some love of reading and writing, my students would take the ball and run with it for the rest of their lives. The first year I was handed some dry old lit texts and ancient grammar books and told to do what I could with them. Mostly I used them for doorstops. I bought my own classroom sets of paperback books—contemporary stuff, classic stuff, *good* stuff. I taught traditional Native American stories right along with the Greek and the Norse. We read contemporary Native American writers along with the writers found on most high school reading lists, and this was long before multicultural curriculum came into vogue. One principal questioned the wisdom of trying to teach Shakespeare and Greek mythology to "these kids." I told him that my students would not be shortchanged. I went back to school and got reading credentials, coupled with my M.S., so that I could teach reading skills along with the literature I loved so much. It's fun to visit with my former students now, see them with their children, reminisce about the old days at Fort Yates. They'll tell me which books they remember best. I've heard *The Odyssey, When Legends Die, Macbeth, Tortilla Flat,* the whole gamut. Oh, the connections we made over those books.

I get wonderful letters from readers who've never clapped eyes on me, never will, but we've made a connection through the written word, and they want to tell me how it affected them. Fiction writing is solitary work, but the writing process is not complete until the work is read. A story does not come to life on the page, but in the reader's mind. The story circle begins with the writer. The reader completes the circle. And I am both writer and reader, coming full circle every day of my life.

I guess I'm not such an outsider after all.

Bob Edwards

Overbooked

When I was a boy, I admired the handsome, glass-doored, antique oak bookcase in the living room of my house. On the top shelf, a foursome of my dad's golf trophies gleamed in eternal midswing. On the next shelf, a pair of ceramic squirrels gamboled amid the bric-a-brac that mom seemed unable to discard. Impractical gifts and some religious items filled the remaining shelves. What the bookcase did not have was a book.

I grew up in a house that had no books. My parents appeared to read every word of two daily newspapers, but they did not read books. Books were for schoolchildren.

Libraries? The nearest public library branch was too far away, and my elementary school didn't have a library until my eighth-grade class established one.

Despite that, reading was my best subject. I often was asked to read aloud because I sounded pretty good at it—which turned out to be one of the incentives to pursue a career in radio.

My older brother was a good reader, too, and brought home interesting books. We shared a room, so I read his books. *Lord of the Flies* and *The Catcher in the Rye* would have been pretty bold stuff for a twelve-year-old in 1959 if I had fully understood their meaning. I took them to be adventure tales.

In high school my teachers assigned novels. The first one was *A Canticle for Leibowitz,* a Cold War tale of life after the nuclear apocalypse and the perfect book to read between civil defense drills. It was a paperback and, unlike my textbooks, was no longer in condition to be recycled or sold. I now owned the book, the first in my personal library.

Then the school library set up a rack of paperbacks for sale. These were the days when paperbacks were still thirty-five cents. With only the slightest lunch money skimming, I could own more books. I could have books that I wanted to read, not books assigned because they were supposed to be good for me. So the first choices reflected the teenaged jock that I was.

After breezing through *Notre Dame Football* and *PT-109* (popular choices among Catholic boys in 1962), I bought a copy of Anne Frank's diary, probably because it was about a teenaged girl. Uh-oh, what had I done? I had stumbled upon something that was literally about life and death. This was not "fun." This was complicated. This had to do with values and the human condition. Yet it was giving me enormous satisfaction. It would be hard to return to *Notre Dame Football*.

By this time, my brother was in college. He was becoming educated. Sibling rivalry dictated that I catch up. I set out to read "the canon." That term was unfamiliar to me in those years before the PC silliness about dead white European males. But the great books were listed in my high school literature text and they included works by a good many dead white European females. I struggled through Austen, Eliot, and the Brontës. I needed Alistair Cooke to teach me about nineteenth-century England, but he wasn't doing that yet. I was on safer ground with Hemingway and Fitzgerald.

It came easier to me in my college years. A wonderful literature course introduced me to Borges, Gide, Camus, Defoe, and Mann. The professor explained the historical and cultural context of each work. I had thought novels were written to entertain me. Now I was learning that writers of fiction could be political activists, historians, social reformers, and journalists. And unlike the professionals in those fields, fiction writers were better able to tell the truth because they were not restricted by the facts.

Once my own journalism career began, I found myself reading more history and biography. Then I started hosting programs which allowed me to interview authors. FREE BOOKS! Dracula working at the blood bank. Not only could I order any book I wanted, I could talk with the person who wrote it. I could explore the creative process and learn what makes a writer write.

Born to a house without books, I now live in a library. Twice I've had to move because I needed more room for all the books. At night we hear the beams and foundations shift under the weight of the books. Bookcases line the clothes closet in my bedroom. That's the biography section. Literary biography A–L is in my daughter's bedroom under her stuffed animals. Literary biography M–Z is in the living room along with poetry, drama, and fiction N–Z. Fiction A–M is in the basement. That's also the repository of history. The media section is in the utility room next to the hot water heater. Books about my native Kentucky take up a wall of the dining room. Sports and music books are in the attic. My wife has a couple of cookbooks in the kitchen but she has declared the county library as the way to go. Painful as it is I've started donating books. We are out of space and can't afford to move. Besides, no mover would have us.

Well, maybe over in the corner of the bedroom I could use that bookcase from my childhood home, but it's not available. My brother convinced our parents that he should have it. Later he gave it to his father-in-law who converted it into a gun rack. It still holds no books.

Gretel Ehrlich

About Reading

When I was a child my father had a woodworking shop in which I made things—doghouses, mostly, but also, grain boxes for broodmares. My interest in carpentry was purely practical and my methods were crude, as they are still. But that early interest, together with a voraciousness for reading, finally merged. Thirty years later when I bought an isolated mountain ranch in northern Wyoming, I finally unpacked all my books and built bookshelves ad nauseum—even in the outhouse. When friends asked if I wasn't lonely up there, I only pointed to walls and walls of literature—those windows into other lives and other worlds.

My family wasn't bookish—we raised horses—but they generously accommodated my interest in reading as well as the other arts. I remember putting a 75 LP on the record player and listening with rapt attention to the whole of Sibelius's *Finlandia* when I was seven. That music inspired what my mother calls my "first book," a "novella"—the story of which I have no recollection, delivered to my parents for Christmas, handwritten and hand-bound. After the novella, came poems and a play in which I acted all the parts.

There were good libraries and bookstores in town and during the dinner hour, we rarely failed to look up something in the encyclopedia, shelved by the dining room table. Television was something we did as a group activity on Saturday nights. Period. Dinners were times of discussions and controversy and the hours after were for reading, homework, painting, and writing.

In my early reading years I loved Robert Louis

Stevenson, all tales about sailing and the South Pacific, and books about animals, especially *Black Beauty* and *The Yearling*. On finishing the latter, I locked myself in my room and cried for two days and two nights. It confirmed all my worst suspicions about the cruelty of human beings and the innocence and goodness of animals.

Poetry was what I turned to most often; it was my daily catechism, a survival guide, an etiquette for the wild mind. I still have an early volume of Langston Hughes and a 1956 edition of the *Uta,* Japanese poems translated by Arthur Whaley, both given to me by my mother when I was a teenager. My mother's older sister gave books every Christmas, and especially memorable was a collection of essays by Loren Eisley. The next year, in Mexico City, where my father had a factory, I bought Octavio Paz's *Piedra de Sol.*

Music and poetry, painting and dance were all of a piece. I did not know then that there would not be enough time in my life to work in all four forms, because I could not see how one could flourish without the other. Later, in the monastic confines of boarding school where I was sent when I was twelve, I decided to pursue my own literary education and began reading one book a night by flashlight, under the covers. During chapel, I lay D. T. Suzuki's book on Zen inside the hymnal and read during the daily drone of sappy Christian songs and sermons.

There was an excellent bookstore near the school and I spent all my allowance there. My reading list was compiled by checking off the "Belles Lettres" listed in the back of Vintage (and other) paperbacks, as well as taking suggestions from the booksellers.

I was, of course, a terrible snob—or maybe, a good snob, and read European and Russian fiction and poetry first—Camus, Gide, Flaubert, Thomas Mann, Tolstoy, Dostoyevsky, Turgenev, Rimbaud, Valéry; then Mexican literature, especially Octavio Paz (still my favorite poet), what there was of Japanese literature in translation—*The Tale of Genji* and Bashō. The Brits and Americans came last—Sherwood Anderson, Steinbeck, Robinson Jeffers, Hemingway, and Faulkner, and of course, D. H. Lawrence, whose early essays about Italy and Mexico held me in a trance, as did his later and wilder novel—*The Plumed Serpent.*

In the classroom, I labored over translations of Virgil, Horace, Ovid, and Catullus and wrote tiny tales in Latin, not because I was any genius, but merely because I was bored. For final papers I wrote long poems. The physical confines of my surroundings and my rage against restraint found deliverance in nightly literary journeys. The life of the mind—though I didn't understand it as such—and the daily discipline of feeding it well, was expanding.

There is no way to describe the naïveté with which I undertook this reading. It was the late fifties and I came from a California family whose holidays were spent skiing, sailing, and riding. I was the only bookworm jock I knew. But reading was the antidote for a strongly felt cerebral loneliness, and it was, for a young person, a passage out of the peculiar, protective constraints prescribed for us by our parents and society as children and teenagers. Literature opened doors but did not slam my fingers. At the same time, it thrummed my heart and mind.

 BARBARA JUSTER ESBENSEN

The Next Book

TO RECALL A TIME when I was not able to read, when I did not have a craving for "something to read," would be impossible for me now. But my earliest memory of loving a book was hearing my mother read *The Tale of Peter Rabbit.* I can still remember my excited anticipation, see the cozy lamplight, and hear my mother's voice begin to read the story: "Once upon a time, there were four little rabbits, and their names were Flopsy, Mopsy, Cottontail, and Peter. They lived with their mother in a sandbank under the root of a very big fir tree." That sandbank home and the family of rabbits, with their clean looking clothes and their sweet faces and little paws made me want to live there with them. I am sure that those long ago evenings in the lamplight began for me the magic that is a book.

For three and a half years, I was an only child, and I was read to every night. It was the thin, pale green book, *When We Were Very Young,* that I asked for night after night, according to my mother. That, and *Now We Are Six.* There was something mysterious about the pictures that went with the poems set out on the pages of these books. The scratchy black-and-white drawings left so much out. I could see that. But I felt that I knew what was going on, beyond the sight of the reader. When I heard "James, James Morrison, Morrison, Weatherby George Dupree . . ." and looked at the pictures, I could hear a streetcar clanging. I can hear it this very minute, as I write these words!

I felt uneasy every time I heard about Mary Jane who wouldn't eat her rice pudding, because of the picture of her, in a high chair, with her crabby little face, her doubled-up body, and her wiry hair scribbled every which way.

Sometime after I had learned to read, my parents bought the six-volume set of *My Bookhouse* from a lady who came to our door. This was a miraculous, gold-edged lineup of thick books, bound in green leatherette. They were wonderfully heavy to hold, and the gold came off on my fingers when I rubbed them along the satiny top edge of the pages. It seemed to me that the paintings on the front covers—six entirely different pictures in rich muted colors—were like doors to what lay inside.

The stories and poems ranged from Mother Goose and simple folktales to legends and biographies. The best thing about these books, I decided as I grew up, was that there was always, in one book or another, something I had missed, some story that was still new to me. I have the whole set of *My Bookhouse* on my shelf and I noticed today that there are stories in them that I don't recall ever having read. To a true booklover, this fact is delightful to think about. It means that even after all this time, I can settle down, any time I choose to, and lose myself once again behind those evocative painted scenes.

Even when I could read by myself, it was lovely to hear a story read aloud. At Lowell School in Madison, Wisconsin, time was set aside every day for our teacher to read to us. Listening to a story allowed me to run it, like a movie, inside my head. *Heidi* came alive for me through the dramatic reading the red-headed Mrs. McKinley brought to it. When Grandfather made that cheese for Heidi, toasting it on a fork over a fire, and then giving it to her with a chunk of crusty bread, Mrs. McKinley brought the very fragrance and texture of that simple food right into the classroom.

Our school had a wonderful library, and the librarian, Mrs. Large, was the perfect librarian. When we went as a class into her library, she was always ready with a stack of books piled in front of her on the shiny dark checkout desk. One by one, she would put her hand on a book and in a leisurely way, bring it over to where we were sitting. First, she would show us the outside. She would run her thin fingers under the title. Then she would ask us what kind of clue the title might give to the story inside. After that, she would tell us about the author.

And finally, when we were all straining forward to see what was inside, she would open the book and read a page or two. The best part was when she would look at each one of us and then say, "I think . . . I think . . . hmmmm . . . I think this is the perfect book for . . ." and with a flourish, she'd hand it to one of us to check out. What a thrill! She was always right, too.

My family caught on early that I loved books. One summer I was sick in bed for two weeks, and my father brought home a new book every couple of days. I smile now, when I remember the books he chose for his ten-year-old daughter. I'm sure these were all books that sounded like ones he'd like to be reading: *Tarzan and the Lost Empire, Robinson Crusoe, Robin Hood,* and Richard Haliburton's gung-ho adventure book, *Seven League Boots!*

Maybe I would have been a writer without ever having read my all-time favorite books, but I really think that Jo March in *Little Women* and the L. M. Montgomery heroines, *Anne of Green Gables, Story Girl,* and *Emily of New Moon* gave me the idea that a real person like myself could actually be an author! I modeled myself after these girls. I thought of myself as a tomboy like Jo and spent a lot of my time in a tree, reading. I used the same words Anne liked: "Scope for imagination," "kindred spirits," and like Emily, I gave names to my room ("Castle Afterglow"), and my favorite tree (a weeping willow I called "Lady Windemere Weep").

At fourteen, when I discovered the huge, two-volume *Autobiography of Lincoln Steffens,* I saw that one could be a journalist. Another possibility for me!

I was fortunate that my best friends were reading addicts too. We bought notebooks and wrote down our stories with characters that became real to each of us. We gave one another books as presents year after year. In eighth grade, my friend Genevieve and I used to go downtown every Saturday and, with fifty cents, buy one another a book. Afterwards we would go have ice cream, if it was summer, or hot chocolate on cold, foggy Saturdays (our favorite "book days" were foggy or rainy). We would write in each other's book, "to . . . from . . ." and the date, and exchange our new treasures across the little table. I still have my purple Nancy Drew book, *The Secret at Lone Tree Cottage,* inscribed to me from Genevieve.

In my sophomore year, I discovered the Wisconsin author August Derleth, and one day, looking in vain for another of his books on the "D" shelf, I came across the lovely title, *Song of the Lark,* by an author I had never heard of. It was sitting there on the shelf, under "C." From the minute I began to read that book, I was hooked on Willa Cather's novels. Her three-dimensional characters and the rich, energetic images showed me again and again what mere words could do. John Steinbeck's books, introduced to me during World War II, had the same effect.

My high school English teacher, Eulalie Beffel, had the most powerful influence on my future. Not only did she tell me, early on, that I was "a writer," but she directed me toward Thomas Mann's *Buddenbrooks* and Stephen Vincent Benét's *John Brown's Body.* Both of them were books that would fill my craving for dozens of characters I could meet and know for the rest of my life. Both of them showed me, once again, how the simplest words set down just right on a page could move the reader.

Why do I read? I read because I want to connect with the next book that is already waiting out there—waiting for me to open its pages, to breathe in that fragrance of paper and binding and ink that signals something exciting and unknown. I read so that I can experience yet again, the miracle that happens when the paper, the ink, the book itself all seem to disappear, and I am journeying somewhere I have never been before on the wings of those magic words so carefully chosen by someone I will never know.

MICHAEL FELDMAN

My Life in Fiction

MY CHARACTER is predominantly fictional. A critic might attribute this to the chronic lack of event, drama, or turning point other than south in my real life, but to that I say, "Ka-pocketa-pocketa-pocketa." The fact is I'm a susceptible reader and have to be very careful what I pick up; I say this as one who would have watched helplessly as Joyce Carol Oates murdered his family had not his eyes already been spooned out by Jerzy Kosinski. I'm a serially monogamous page turner, and have to really like an author before I'll crack his book, let alone go all the way. Whenever I've tried juggling several authors one of us always gets hurt. But once I like a guy, I'll pretty much do his oeuvre until I beg for mercy (begging off only on Updike's heartbreaking psoriasis diary and the Nabokov with butterflies, Russian artistocrats and blank verse) so it's helpful if the author's either dead or Salinger so I can get on with my life. Oh, I've made my mistakes (McInerney, Kotzwinkle, post-Yossarian Heller), but very rarely will I read someone I don't deeply care for or think I could, and you've got to admire that.

I've often thought that if Stuart Mill had been my dad I could have been a utilitarian today, or, barring that, at least have had a more overarching literary/intellectual education, instead of the cold start of a Dairyland household where the bulk of the available reading matter recounted the percentage of fibers in the fill and the small comfort of a land grant university closed by riots right in the middle of the lake poets. This happenstance (a word we don't hear nearly often enough today) abetted by a lack of oral tradition (well, I guess Dad's asides were oral, but the narrative "Putterman" would never have been mistaken for *Beowulf*) and a library overrepresented by Mickey Spillane (I can still mentally retrieve the cover of *I, The Jury,* and do), *National Geographic* (which, like myself, found no bare-breasted women in its look at Milwaukee), and the poorly concealed copy of Paolo Mantegazza's 1925 groundbreaker, *The Sexual Habits of Mankind,* made for an environment that would have pinned Mortimer Adler for the count. We did have a bound set of Twain, but that was for pressing pansies.

With this apology for my life as a reader (I'll apologize for the rest of it later if you have time), here is my literary history: *Danny Dunn and the Anti-Gravity Paint* made me an early believer in technology and one-coat latex, while *Dr. Doolittle* startled me with the revelation not so much that it was possible to talk to animals but that, unlike humans, they might answer. Perelman bridged the gap between intellect and whoopee cushion. Maybe I got to it at the wrong stage of adolescence, but *The Catcher in the Rye* only made me want to assassinate Paul Anka. During junior high school I awoke morning after morning to find I had not been transformed into a giant dung beetle but could not say the same for my brother Arthur. Thurber fleshed out my father's rather bare bones muttering on the opposite sex ("Women!") and for a time convinced me both that I was going blind and could draw. Twain made it clear that you've really got to be good to write dialect, and Faulkner that you've really got to be good to live somewhere where they speak in it.

As I think back on it, it may have been Henry Miller and not me making impromptu and violent love on a radiator in the hallway of a Parisian apartment house in 1923; I'll have to check Anais's diary. Kafka was kind enough to render high school meaningless, Beckett made meaninglessness meaningless, and I'm forever indebted to William Carlos Williams for proving a piece of paper about the size and shape of a man was not a man by driving over it. I've had days like Raskolnikov, but without the resolution, and unlike Gogol's character, if I saw my nose on another person I would not pursue it but gladly let it go.

My great love for the Protestant people, more specifically their women, comes to me by way of Cheever and Updike, who convinced me that a Jew might hold up pretty well against these guys despite their good teeth, although Fitzgerald caused me to marry in the faith. I have not even seen the best minds of my generation let alone in the condition Ginsberg found his, so I guess it's a trade-off. Early on, Roth and I pulled in tandem, although he got a lot further with his. Currently Martin Amis reassures me that a dismal view of human nature and an impenetrably bleak worldview need not keep you from being a laugh a minute.

Max Garland

The Inwards

In the memory I've concocted for myself, as opposed to the way things happened, my earliest reading experience was the King James Bible. Of course, I rhymed my way through the alphabet first, I suppose; barked out *boy* and *ball,* and eventually advanced into multiple syllables. And there is a vague, soapy recollection of small waterproof books in which pigs owned houses and wolves pursued dutiful young girls. Later, I even recall a few paperback Westerns belonging to my father. Nothing as fancy as Zane Grey; just dogeared stories in which strangers drifted through chapter after dusty chapter, getting wounded in the shoulder, eventually being provoked into righteous killing sprees. Occasionally, a woman's bosom was mentioned. It rose and fell, as I recall.

But those were just books. King James was *The Book.* I knew that because it resided on the living room coffee table—leather-bound, gilt-edged, thumb indexed, with the words of Jesus highlighted in bloodred ink. It rested there like God's anchor, right next to the dish of hard candy and a huge ashtray of nautical design.

And what, after all, were mere home-owning pigs or bonneted wolves compared to the speaking-into-existence of all animals, the thundering down of commandments, sticks into serpents, rain of frogs? And what were simple declarative sentences—*The third little pig was a sober little pig*—next to the antique structures of King James—*Wherefore . . . O Thou of . . . Ye shall . . . ?*

Of course, it helped to hear the words pounded down

Sunday after Sunday from the Baptist and Methodist pulpits of western Kentucky (we had relatives of both denominations, and like professional lobbyists, we knew enough to hedge our bets). Until you've heard Elizabethan English spoken with a pre-TV western Kentucky accent, you can't fully appreciate the number of uncharted vowel sounds contained in the single word *Jesus*.

It's not even that I was a particularly devout child, nor remotely understood the Bible, for that matter. What does a grade-schooler make of *and the fat of the bullock and of the ram, the rump, and that which covereth the inwards, and the kidneys, and the caul above the liver*? But what is textual understanding, anyway, compared to the simple authority of the Bible's presence there, right next to the candy dish and ashtray from the deep? Something was coming through as I riffled the pages and sounded out the names and admonitions—the written word as ornament and pivot, and something beyond that.

I mention this now, not as a middle-aged promotion of some back-to-the-Bible program. Personally, I think the Bible could have used one of those legendary New York editors, the ones before conglomeration set in. Doesn't the Bible *tell* a little more than *show*, after all? I mention those early years of bibliolatry because I often find myself shrinking into a bout of regret—a too unlettered childhood—no stacks of classics, no long winter afternoons following Pip or Huck or even Spin and Marty. There is that continual sense of needing to catch up, make up for all the books not read in childhood. But in the midst of such hand-wringing, I think now of the book that *was* there, and find myself not ungrateful for that initial sense of the written word as eternal presence, as conveyor of ultimate concern. It's a high-minded and decidedly un-postmodern notion. As a writer, it's something you generally want to keep under your hat, in fact. I can see my father's paperback cowboy squinting disdainfully down the bar, ordering another double for the flame in his shoulder. I agree. When it comes to ambition, it's generally better to play it close to the vest. What gets talked about too much gets stolen, or at least must be defended with gunplay.

Still, in the memory I've concocted for myself, there it lies, that early idea that words have power, and beyond that, the sense that the written word, story, poem, is the trail of some animating spirit, and reading is how you follow, no matter how it might meander, or double back upon itself. Whatever else I've come to doubt or believe, some remnant of that early encounter remains when I pick up a book. Of course, this is not the thought of a grade-schooler (the memory is concocted, after all). The grade-schooler is long gone, back there with the inedible candy and bowl of ashes. But I'm stuck with the idea of book as Bible, and I guess I have the Baptists to thank for that. Not to leave out, of course, those good people, the Methodists.

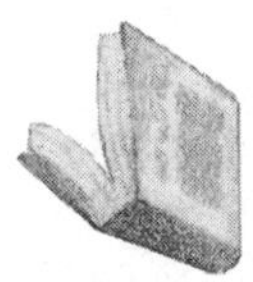

David Gates

"It's Agony, Betty! Agony!"

1

A is the Apple for Jimmy to bite;
B is the Bed that he sleeps in at night.

THESE MAY NOT really be the first words I ever heard read to me, though their primal appropriateness makes me want to think so. But they remind me that even before I could read I could misread—both in Harold Bloom's agonistic sense of armtwisting a text to my own uses and in the everyday sense of just plain getting the thing wrong. I remember hating Jimmy, and the scheme of things in which he bit his Apple and slept in his Bed; maybe I was just resisting toilet training, or maybe I felt that only David should have an Apple to bite or a Bed to sleep in. Whatever the problem was, I resisted that doggerel rhythm piledriving the implicit assertion that A stands for Apple and nothing but Apple—A *is* the apple—and B for nothing but Bed. It felt as oppressive to me as I'd like to think *The New England Primer* felt to my swamp-Yankee ancestors:

The Dog will bite
The Thief at night.

Assuming any of them were privileged enough to be looked at down the nose of some small town Jonathan Edwards manqué schoolmaster in the first place.

Of course my parents must have thought this harmless alphabet rhyme was sweet and comforting: any parent would. And despite what I've just said, it was. I found just about anything read to me comforting—except for some storybook that had a scary fox peeping out of a hole in a hollow tree, which made me terrified of the stovepipe damper in my grandmother's house. My parents, who read a lot, read to me a lot. And I could read myself before I started school, or so I'm told. One much-repeated story has the first-grade teacher showing a picture of a bottle and me coming up with a letter C (for "champagne") instead of the expected B. Reading—including the inner dramas of misreading—has always been a comfort to me, whatever else it's been.

2

Graham Greene claimed that "it is only in childhood that books have any deep influence on our lives." I'm not convinced *The Saggy Baggy Elephant* changed my life as much as reading Beckett, Nabokov and Barthelme in my twenties, or Jack Kerouac and Allen Ginsberg in my teens. But any important reading I may have done way back when was done at home. Not that I hated school: far from it. I remember my satisfaction in being chosen for the top reading group in third grade and getting to sit in a circle with pretty girls I considered my social betters; I just can't remember what we took turns reading. Until seventh or eighth grade, when we had *Silas Marner* and an edition of *Julius Caesar* illustrated with photos of Marlon Brando and John Gielgud, all I can recall was some insipid story about a boy coincidentally named David Gates who had a little red wagon. If he'd been named anything else, he'd be gone with all the rest of whatever it was.

But the books I had at home have stuck with me, though not always much of them. I loved some book with eighth-inch-thick pages, but I remember only the pages. I loved Little Golden Books, too, but I mostly remember the look of the gold, vine-embossed spines, the smell of the paper, and the security of ownership. (These are the same atavistic, extraliterary pleasures I still get from books. The sweet tobacco-ish smell of the Penguin *Little Dorrit,* the sharper, inkier scent of the Ballantine paperback *Stories of John Cheever*—the same smell as my old copy of Sartre's *Saint Genet, Actor and Martyr,* which I lost track of twenty years ago. And the look of familiar spines on the shelves, dearer than any painting, print, or photograph.) My father reminded me the other day that I loved one tall narrow book, but all either of us could recall was that it was tall and narrow. Could have been Mother Goose. Or maybe it was the source of some of the stories—the "Three Billy Goats Gruff," "Jack and the Beanstalk," "Goldilocks and the Three Bears," "Teeny Tiny"—I seem never not to have known.

I used to think our family was giving itself airs by calling the room where we watched TV the library. (I wasted many more hours watching than my parents did.) But it *was* a library: two walls of bookshelves and a giant old mahogany desk and leather-upholstered swivel chair that had been in the office of the president of my father's company. I used to sit in that chair and sample. *The D.A.'s Man,* by Harold R. (Dan) Danforth, an investigator's tales of his adventures in Harlem dope dens and the "twilight world" of homosexuals; I believed the part about how he simulated smoking a reefer by blowing into it to make the tip glow, and I was probably right. *The Decameron* and the *Arabian Nights* packaged as ribald classics, with tits-and-ass illustrations by Rockwell Kent. Bennett Cerf's *Try and Stop Me,* a collection of anecdotes whose secret theme (unless I was misreading) was that among writers, actors, and such, excessive behavior was amusing and endearing; it had no good effect on my character. Three-to-a-volume condensed mysteries, one of which *(The Frightened Murderer,* by Nancy Rutledge) I lazily made the subject of a seventh-grade book report, omitting to mention that it was condensed. I got an A-plus and a note from my English teacher to the effect that I might some day be able to make a living at writing. This episode, too, now seems an ambivalent portent.

I approached my parents' library with a now-unrecoverable freshness. I picked up a book bound in old green cloth that said *Oliver Twist* in antique gold lettering, and was depressed and terrified by the story of a boy starved, emotionally abused, and fallen in with a gang of thieves who wanted to incriminate him and ruin him with the only decent people he'd ever known. This was supposed to be fun? A small, thick, blue-bound volume with *Paradise Lost* in silver on the spine was the most sublime thing I'd ever read—scary, too—but after the first couple of books enough was enough. And this thing *The Iliad of Homer* (a prose translation in a book-club edition). It seemed pretty modernistic, starting off right in the middle of the story, and the dead guys on chariots with their spears scribbling in the dust promised blood-and-guts action. But I soon gave up on that, too, because half the time I couldn't figure out who they were talking about and couldn't tell which army was the good guys.

3

When people reminisce about their early reading, they're often covertly praising their own precocious wonderfulness, whether their tastes were intimidatingly catholic (Rex Stout's alleged thousands of volumes before the age of whatever) or transcendently humdrum (W. H. Auden's impossible-to-top mania for books about lead mining). But it's a species of self-praise that's inadvertently accurate. We are what we read, and the world on the page is temporarily at one with our own. One purpose of reading is to learn what the outside world offers and threatens, what the possibilities out there might be. But we keep meeting ourselves in the characters we read about, whether imaginary or historical (that is, only partly imaginary). So readerly people, and probably writers above all, tend to be loyal to their first books, and wouldn't wish them to have been any different. Just these texts and no others told them who they are.

It's tricky, therefore, to push your childhood favorites on your own children. Some books may take, some may bomb. (And some you may have better sense than to offer in the first place, knowing that your loyalty is purely personal and undeserved.) It's painfully apparent that my stepdaughter doesn't have quite the appetite I had for Kipling's *Just So Stories,* even though I found her the same 1952 Garden City Books edition with jazzy, spooky color illustrations by one "Nicholas" (no other name given) instead of Kipling's own, which I approve of as a purist, but discovered too late to love. Yet even the books that take necessarily take in a different way: that is, in a different person. My stepdaughter is as obsessed as I was with Thornton W. Burgess's bedtime storybooks. Maybe more: she's now read more of them than I ever did. But her experience of the Burgess books is necessarily different from mine. My grandmother Gates talked in something like Burgess's old-fashioned, matter-of-factly garrulous, gently didactic narrative voice: my stepdaughter has heard this voice only in books. If she pictures Burgess's Green Forest it's more apt to be like the deciduous woods around our house in upstate New York rather than the pinier woods I used to know in northwestern Massachusetts. And she doesn't have the enriching coincidence of a neighbor named Bill Brown at the farmhouse down the road, whom I conflated with Burgess's Farmer Brown even though I knew better. On the other hand, I didn't have what she has: a short, slight schoolmate named Danny with whom to conflate Danny Meadow Mouse—though this is a matter private enough that to ask her about it would be intrusive and crazy.

Charles Olson once said no child was properly brought up without the Burgess books. But these days bibliophiles are more apt to know them than kids are, though some company does paperback reprints, with poor, innocent Bobby Coon politically overcorrected to Bobby Raccoon. Probably few kids were reading them even when I was young. They were first published in the teens and twenties; by the fifties they were already antiquated, though still reprinted by Grosset and Dunlap. Each book has its individual charms—especially such white-knuckle adventures as those of Chatterer the Red Squirrel, caged by Farmer Brown's boy after being trapped in the corncrib, or Bowser the Hound, led far from home by crafty Old Man Coyote. But each book was also a separate window into the same timeless world, which didn't get more real the more you read—it was real right from the first—but opened out, like Yoknapatawpha County, extended the relations among characters like the novels of Galsworthy, and always repeated the same familiar information in the same incantatory language. Jolly, round, red Mr. Sun always goes to bed behind the Purple Hills and the Dear Old Briar Patch and Smiling Pool are always there, like Nero Wolfe's townhouse on West 35th Street, with the orchids on the roof and the office with the trick picture of a waterfall.

4

Still, as I remember it now, much of my experience of reading was confusion and incomprehension. Not what I'd recommend for a child, but for some reason it hooked *me* in. With my gift for misreading, I'd feel alienated when Thornton W. Burgess was trying to make me feel included:

> When Bobby Coon left Unc' Billy Possum's hollow tree, he went fishing. You know he is very fond of fishing.

Well, I *didn't* know it, until that second, and I worried that I was a little faker because Burgess thought I did know it, as all his other, smarter readers clearly did. Agony—though still a form of comfort. Speaking of which, I remember reading an *Archie* comic aloud to an older cousin and being scoffed at for screwing up the line "It's agony, Betty! Agony!" I had no idea what agony was, and figured it must be pronounced *a-GO-ny*. And I puzzled over Bennett Cerf's retelling of the original shaggy dog story, in which a Kansas City barfly somehow sees a *London Times* ad offering a reward for the return of a very shaggy dog. He finds such a dog, goes to England, and rings the lady's bell.

> "Good heavens, no," she snapped. "It wasn't that shaggy"—and slammed the door in his face.

I misread the dash (which I now see is outside the quotation marks) to mean an ellipsis, which made me think a dirty word ("bitch," surely) had been left out. The joke didn't seem howlingly funny, but it was daring and sophisticated, and I retold it to my friends suggestively drawing out the word *shaggy*.

Often I was content simply to savor the sounds and cadences of adult language, the better for being mysterious. I loved this passage in Kipling's story "How the Whale Got His Throat":

> Then he recited the following Sloka, which, as you have not heard it, I will now proceed to relate—
>
> By means of a grating
> I have stopped your ating.
>
> For the Mariner he was also an Hi-ber-ni-an.

Now this seems flat and jokey, a dig in the ribs to grown-ups with maybe a little sideways sneer at the Irish. Back then I barely knew what a mariner was; "Hibernian" was simply another *Just So Stories* nonsense word, like "equinox" or

"Limpopo." ("Sloka," for some reason, I took in stride.) And its nonsensicalness made that *For* hilarious: an explanation that explained nothing. My kind of shaggy-dog story.

5

As nearly as I can reconstruct, I became an obsessive reader in fourth grade, when I was nine or ten years old. Well, probably earlier. But that must have been when I began reading, on my own, about more-or-less adult matters. Some of what I read was pitched at kid level: the mild crimes (which mostly turned out to be misunderstandings) in the Nancy Drew mysteries, the Signature Books series of childhood-centered biographies, several by a woman with the ultra-authorly name of Enid Lamont Meadowcroft. But more and more I tended to read books written for grown-ups: that was where you could find the stuff it wasn't yet appropriate for you to know, in language you couldn't quite understand.

The more metaphor-encrusted the writing, the more I was impressed. It was a thrill to be in on the grown-upness of such passages as this, from John and Alice Durant's *Pictorial History of American Presidents:*

> But the genial Taft was no Roosevelt. The minute Teddy was gone the standpatters took the tiller from Taft's uncertain hands and steered a reactionary course.

I didn't care particularly about deciphering this; learning about political infighting during the Taft administration wasn't the point exactly. I did enjoy the fleeting image of people with flat feet grabbing at a ship's wheel with fat Taft looking on helpless and aghast, but it was the sound, the rhythm, and most of all the fake sophistication that kept me rereading it. The metaphorical bombast gave a sense of mystery, of a meaning out of my reach: a vision of knowledge that no real, specific knowledge could match.

I found something to fascinate me on just about every page of *Pictorial History of American Presidents,* from the wig-powder that portrait painter Adolf Ulric Wertmuller showed on the shoulders of George Washington's velvet coat to a cartoon of a big-headed President Eisenhower (the book was published in 1955) about to whack a baseball with a golf club as Washington Senators' owner Clark Griffith (with "Griff" helpfully lettered across his chest) races, tie over shoulder, across the White House lawn to stop him. "You mean I'm supposed to THROW it out?" Ike is saying. I got this, at least: President Eisenhower liked golf. This was the book from which I learned the word "skulk": whenever I read or write it, I still see the cartoon in which a scowling William Jennings Bryan, with straw hat and pitchfork, "skulks off to his Nebraska farm carrying the full dinner pail of Republican prosperity."

Best of all, *Pictorial History of American Presidents* had enough sinister and violent stuff to satisfy a ten-year-old boy. The barefoot Chinese executioner during the Boxer Rebellion, squatting with long, stained sword over a pile of severed heads. Joe McCarthy and Roy Cohn looking like a pair of mobsters. The hanging of the conspirators in Lincoln's assassinaton. We'd only had the three assassinated Presidents back then, and I'd linger over the pictures of Guiteau shooting a wincing Garfield in what appeared to be the kidneys, Czolgosz (whose name I had no idea how to pronounce) sticking a hanky-covered pistol into McKinley's ample white-shirted belly, Booth blowing out Lincoln's brains. This last inspired me to write, direct, and star in a play. I was Lincoln; as Booth, Jay Stannard (the other tall boy in Miss Troshkin's fourth-grade class) leapt at me out of the coat closet, and the girls sang "Glory, glory, hallelujah" as I lay in state on a couple of desks under stapled-together sheets of white paper.

6

My old copy of *The Fireside Book of Baseball,* edited by Charles Einstein, is inscribed "Christmas 1956. Uncle Philip & Aunt Bettie." That was two weeks before I turned ten. The book had just come out that year; my aunt and uncle couldn't have chosen better for me (had some consultation gone on?) and I still think it's an anthology full of marvels. (Einstein's *The Second Fireside Book of Baseball,* published two years later, is equally marvellous, even though he'd already used Ring Lardner's "Alibi Ike" and James Thurber's "You Could Look It Up.") Einstein favored complexity and eccentricity over rock-jawed heroics, and included profiles of such iconic odd-balls as Babe Herman, Satchel Paige, Dizzy Dean, and Branch Rickey. ("'Pooh,' said Rickey into the phone after a moment. 'Three poohs. Pooh-bah.' He hung up.") Better still, Einstein seemed to relish (as I did) outright pathology. An excerpt from the clinical report on the young woman who shot Philadelphia Phillies first baseman Eddie Waitkus in 1949; "As a child she was gay and happy," it began ominously. An excerpt from Jim Piersall's account (ghost-written by Al Hirschberg) of his nervous breakdown, *Fear Strikes Out;* "I was with the Barons exactly twenty days," it began ominously. Collie Small's "The Man Who Hated Southpaws," a profile of a gifted old-time minor-leaguer undone by his obsession with lefthanded people; "I'm old John King," ran the pullquote above the title. "Men walk around me like I was a swamp."

As any anthologist of classic sportswriting must, Einstein also shared my taste for the cheesy and the pseudoliterary. Grantland Rice's poem on the death of Babe Ruth:

> The Big Guy's gone—by land or sky or foam.
> May the Great Umpire call him "safe at home."

Damon Runyon's 1923 report of then-Giants outfielder Casey Stengel's World Series home run:

> This is the way old Casey Stengel ran yesterday afternoon, running his home run home.
>
> This is the way old Casey Stengel ran running his home run home to a Giant victory by a score of 5 to 4 in the first game of the World Series of 1923.
>
> This is the way old Casey Stengel ran, running his home run home, when two were out in the ninth inning. . . .

A lot of stuff was over my head, like the first sentence of the Heywood Broun piece that read "The Ruth is mighty and shall prevail." This passage, by onetime Pittsburgh Pirates manager Bobby Bragan ("as told to Stanley Frank"), is *still* over my head:

> A weak sister occasionally goes crazy with the heat for a while and threatens to upset the dope, but it's all a snare and a delusion.

He's talking about underdog teams winning games in mid-season, but it now seems like a surreal amount of spin to put on a simple assertion. Back then it seemed surreal, period.

But I was most amazed by the excerpt from Arnold Hano's *A Day in the Bleachers:* his eyewitness account of one of baseball's legendary moments, Willie Mays's catching Vic Wertz's long line drive in the 1954 World Series. It takes Hano more than three double-columned pages to tell everything he saw in those six or seven seconds, and even then he admits it's a partial acount.

> There is no perfect whole, of course, to a play in baseball. If there was, it would require a God to take it all in. For instance, on such a play, I would like to know what Manager

> Durocher is doing—leaping to the outer lip of the sunken dugout, bent forward, frozen in anxious fear?

Years later, *To the Lighthouse* seemed to me no more than a superior example of realist fiction. The notion of a universe of inner and outer events contained in a few seconds of time continues to affect my own writing—for better and worse—and *A Day in the Bleachers* suggests most of what I still believe about the powers and the limitations of literary representation. All I've brought to the party, really, is my own incomprehension and misapprehension: the subjectivity that limits the possibilities of representation still further, yet also opens them up boundlessly. Though I don't know about "boundlessly." And I had to read Samuel Beckett to grasp the idea that impotence and ignorance could be literary virtues. Though I guess I was ripe for it.

Poe, whose young mother died when he was two, claimed the poet's ideal subject was the death of a beautiful young woman. I'd say the writer's ideal subject is people misreading each other and themselves—assuming we could ever decide what's reading and what's misreading—though the stuff I've just been telling on myself makes my ideal as easy to dismiss as Poe's. Yet unless I'm misreading everybody from Shakespeare to Raymond Carver, something like my penny-ante traumas of isolation and miscommunication are normative; personal disasters like Poe's are simply the icing on some people's cakes. Which literary ideal is more cheerless? Six of one. But words, necessarily misconceived and misperceived, at least serve to break the silence and to say someone else is there. That in itself may be some comfort.

Doris Grumbach

To Write—To Read and Vice Versa

My mother had a unique method for teaching me to read. She said she started when I was a little more than three and she was about to have another child. She told me she had grown tired of my constant demands to be read to. She thought it time I read to myself. So she began her tutelage by pointing to a simple word on the page and repeating it to me again and again, making me look at it and repeat it to her. Then she made me write the word again and again in my large, awful block letters, so that, very early, I associated the printed page with writing. I think I believed that in order to read I had to be able to write, and vice versa. In this way, I suppose, I could write almost before I could read.

I seem to remember that the first word I knew, via this method, was READ. But that may be a fiction I've chosen to recall. In any event, by the time I got to kindergarten I was a practiced reader and showed off by reading to my peers while the teacher was cleaning the blackboards, or some such thing.

My first grade school, Public School 9 in Manhattan, was three city blocks from the St. Agnes branch of the New York Public Library. Once a week on Friday afternoon, my mother would meet me at school, take me to Schraffts for an ice cream soda, and then to the library. From the overflowing tables and chaotic shelves of thin children's books I was allowed to take seven up to the desk where the librarian stamped with the date due my proudest possession at the time, my own library card. When that card was filled, front and back, she would issue me another. Those cards meant I was something more than a child, somehow, even though I was six and the stamps on the cards only represented quantity.

I remember developing a fondness for some of these borrowed treasures and I hated to return them. But once I was eight or nine, and my mother trusted me to navigate the streets between the school, the library, and our apartment, I would stop daily at the library, return the book reluctantly, and take another. Sometimes I tried to find a favorite from the week before and would be resentful if some other reader had taken it out. When I did find it again I learned the pleasures of rereading, a pleasure I have had now for seventy years.

I think I was ten or eleven when I was sent upstairs to the adult floor because I had exhausted the resources of the children's section. I remember my surprise at how orderly everything was up there. The books were arranged by author, beginning with A. I must have decided that this order was both alphabetical and compulsory because I began to take books out in the order I found them there, for months, that is, until the librarian wondered why a girl of ten was reading all of Sherwood Anderson and Gertrude Atherton. She released me from the alphabetical imperative, and led me over, I believe, to the "L"s where she suggested I try the confections of William J. Locke.

My mother did not believe in owning books. Libraries were there for the purpose of forestalling that desire, and furthermore, she thought, books in the house created disorder on tables and most shelves. (I was an adult with my own apartment before I owned any books, and then the first ones I wanted and bought were books I first became acquainted with in the library.)

But I should acknowledge my possession of one priceless set, *The Book of Knowledge*. These twenty volumes were permitted in the house because with their neat, gold-stamped bindings they sat ordered on shelves in the breakfront which otherwise were occupied by pieces of oriental porcelain and commemorative plates. This was not an encyclopedia but a set of entertaining and informative books with a motley arrangement of short essays (and large illustrations) on many subjects, all jumbled together in each volume: the earth, poetry, men and women, plant and animal life, myths, literature, countries, etc. I read these volumes hungrily, obsessively, avidly; they were always *there,* while library books came and went. I am stunned to find, after all this time, how much of my education seems to have come from them, which may account for the amount of misinformation programmed into the personal computer that is my head.

Public school was my teacher, but the public library was my supplier of mind-expanding and exhilarating drugs of the imagination and intellect. In my early years I believed that by the end of my life I would be able to read everything printed, and that it was all there, on the shelves of the St. Agnes branch of the library. As I approach eighty I have been sadly disabused of these convictions, but not of the lifelong pleasure that what I *have* read has afforded me.

Thom Gunn

A Letter to Mark Rudman

The "formative encounter"—that's easy. The house was full of books, as it usually is for those who are going to depend on books the rest of their lives for part of their living. The exceptions, by their own accounts, were the childhood homes of the English Alan Sillitoe and the American Gary Soto, which were both bare of books. They had to form their attachments later, more difficultly. But books already gave me a lot of pleasure, in 1934, when I was four. My mother would take me round to the local newsagent and we would get another book by Beatrix Potter—evidently it was also a modest kind of bookstore in that upper middle-class neighborhood in London. I thought that the rather colorless woman who sold us the books was also the author of them, Beatrick Spotter I thought was her name. Then this, and all the other children's classics, were read to me at bedtime. But I could see that books were more absorbing, more private and involving than such communal sharings. I do remember my mother reading and reading at a big book, and I realized it was something, reading, that was an important and adult activity that I would get to do myself one day. "What is it all about?" "All the terrible things that people do to each other in wars, killing and maiming and sadness." "What is it called?" "*Gone With the Wind,*" said my mother, and do you know, in spite of the fact that this *was* the formative encounter, I have never even opened that book in adult life.

There have been books that I have devoured in enormous sittings, barely stopping to sleep, *The Hobbit* when it first came out, and later *The Executioner's Song,* but I have mostly been a slow reader, and since I have read a lot of poetry, I have studied to make myself a slower reader. When I now read *Ulysses* again, I read much of it "aloud," mouthing it to myself so that I hear it in my mind, as if it *were* poetry. And also I reread a lot—and I am fascinated by the way that books change with each rereading. *Hamlet* certainly has—when I first read it, I identified with the hero as the moony adolescent I was, and now I see him as a selfish self-absorbed pig, with whom I also identify; and I first read *What Masie Knew,* fascinated, at nineteen, without a smile: I have read it several times since then, each time laughing more. You can quarrel with books, or come to love them more, rather as if they were people. The quarrels and reconciliations I have been through with Yeats and Eliot!

Certain books I return to again and again. I remember my first reading of *The Brothers Karamazov:* I was nineteen then, too, doing my National Service in the army, and hating it. But this was the beginning of a *weekend:* I was in my thick, prickly, unlovely army uniform, got on the train at Arborfield, going to London for the rest of Saturday and the whole of Sunday, under an hour's trip, I suppose. It was one of the old trains they no longer have in England, where each carriage was composed of separate compartments. I got a corner seat, and the autumn sunshine shone on my book, mixed up with the shadows of trees, I remember clearly. I was just into it, this was the part where they consult with Father Zosima. My excitement at getting away from the base for a little was folded into my excitement with the book. . . . We *all* have this kind of experience, in which our experience of the book is inextricably confused with the experience of reading it for the first time (Wallace Stevens has a beautiful poem about it, "The house was quiet and the world was calm"). That's what reading is—an inextricable part of our lives, what we experience, what we learn from—anything but a decoration, an extractable and finally irrelevant pleasure like eating a Mars Bar or watching *Melrose Place*.

Now, for Dostoyevsky's book, and then I'll stop this impossibly un-letter-like letter. I don't think I would have gotten along with F. D. himself *at all*, his feelings about country, and so on, and he was a very *spiritual* person, and I'm not spiritual at all. And yet I come back to this and others of his novels again and again: it is something I live through, I share the extraordinary alien life and it becomes an intimate part of mine. How to put it more clearly? It is experience and it is learning from experience, it is being in Russia and Berkshire in the 1880s and 1940s and 1990s all at the same time, it is learning about God while not believing in God—all extraordinarily complex, as far from learning the rules of grammar as it is from eating a Mars Bar.

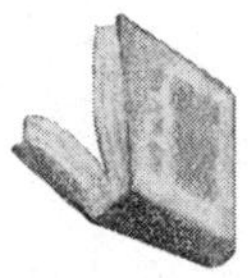

RACHEL HADAS

Reading, Being Read To, and Reading Together

READING IS and is not a solitary activity. My adolescent discovery of Dickens and Shakespeare's sonnets and, a little later, Proust was a succession of lone forays into enchanting territory. But earlier, reading was associated for me with a beloved voice: chiefly my mother's, but also my father's, my half-brother's, even my grandmother's. Unexpected echoes can still call up these memories. Reading "The Pobble Who Has No Toes" aloud to my son, I suddenly hear my grandmother's deep Virginia voice saying the words. She died when I was no more than six, and just about my only memory of her is this one. The other night I rediscovered the poem about the Bandar-Log that follows the chapter "Kaa's Hunting" in *The Jungle Book*. And I could hear my mother's voice: "Brother, thy tail hangs down behind."

Not so solitary, then. And—since I've been a mother for the past twelve years and a teacher for fifteen—not so solitary now either, since my job in the classroom is to enact, evoke, essentially share the book, surely in order to equip the listeners to go off on their own. Beside me on the desk as I write is a bookmark, a gift from the Vermont Council on the Humanities. Two children are silhouetted on it facing each other; one holds a book. "Read with Me," says the logo. A contradiction in terms; one reads perhaps to another person, but *with?* And yet my most vivid memories of reading are emphatically of reading *with*. What follows is a small collection of such memories, excerpted from my 1988 essay "The Cradle and the Bookcase," which takes its title from the first line of Baudelaire's poem "*La Voix:*" *Mon berceau s'adossait a la bibliothèque.* Or if not my cradle, my son's; or if not a cradle, then a hammock. . . .

In my family, and especially since my son has become a greedy readee, the pleasure of sharing books is also the pleasure of leaping the generation gap. It occurred to me the other night that Jonathan (aged four and a half) was ready to be read "Rikki-Tikki-Tavi." My husband and my mother would both have loved to read him the story; since I was the lucky reader, they listened with, inevitably, more pleasure than the child hearing it for the first time. A good deal of Jonathan's pleasure was a reflection of our excitement at the prospect of his discovering Kipling's story. As he helped me look for *The Jungle Book* in the attic, we found that we had two copies of it: one belonging originally to my sister and one with my father-in-law's name on its flyleaf. I told Jonathan of these two prior owners. "Were they friends?" he asked.

All this is not to say that children automatically devour what their elders assure them is delicious. Note the food metaphor, which proves pervasive in discussions of reading, from the fickle browser to the voracious gulper. Orwell tells us in his essay on Dickens that "forced feeding" of Dickens to him as a child initially caused "rebellion and vomiting": he ponders the irony of having *David Copperfield* "ladled down my throat by masters in whom even then [he] could see a resemblance to Mr. Creakle." The mysterious process of forming—consciously or not—a child's taste is probably often slow and indirect, just as our own tastes are gradually and often painfully acquired.

The epitome of shared pleasure in reading is the slippery business of reading aloud, and it is here that the analogy with food and feeding comes into its own. To spoon-feed an adult is an act of tenderness and patience (or so one hopes; condescension and power-mongering are strong possibilities too), but it is also a sad necessity for both the feeder and, above all, the one being fed. Nursing a baby or feeding a small child, on the contrary, is a quintessential icon of the sustaining reciprocal love that nurtures both the one who feeds and the one who is fed. The issue of power, and later of individual taste, comes up here too, the moment we move away from the haloed image of a nursing mother, for the further the child moves from babyhood, the greater the range of choices, possibilities, and attendant problems. Still, it's considered natural for a mother to choose, provide, and prepare the food she then helps the baby to eat. If one of the joys of adulthood—as great, for me, as never having to take a math course again—is reading what one chooses when one wants, then one of the joys of childhood, long past the age of weaning, is being lovingly provided with another kind of fare: books. There will be time for the inevitable rebellion or disaffection later; but in my experience as child and now as mother, to reject books is to reject love.

Jonathan prefers to snuggle cozily against whoever is reading to him—in a recliner, or lying down before the lights are turned out at bedtime, or (this summer's hit) swinging lazily with the reader in a big hammock. Horizontally suspended, the reader and the one being read to share the illusion of having escaped gravity, as the gentle pendulum of the hammock's swing (a motion deliciously evoked in James Merrill's poem "A Timepiece") marks the time.

In the absence or abeyance of vertical busyness, of scurrying hither and thither, the time which the hammock's pendulum marks is all the freer to cluster, almost like drops of moisture, around the dream of the book. Of the essence here is *otium,* the empty time needed to read, to snuggle, to dream. *Otium* is also an important ingredient of the kind of patience needed to create any book worth spending time over.

Still in the hammock. I consider how reading takes over

with exquisite tact from the other kinds of nurturance—being fed, changed, carried—that a four-year-old has outgrown. Think of Wilbur in *Charlotte's Web.* Miserably lonely in the strange barn and then at the fairgrounds, the pig begs Charlotte to tell him a story before he goes to sleep. Wilbur is, to say the least, well fed by the Zuckermans, but only Charlotte's attention can feed his hungry heart—and her attention, since it cannot be directly physical, consists of the tales (as well as epithets) she spins for him.

I thought of Charlotte one hot afternoon recently. Reading in the hammock, Jonathan and I noticed a couple of small spiders delicately lowering themselves from the larch boughs above our heads, swaying on their almost invisible strings a few inches above the pages of our book, which happened to be Howard Pyle's *The Wonder Clock.* Apparently it was Charlotte's turn to be read to.

I wonder whether Jonathan will remember those spiders and fairy tales, that hazy July afternoon. Probably not. Yet many of the memories of reading I still retain have the glamor of a slight strangeness—an unusual location, a shared response. Memories float up from childhood; also from various layers of my adult life.

I'm in Athens, reading through *The Inferno* and some of *The Purgatorio* (in Italian with facing-page translation) with Alan Ansen, in his tall apartment in a house that now no longer exists on Alopekis Street. Alan's sonorous declamations stay with me, as does our having gotten as far as the interrupted pageant in the Purgatory sometime around Lent. I kept trying to draw that pageant in order to be able to visualize it, and finally gave Alan the resulting watercolor for Valentine's Day. We had our *quel giorno piu,* one of literature's most celebrated and rueful tributes to the power of reading together.

I'm in a cafe in Karlovasi, on the island of Samos, waiting while Stavros does some errand connected with the olive press. It's noon. I'm hungry, I've ordered some *meze*—probably wine and olives and bread. But what I'm really devouring are the brand new, posthumously published volumes (this is 1971) of Sylvia Plath's *Crossing the Water* and *Winter Trees,* which have just arrived from Blackwells.

Back in Athens a few years later, I was one of a dozen people lucky enough to hear James Merrill read aloud his just-completed poem "The Book of Ephraim," now of course the first volume of the Sandover trilogy but then a self-contained (in a fat spring-form binder) and wholly enthralling feast in itself. We were also entertained with food: the evening, as I recall, was divided into drinks/reading, dinner/reading, dessert/reading. Except for some kind of pâté, the menu has faded from my memory; the poem, on the other hand, I can and do consult, frequently and with delight, noting my favorite passages and some minor revisions made since that reading.

Not all the memories are of Greece, which seems to have been the scene of an early second childhood—the third childhood is now that I *have* a child. One of those summers in Vermont when my half-brother and his family shared the house with us, my sister and I were lucky enough to be read *David Copperfield* by our half-brother David, twenty years our senior. We were old enough to have read it ourselves, but there was no comparison between the book we would have evoked and the ferocious Mr. Murdstone David enacted for us. A couple of summers later, Beth and I, now at the advanced ages of thirteen and ten, were read *Pride and Prejudice* by our mother.

There are winter memories too: notably reading Cicero's *De Senectute* with my father—both of us home from school, tired, lying down (though not in a hammock), enjoying puzzling out the syntax. I recall something about metaphorical manure-spreading, no doubt to signify some sort of spiritual enrichment of old age: *stercorandi*. In another year or so, I would be off to college. My father had only two more years to live.

I don't think it's claiming too much to say that every one of these memories, each of which casts a halo over both the reader and the text, signifies love. And not a vague floundering love, but affection in a highly concentrated, focused shape. It sounds paradoxical, but I'm thinking of *otium* again, of that sense of literate leisure favorable not only to visitations from the Muses but also to their worship, in the form of reading.

JUANITA HAVILL

Journey of a Lifetime

I CONSIDER MYSELF LUCKY. I am in my second childhood of reading. The first began in earnest when I was five, and the second started after the birth of my daughter. The first was marked by discovery of books, any books, not necessarily those written for young readers, while the second resulted from motherhood and my desire to write for children. I simply plunged headfirst into the vast sea of children's literature at the age of twenty-eight. It was exhilarating and I continue to swim there often.

Reading was a slow burning passion for me. I don't remember, as some readers do, that moment when sound and sight united into meaning. I memorized books before I could read them. The wonderful flow of words, their rhythm and rhyme, captured me. That letters should flow together to make words was mysterious and at the same time natural like lightning, wind, or the current of the Wabash River in which my brothers and I swam when we were children. The words, like the river, took me someplace. There was a thrill in being lifted and carried away by a power I couldn't see and couldn't understand. Long before I met Huck Finn, I dreamed of floating down the Wabash River on a wooden raft. It would take me far away to wider rivers, the Ohio, the Mississippi, to the Gulf of Mexico, and even to other lands. I never took that trip on the river. Although my parents sympathized, they wouldn't let me go. But I did take another journey—a lifetime journey. I read.

There were books in the house on Mulberry Street in the small town where I grew up. There were no bookstores in town—there still aren't—but my mother ordered from book clubs, and on the bookshelves around the house I read titles such as *Barefoot Boy with Cheek, World Enough and Time, Mary Queen of Scots,* and *Gone With the Wind.* My mother collected art books, too, with works from the Louvre, the Jeu de Paume, full-color prints of Audubon's birds, and a book of photographs from the Civil War. The Civil War book both fascinated and repulsed me. I had a glimpse of horror for the first time when I was seven years old and came upon the photos of war-ravaged prisoners at Andersonville. What had happened to those soldiers? Why did they look like that? Who did this to them? I couldn't help staring, couldn't forget their faces, and could never again feel secure as I once had in my safe world.

My father's books were not as varied. He had several civil engineering textbooks and a book or two on oil production. I never saw him read them or anything else but the local and tri-state newspapers, the *Wall Street Journal,* and mysteries. He didn't care which mystery he read, and because he forgot them immediately after finishing, he could read the same mystery again and again. My father read to fall asleep.

My mother read as if her life depended upon it. Sitting on the living room sofa behind the cofee table piled high with library books, she would open a book and disappear. She didn't fidget or nibble snacks or look up. While reading, she had an expression of calm, transported by the story to another place. One day I saw her sitting at a table bent over a book with her elbows firmly planted. She was frozen, motionless except to turn the pages. I walked by her again several hours later. She closed the 350-page book, looked up, and said, "That was a great book!" I share my mother's attitude toward reading.

I learned early that books did not have to be on the shelves in my room for them to belong to me. I did not have to buy them in order to claim them. I had only to read them. I claimed hundreds of books as a child. I have certificates from the summer library reading program to prove it, certificates accompanied by long lists of slim volumes and a blue or red ribbon awarded during a cookie and lemonade party in August. From all of the books, I remember three in particular which became part of my life and influenced the way I look at the world. Not one of these books was mine.

The first was an illustrated book of myths and legends and was a gift to my brother from, I believe, my grandmother, who sometimes sent us books at Christmas. In fact, she sent me a copy of Raggedy Ann stories, but these never generated in me the excitement produced by the tales of Beowulf and Grendel, Roland and Charlemagne, or Tristan and Isolde, dark, sometimes violent stories of life and death, love and fate. These were stories about heroes and reading them, eight-year-old girl that I was, it never occurred to me that I couldn't be a hero, too. I think this fact is often lost on adults recommending books to young readers today based on their reading level, gender, and background as well as what is perceived as socially, politically, culturally, or morally correct.

The second book I remember but never owned as a child was Charles and Mary Lamb's *Tales from Shakespeare,* an old edition bound in blackened leather and illustrated with engravings of women with rosebud mouths and men with noble profiles. The book belonged to Elizabeth Wade, my fifth-grade teacher. She allowed me to do something that no teacher before or since ever let me do. At recess, when I complained, not very convincingly, of a stomachache or sore throat, she didn't send me to the nurse's office. She simply let me stay in and read. For several weeks I chose *Tales from Shakespeare.* One Friday I was reading *Twelfth Night.* I got caught up in Viola's masquerade as a male and was wondering how she would be found out when the bell rang. My disappointment must have been obvious to Mrs. Wade. She suggested that I take her precious volume home that weekend, and for two and a half days I owned the most beautiful book in the world. I read it from cover to cover. I have since bought other edition of the *Tales,* but none can compare with Mrs. Wade's.

I read the third book when I was nine years old. I borrowed it from the Carnegie Library in town, and I read it in one afternoon, in one sitting after school. I don't remember the name of the book or the author, but I recall that it had one of those sturdy blue-gray library bindings. I remember the protagonist, a sickly ten-year-old Welsh boy whose father worked in the mines. His protective mother refused to let him go down into the mines with his father and uncle and older brothers, but the boy remained determined to be a miner. An accident and explosion occurred, followed by a cave-in. Because he was small enough to get through with a lantern and medical supplies, the boy helped save some of the miners, including his brothers and uncles, but not his father. I identified totally with this boy from another time and place, and although the story didn't spell it out, I knew he would become a miner like his father. It was not a particularly happy ending. I remember when I finished the book, my mother asked me why I was crying and I couldn't explain it. So closely had I identified with the miner's son that when I wiped the tears off my cheek, I looked at my fingers to see if they had been blackened by coal dust.

Books have the same overwhelming power for me now that I am in my second childhood of reading. I still get lost in a book. I still meet unforgettable characters, Charlotte the spider and Curious George, Ramona Quimby and Maniac Magee. I have learned to read as an adult who can analyze and reflect from life's experiences. But I have not forgotten how to read as a child for whom characters are living and breathing and who participates in the unfolding of a story without reservation.

A college English professor once told me that he had always believed as a child that books on the library shelves came to life when everyone left. The characters and the authors slipped from their volumes and spent the midnight hours discussing, dancing, partying, and doing all the things that real, live people do. It's a joyful image and it comes to my mind whenever I read another futurist describing the demise of the book. Yes, I know, in our new technological world we are told that books will not be needed. The book as we know it will be dead. Then I see Beowulf and the Welsh miner's son, Viola and Mrs. Tiggy-Winkle, Mark Twain telling Ramona to sit still, and Curious George hanging from the ceiling with a few of the Wild Things, and I imagine their reaction. "Dead?" they exclaim. "People are saying we are dead!" And they burst out lauging.

URSULA HEGI

Kafka & the Titanic

AS FAR BACK as I can remember, there were stories. How I loved to disappear into those stories when my mother told them to me or read them from books. One I asked for again and again was that of Joseph and the coat and the pharaoh. When I think of my mother telling me that story, it seems to span the first five years of my life.

Evenings, after she'd turn off the light, I would tell my version of those stories to my younger sister who shared the bedroom with me. Of course I'd make up some of my own. I didn't know that I had another audience until years later when my mother would tell me that she and my father used to stand outside that door, listening.

I learned how to read when I was five, and by the time I was six, I had figured out that the only thing that could possibly be more exciting than reading would be writing. But I didn't know anyone else who wrote. It seemed a weird thing to do. I'd walk along the Rhein by myself, sit on the jetties, write poetry. I wrote stories. Began a novel. Finished half of it on lined paper.

I read whatever I could find at home, in the library of the Catholic church, and beneath the cover of our ironing board, where our housekeeper hid the trashy romances that she borrowed from the pay-library. More than three decades later, I would give my reading experiences to the girl Hanna in my novel *Floating in my Mother's Palm:* "When our housekeeper, Klara Brocker, was alone in our apartment, she read romances that she borrowed from Trudi Montag's pay-library. Except for names and settings the novels were alike and invariably ended with promises of eternal love and weddings. . . . Frau Brocker hid the romances under the cover of our ironing board from where I retrieved them late at night and, with a flashlight under my blanket, read about women in distress and the men who rescued them. Each book jacket showed a beautiful woman leaning against something while she looked up at a man who wasn't leaning against anything. . . . I was careful not to move the folded tissue Frau Brocker kept inserted as a bookmark, and if she ever suspected I read her romances, she didn't say."

Just like Hanna, I read with a flashlight beneath my blanket. By the time I was twelve, I'd gone through nearly everything my parents had on the shelves in the living room—Kafka and tales of saints; Edgar Wallace mysteries and Goethe; Dostoyevsky and the catechism. I loved Thomas Mann as much as young girls' adventure series.

Reading and rebellion were closely linked for me during my adolescence. Since my mother did not allow me to have comic books—she believed they stunt your imagination by feeding you pictures along with the words—I read comics at my friends' houses. Also taboo were books that had even the slightest bit to do with sex. Those were locked up in a glass case in our living room. Once I found out where the key was, I sneaked in there whenever my parents were out for the evening. The one I remember most vividly was about the *Titanic*. I can't recall its title or author—only that it had at least five unchaste scenes of women and men inside their cabins in the hours *before* the *Titanic* sank. Soon, I had memorized those page numbers, and then, of course, I got to relive those pages when I knelt in the confessional and whispered to the priest about the impure thoughts generated by the *Titanic*.

I was a greedy reader, a fast reader. I would read four or five hours a day, and what I looked for then—just as I do now—were books that sucked me into their pages, books that let me identify with their characters, books that made me forget my surroundings and even the fact that I was linking words and turning pages. The passion of words. I was a Christian martyr in Rome. A murderer in Russia. A grandmother in Norway. I gave birth a decade before I ever became pregnant. Rode a horse through the American West years before I arrived here as an eighteen-year-old immigrant.

I feel fortunate to live a life that's so deeply connected to books—I read them, write them, review them, teach them. Yet, since so much of my reading has to do with responding to what I've read, the magic of being sucked into the pages happens less frequently. Whenever it does, though, I know what it's all about—like that day when I stood in a bookstore three hundred miles from home and opened Isabel Allende's *Eva Luna*. Within the first few words I forgot where I was. After I bought the book, I stood reading on the sidewalk. Throughout the long drive home, I sat in the passenger seat, reading—even though reading in a car makes me nauseous. But I would close the book just before I'd get ill, wait for it to pass. After we got home, I stayed up till I'd finished *Eva Luna* at dawn.

I tell my graduate students how to re-create that magic for themselves. At the library or a bookstore, they scan fifty first paragraphs by writers whose work they don't know. After they choose three writers who affect them the strongest, they go with the one who makes them vanish into the pages, and then they read everything that writer has written. I teach them how essential it is to give ourselves time for the silent and greedy reading we discovered as children, the reading we do just for ourselves, the reading that lets us emerge from a book dazed. Awed. Transformed.

Bill Holm

More Shelf Space

Here in the harsh north, today, April 17 is the first flicker of something like spring. The plastic comes off the windows and the wind makes its first appearance inside my old house since October. The new fresh air blows up aureoles of dust from the piles of books in window ledges, on coffee tables, rising from the floor in cobwebby corners. The piano and the harpsichord are heaped with two-foot stacks of scores: Haydn, Clementi, Fats Waller, the Hamburg Bach, James P. Johnson. In the front hall sit a couple of cases of fresh books waiting to be unloaded. Maybe the kitchen table? We can always eat out. . . . In his fifty-second year, a man needs a motto for his life to sew it together with some sense of direction. Here's mine: he ran out of shelf space—again.

As you wander from room to room, notice that no bed or couch is without both a shelf and an extra pile of books in arm's length. Both bathrooms are well stocked. There's a couple hundred cookbooks in the kitchen, plus the current piles of Chinese history and poetry waiting on the old oak hutch to be read today. All these tons of heavy books live precariously on top of an old cracked foundation built right over the tall grass prairie. The century-old beams of the house lean toward each other wearily, making crooked doorways, floors that slant toward the center. The bookcases are all shimmed and jerry-rigged to keep them upright. Each day new books arrive by mail, or after little side trips to library sales or used bookstores for bargains too good to be ignored. What's not here? Computer, printer, TV, fax.

There's a non-touchtone phone, often unplugged or ignored. This is an unashamed Luddite house that ignores its own century and its passing whims, and longs instead for more shelf space.

Since I live in this chaos of print, I must always have wanted it. The nest we make is the mirror of our soul. Indeed my first bedroom in an old farmhouse eight miles north was clotted with books too. A neighbor stored my bedroom furniture when my mother and father moved off the farm thirty-five years ago. She returned the bed and table last year. I opened the drawer and found it full of paper left there since 1961. *The Complete Poems of Poe,* a Gideon *New Testament* (to gather ammunition for argument), Unitarian pamphlets, *100 Best-Loved Poems,* a 1960 Yale catalog (I had big dreams . . .), and small notebooks full of poems, essays, and quotations. This was a teenager not likely to love Nixon, serve in Vietnam gladly, make any money, or amount to much in the American scheme of things. He didn't. The drawer told the truth. But he gathered books and scores by the thousands, and now finds himself at fifty-two almost buried by them. He is out of shelf space again.

I loved books in two ways. First, I read them like an addict. A day—even an hour or two—without print makes me edgy and hungry. I hide books in my car, both trunk and cubbyhole, in my office drawers, in side pockets of duffel bags. I buy small books to carry in my shirt pocket, just in case. The vision of jail with a good library is not so bad. With no books, I'd be a fine candidate for suicide. I became a teacher of literature because I could think of nothing else that gave me an excuse to read for money—albeit a pittance. My chief misery as a teacher is to have lived to teach in rooms full of Americans for whom books are not a matter of life and death, but only a trifle, a boring nuisance to be endured on the way to the computer lab and an office job. Books contain the seven basic food groups of the soul.

Ignore them and you starve inside; you die with a malnourished, shrivelled, bony spirit. Your computer will not feed you. Montaigne and Walt Whitman and Willa Cather will serve you elegant and nourishing dishes. Take and Eat.

But I love books also as they might be loved by an illiterate sensualist. I love the bite of lead type on heavy rag paper, the sexy swirls of marbled endpapers, the gleam and velvety smoothness of Morocco calf, the delicate India paper covering the heavy etching of the frontispiece, the grand heft of Gibbon or some collected works, the faint perfume of mildew in old English editions, the ghost smells of ink and the glue in bindings. I feel my books. I run my hands over them as over skin or fur. I stroke them and sniff them and admire them from various angles in various light. The first time I visited a Russian Orthodox church (in Sitka, Alaska), I watched the black moustached Metropolitan emerge from behind his gold doors in a great cloud of incense. The choir surged louder in four almost-in-tune parts. The Metropolitan bent ceremoniously down and kissed the Book. That's right, I thought! The right thing to do with a book! I will go home to Minneota and light a candle and every night I will kiss a book. Tomorrow *Leaves of Grass,* and after that *The Iliad* and after that the *Well-Tempered Clavier* and after that some random shelfless book from the top of a dusty pile that's lonesome for the living breath of a human being. More shelf space, says the Universe, more shelf space!

Ellen Howard

The Magic of Reading

IT IS A PUZZLING QUESTION. What *was* it that made me a reader? What was it that gave me my love of books?

My mother says that, as a toddler, I was perfectly happy to be tucked into a corner of the sofa with a book on my lap. I would turn the pages carefully, gazing as though hypnotized by the pictures and the words which I could not read. When my father presented me with my first tricycle, it was not long before I was discovered sitting on the front steps, turning the pages of a picture book. The child next door was riding my new trike up and down the sidewalk. We had made a trade!

I did not learn to read until first grade, but it seems to me now that Mrs. Lindholm had only to present me with a "magic decoder" in those first weeks of school, and I was reading. I have been reading ever since.

A typical day from my childhood: My grandmother's voice calls up the stairwell, "Breakfast is ready." I pull on my underpants and read a page. "Your breakfast is getting cold," Granny calls. I put on a sock and read a page. "Get down to breakfast RIGHT NOW!" I can hear the shrillness in her voice. I put on the other sock *and* a shoe. I even tie the shoe. But then I *must* just read one more page!

I read as I walk to school, only glancing up momentarily as I cross the street. I hurry through my classwork so I can read my library book. I read as I eat my lunch. I read during recess, hiding beneath the bleachers so the P.E. teacher won't force me into a game. I read when I should be cleaning my room. I read at night when I should be asleep.

On Thursdays my friend Christie and I walk the twenty-six blocks to the library where we each check out the children's limit—five books apiece. We both read all ten before the next Thursday.

In high school, I am taunted by names, "Bookworm" and "Brain." The reading is worth it!

Why? Why do I love to read so much?

Surely it had something to do with Mother. (Another family story tells of the day that my father went to work, leaving Mother in her nightgown at the breakfast table, reading. When he returned that evening, she was still there, the breakfast dishes unnoticed all about her, just finishing her book.) She read to us children from our infancies. Until we were old enough to understand the words, she read aloud to us whatever she was reading. But later she began sharing her own favorite children's stories. She had been brought up on the *My Book House* books, edited by Olive Beaupré Miller, so we were brought up on them too. Those six weighty black volumes, illustrated with intricate drawings, contained nursery rhymes and stories, fairy and folktales, excerpts from the classics, poetry and biographies. I know that her love of those stories, her delight in the printed word, her own passion for reading must have been conveyed to us from our first days.

I'm sure it had also to do with my grandmother, with her innate sense of the beauty of language. She could recite all the English nursery rhymes, quote from the Bible, and sing the old hymns from memory as she worked. The telling and hearing of family stories was her chief entertainment. I can remember sitting under the kitchen table, where I was out from underfoot, listening to Granny and her sisters and daughters and nieces tell those stories as they washed dishes after a holiday meal.

It also had to do, I am certain, with the reverence my

family showed for books. They were considered precious, handled carefully, hoarded with pride.

Perhaps it had something to do with the fact that, until I was nine years old, we had no television. I was well-addicted to books before the distraction of TV entered our home.

But all these influences do not sufficiently explain my seemingly instinctive attraction to books, the ease with which I learned to read them, my preference for stories over real, everyday life.

My brother and sister were only slightly younger than me. All the influences that worked on me must have worked on them. Yet, though they too loved stories as all children do, when he was little my brother would as soon dismantle a book as look at it. My sister much preferred her dolls and toys.

Learning to read for them was agony. They found no "magic decoders" at school. Though both are competent and intelligent people, neither learned to read with any fluency until adulthood. "I can't understand why Dan gives such beautiful oral reports when a written one seems beyond him," his teachers would say. "Kathy understands perfectly when something is told to her," her teachers would complain, "but she doesn't seem to understand written information." To this day, reading is not *their* joy.

Reading ability is necessary to all of us in the modern world, but I must conclude from my own family's experience that a *love* of reading is a special inborn gift. Reading can, and should, be nurtured by early happy experiences with books and stories. It can, and should, be competently and creatively taught. It can, and should, be treated with the respect due it as a source of information and entertainment and insight.

But the *joy* of reading, I believe, is a gift. It has to do with who we are and to what we aspire. It has to do with our individual weaknesses and strengths. I do not love mathematics or mechanics or sports, though to live fully I need some understanding of these things. I do not believe that *everyone* can, or even should, *love* to read. But everyone, I believe, needs, at least, to know *how* to read.

After that, it is up to the books themselves to work their magic where they will. For me, they always have.

Susan Kenney

A House of Books: My Book House

I don't remember it not being there—the series of twelve tall, slim volumes, ranging in color from pea-green through grass to emerald to deep forest, changing over at volume eight to navy blue, cobalt, teal, then up through ever-lighter shades of blue, until the last, a rich cerulean that matched the color of the deepest blue sky overhead. I say "it" because I never thought of them as separate volumes but as parts of a whole, just as bands of different-colored light make up the rainbow. This was *My Book House,* an anthology of great works of literature edited and arranged for children by Olive Beaupré Miller, from Aesop to Israel Zangwill, "Ring Around a Rosy" to "The Rose and the Ring"—literature from the ground up. For me it was a house of many mansions, as I read my way steadily upward through my childhood from palest green to heavenly blue.

Of course, at the time I knew nothing of this inspirational onward and upward motif, much less the concept of graded reading. According to my mother, I was too busy fueling my soon-to-be five-year-old imagination with the trials and tribulations of Helen Trent, Just Plain Bill, and Mary Noble, Backstage Wife. Hoping to wean me from my preternatural addiction to afternoon soap operas, in desperation she invested the not inconsiderable sum of fifty dollars in a set of books recommended by an aunt who was an educator, and presented it to me one day while we were still living in Pittsburgh. Here was something that would be much better for my young mind than listening to those lurid fifteen-minute radio dramas. She pointed out that there were short, easy things to read in the beginning and harder ones at the end, but that as I grew up, the stories would grow with me. Or was it the other way around? In any case, there it was: The Rainbow Edition of *My Book House,* in twelve colorful, imposing volumes. At an inch a pop, one whole linear foot of books.

Well, fine. I could see it would take me a while, particularly since I did not yet know how to read, but somehow I got the idea that the faster I worked my way from the green end to the blue, the quicker I would be grown up and in charge of my own life. In an attempt to finesse the initial inch, I instantly declared myself too old for the first volume, *In the Nursery,* with its baby rhymes and jingles and large, brightly-colored pictures of Goosey Gander and Wee Willie Winkie. After all, I was a kindergartner, and when it came to picture stories, preferred to stick to *Mickey Mouse* and other comic books my father read to me each night before I went to bed. Give me Little Lulu over Little Miss Muffet any day. Somewhat to my surprise my father concurred, and despite my mother's protests, *Tom and Jerry* won out over "Tom, Tom, the Piper's Son."

It seemed we were at a bit of an impasse as far as my educational reading went. But now that the plug had been yanked on my afternoon soap opera regimen, for lack of anything better to do I would often listen over my mother's shoulder as she read Mother Goose rhymes to my baby sister. This secretly sparked my interest, and since the entire *My Book House* had been shelved in the bookcase in my room, sometimes when I was supposed to be napping I would pick up the rejected pea-soup volume and leaf through the pages near the end. One day I came across a picture that showed a pair of rubbers and a huge umbrella marching along the sidewalk all by themselves. The black-and-white drawings accompanying the story illustrated the simple text so closely that by sounding out the letters, I could work out for myself the story that began: "Once there was a great big umbrella and once there was a little pair of rubbers. And the great big umbrella and the little pair of rubbers belonged to Barbara Ann." I was so enchanted with the image of the little girl hidden under an umbrella bigger than she was that for a while I went around calling myself Barbara (pronounced, until my mother corrected me, Bah-R-Bah-R-ah) Ann.

Browsing further, I discovered more scenes that reminded me of my own life, as in "The Elevator," "Good Morning, Peter," or "The Big Street in the Big City," and "The Police Cop Man." They were easy to read; in fact I was not even aware I was reading; it seemed to me I was telling myself the story that went with the pictures, just like the comics my father read to me each night, except that the words weren't in balloons.

So that was the beginning. I had discovered something magic; that words on the page made pictures in your mind, and you could take in a story with your eyes as well as through your ears.

The moss-green second volume also had lots of pictures—Peter Rabbit, the City Mouse and the Country Mouse, Krazy Kat, the Purple Cow—but not nearly as many in full color, and not so many to a page. In fact, there were whole pages, sometimes even two together, with just the words. This was more than I could tackle on my own, so one night I cajoled my father into reading to me out of *Story Time* instead of *Looney Tunes* at bedtime. This was how I learned about authors and titles, for my father did not begin at the beginning and read straight through. Each night he would run his finger down the table of contents, alphabetical by title, and say "How about this one?" Mostly we skipped the poetry, except for Edward Lear's nonsense rhymes, and read and reread "The Little Engine That Could," "The Ugly Duckling," or one of the many folktales from different lands. My favorite story of all was Carl Sandburg's Rutabaga story, "The Village of the Cream Puffs," featuring a little girl inexplicably named Wing Tip, who looked exactly like me with her braids, blue eyes, and freckles on her chin. How I envied Wing Tip, with her air of independence and the cool aplomb with which she bossed her silly uncles. When she described the Village of Cream Puffs as looking from "a long ways off like a little hat you could wear on the end of your thumb to keep the rain off," there was a picture of a thumb with a face grinning under a rain hat right next to the words. Although I could draw a face on my thumbnail, I never found a rain hat small enough to fit.

Soon it was time to move on to the next volume, grass-green *Up One Pair of Stairs.* Right away I knew we were on different turf, for the picture on the cover showed a girl sitting alone in a chair about to turn the page of the book on her lap, her doll some distance away on the floor with a book in her lap too. Obviously the doll over there in the corner couldn't read, but the little girl could. Was this a hint? Furthermore, instead of green silhouettes of Henny Penny and other baby barnyard creatures, the endpapers showed a detailed scene of a turreted castle far away in the distance, with a winding path and a group of children making their way toward it, and no adults in sight.

But the most striking change was in the illustrations. There were still lots of them, but they were all either plain black and white or colored in distinctive shades of orange and blue, so to this day I cannot pass a Howard Johnson's without being reminded of them. The stories themselves were much longer and more exciting, and I could hardly wait for my father to get down to the bottom of the page so we could turn over and find out what happened next. Thus it was by sneaking a peek underneath my father's fingers that I inadvertently let on what I had been keeping from my parents for some time: I could now read to myself faster then they could read to me aloud. It was just as well, for by now my mother had two babies, and my father's help was needed in putting them to bed. Though my father and I still looked at comic books together, as far as reading actual stories went, *My Book House* and I were on our own.

And so it went, in one book and out the next, *Through the Gate, Over the Hills, Through Fairy Halls, The Magic Garden,* from "The Cap That Mother Made" to "Verses on Kingsley's Water Babies," "The Peddler's Caravan" to "The Pert Fire Engine," "The Story of Tom Thumb" to "Thumbelisa." I remember being warmed by "The Nuremburg Stove" and chilled by "The Snow Queen." Little did I know when I first chanted it aloud that the song of "The Raggle Taggle Gypsies" would haunt me for the rest of my life, acquiring a new and personal meaning when I graduated into the first blue volume—number 8, *Flying Sails*—and read "Maggie Tulliver Goes to Live with the Gypsies." Life and fiction blurred as, furious with my mother, I proceeded to cut off my own hair, pack my little suitcase, and run away from home. Because my route was somewhat limited by the fact that I was not allowed to cross the street, I did not get far before she came and found me, sitting by a fence around the block. But both the theme and the action would persist in my imagination, and recur time and again in my own life and work, as would other images from the diverse pages of *My Book House.*

With the change of hue came more stylized endpapers, all black and orange and turquoise with stylized knights on horseback riding along a moat with a fierce-looking Viking ship in full sail and a castle wall in the background, its design vaguely reminiscent of Rockefeller Center. The tables of contents got shorter, the print smaller, and the stories even longer and more sophisticated. After *Flying Sails* came *The Treasure Chest, From the Tower Window, In Shining Armor,* and finally *Halls of Fame.* I was bored by the story of Daniel Boone (though the N. C. Wyeth cover illustration on volume 9 was certainly the best of the lot) and skipped ahead, determined to get through the fifty-odd pages of William Thackeray's *The Rose and the Ring,* the longest story of all, with its strangely formal language and even stranger drawings done by the author himself.

On the first page of *From the Tower Window,* with what looked to be Prince Valiant and a haughty lady on the cover, I was greeted by Chaucer's "A knyght ther was, and that a worthy man," in some very oddly spelled English. Here were El Cid, Lohengrin, Roland, Beowulf, Igor—Igor?—heroes, heroes, and more heroes with hardly a distressed damsel in sight; pretty musty material for a growing girl. Anyway, by now I could read whole story books at a single blow, and these epics were mostly ho-hum versions "retold from." The truth was, they could not hold my attention; I was bored. Though I would occasionally go back and dip into the chivalric tales, the historic sketches in the later volumes (but *not* the speech by Woodrow Wilson), and the biographies of famous authors, my pilgrimage through *My Book House* had run its course. There was no dearth of reading material in our house, for we had always been a bookish lot, so I headed straight for the bookshelves my father built and began reading my way through them—Louisa May Alcott, John Kendrick Bangs, J. M. Barrie, L. Frank Baum, and so on—alphabetically by author, of course, for I would never quite get over the systematic approach to reading that *My Book House* had instilled in me.

Just as I don't remember *My Book House* not being there, I don't really recall exactly when it disappeared. Perhaps it was given away, or sold, or merely lost in the years of upheaval after my father's sudden death, and our subsequent moves from one house to the next and back again, shedding toys and books and other childish possessions like so many unconsidered trifles. But even though the set itself had vanished, the stories and images, most particularly the illustrations in their distinctive HoJo colors, stayed in the landscape of my memory, to be recalled now and then when I come across one of the familiar stories in their original form—*Gulliver's Travels, The Mill on the Floss,* Spenser's *The Faerie Queen.* But in time those too began to fade. Out of print and out of favor—after all what was it but a bunch of excerpts and adaptations edited for young readers by some old biddie whose educational philosophy had long since been outmoded?—like Tinkerbell, *My Book House* might well have languished into oblivion, its magic dissipated by neglect.

Except that in odd ways, it kept turning up.

Fast forward twenty years. Two Ph.D.s in literature, two jobs teaching English in a small liberal arts college in Maine, and two kids later, my husband and I rent a house for our sabbatical in Ithaca, New York. I mount the stairs, suitcase and baby in hand—and there it is. Twelve volumes from pea-green to heavenly blue—stacked like crayons in a shelf full of children's books in the hall. Swamped by nostalgia, in my haste to verify this vision, fortunately I drop the suitcase and not the baby. But yes, it is identical, the very same Rainbow edition, so much so that I even check the flyleaf to see if by chance it has my name on it, but no such luck. Also no luck with enchanting my own children, glued as they are to their afternoon regimen of cartoons, so I end up spending the year reading the whole thing over to myself. But as much as I would like to, I can't take it with me, so that's that.

Or so I think. A year or so later, I'm sitting in the living room of my friend who teaches nursery school, when I notice on the bookshelf over her TV several tall dark blue volumes with a faded but familiar configuration of titles and numbers on the spines. Could it be? It is. To be sure, hers is an earlier all blue edition with fewer volumes, several missing; still, inside it is the same old *My Book House.* Leafing through volume 5, I come across the orange-and-turquoise pictures of Tom Thumb and Thumbelisa, and realize with a jolt of recognition that these are the "tiny real people, small enough to sit in my hand" that young Sara wishes for in a story I've just written called "Mirrors."

And yet again. A new friend and I are reciting a litany of favorite childhood books we have in common despite our diverse backgrounds—*The Tales of Mrs. Tiggy-Winkle, Uncle Wiggily, Mrs. Wiggs of the Cabbage Patch,* and—*"My Book House?"* she shrieks. "My dear, of course! And I still have it!" But hers is no mere collection of dull blue volumes, nor is it a graduated set of green to blue. It is the deluxe original edition; six fancy gray-green volumes ranged like pillars in their own little foot-high wooden house with a peaked roof and red chimneys, three taller companion books with tales and pictures from around the world shelved in a portico on the left-hand side—literally a House of Books.

I am consumed with envy. Of course I don't really need the house; I'd gladly settle for a plain old twelve-volume set like my long lost one in good condition. But though I search out the odd volume now and then in dusty backrooms of used bookstores and buy it for the friend who's missing several, I never even lay eyes on an intact set, and it seems the chance of ever replacing the one I lost is nil. Besides, it's too late to share the magic anyway; my kids are reading Dr. Seuss and C. S. Lewis—when they're not watching the tube. To spend both time and money acquiring some useless, moldy relic of my childhood seems sheer self-indulgence at best. After all, we have a whole house full of books, yards and yards of every shape and size and color, who needs one more cool-end-of-the-spectrum-colored foot? So I gave up on *My Book House* once and for all.

But it didn't give up on me.

The next fall I am at the annual AAUW book sale in our town, a big event for book collectors or just plain readers, and a major dumping ground for beat-up, outdated, no-longer-wanted, as well as perfectly fine used books. A whole gymnasium full of books, books, books. I've brought in my own lot to donate, and am on my way to the mystery section when I catch a familiar flash of shape and color out of the corner of my eye. I turn, and catch my breath. There on the bleachers, flat on its back among the ragged assortment of loved-to-death children's books, I spy a ship in full sail against a background of cobalt blue. I fall upon it; sure enough, it's good old volume 8. But wait, here's yet another; the unmistakable Prince Valiant and his snooty Lady. I look around in disbelief, and spot a green one here, another blue one there. Spread out at random for the picking, each one priced separately at a dollar (pricey for this sale, but after all, they are hardcovers, with nice pictures, and in good shape); it seems as though no one has even realized they are in fact a set.

Except for me. Someone has not only unloaded an entire *My Book House,* but the very same edition that had captivated me all those years ago with its progression from green to blue. I clap my hands in gratitude; clearly it is meant.

I get to work and gather up all the ones I see—volumes 2, 6, 4, 3, 7—pile them up in the care of my next door neighbors Punch and Polly Grow, who are in charge of the whole affair, and head back into the fray to find the rest. Rummaging through more piles, I unearth 5, 9, 11, 8, and 10. My pile is growing, but two volumes still elude me. I tell my neighbors the story, and together we go hunt. But missing they remain, the two that bracket the rest, the end and the beginning—*In the Nursery* and *Halls of Fame.* Someone must have bought them before I got there, so I must content myself with just the ten.

And so I did; who needs nursery rhymes and an index

anyway? Once again *My Book House* would take its place of honor on the bookshelf, minus lightest green and brightest blue to be sure, but no matter; the rest of it was there for my children to dip into if they still had a mind to, for me to browse through and call up images at will—Old Stormalong, Maggie and the Gypsies, The Little Engine That Could. No Barbara Ann, no Hans Christian Andersen, but here was Wing Tip of the cream-puff-shaped freckles, straightening out her uncles as deftly as ever. I could almost hear Pecos Bill strumming "Ten Out of Twelve Ain't Bad." As I have written elsewhere in a more serious context: perfect is the enemy of good.

You would think that's the end of the story, but it's not. I have always thought that what happened next was true *Book House* magic, but then it seems to me that's what reading is.

Snow falls, spring comes, then summer, and another fall, almost time for the AAUW book sale again. A knock on the door: it's my neighbors. They have a couple of books for me, they say, looking—well, pleased as Punch. And, what are they? None other than—the missing volumes 1 and 12 of *My Book House:* the very same.

A miracle? Not really. Before going to live with her daughter in California, the previous owner had cleaned out and donated all her books to the AAUW—or so she thought. When she finally got down to unpacking her last few boxes, she found the two stray volumes, and had shipped them off, with a brief note, to Polly. The note read: "I'm sending these to you on the remote chance you may know who got the others. If so, please pass them on. Whoever has the rest will want these too." Thank you, Betty Desmond, wherever you are.

So the two fugitive volumes took their place at each end of the blue-green spectrum, the set once more complete. And so it will stay, to be passed down to my children and their children—for as it turns out, all those years when I wasn't looking, they were busy thumbing their way through the crowded pages, taking in all the old stories with those strangely compelling illustrations in eye-catching orange and blue.

Postscript. Last summer in an antique flea market I ran across an intact earlier edition of *My Book House,* complete with house. The volumes were rubbed and a little whiffy, and the house had seen better days, but still, there it was. I stood there for a long time, glancing through the familiar pages, wondering if I should buy it. True, I already had a *My Book House,* but wouldn't it be fun to have one that actually came with the house? Should I become a collector?

No. Let someone else discover the magic. And so I passed it by.

Perri Klass

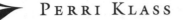

Years in The Life

Because my father was an anthropologist, and my family spent the year in a small village in India, I avoided Dick and Jane. I was five, and eager to read; my parents brought along flash cards to help me learn. But after I had memorized the flash cards, my father tried me out on a book he had brought to read aloud, a paperback copy of *The Wizard of Oz*. He helped me over the hard words, encouraging me along, trying to make me see that individual words, learned off file cards, were what books were made of. I have a very vivid memory of making my way slowly through the first page, word by word by word. "There . . . were . . . four . . . walls . . . a . . . floor . . . and . . . a . . . roof . . . which . . . made . . . one . . . room . . . and . . . this . . . room . . ." There was a long and unfamiliar word looming up in front of me; my father would have to supply it. Then something clicked inside my head: "Contained . . ." I said, and kept right on going, ignoring my father's approving noises. The first time I ever figured out a new two-syllable word from context, the beginning of the end of "sounding out" words.

It was the first paragraph of the first page not only of my first real chapter book, but also the first paragraph of the first page of my first series. When we got back to New York City, I would find all the Oz books in the Morningside Heights Public Library, and I would solemnly chomp my way through them, not once, but many many times. The fourteen L. Frank Baum books—some people think he stopped after *The Wizard of Oz*. They know nothing of Tik-Tok and Rinkitink and the Lost Princess. And then there was

Ruth Plumly Thompson, who picked up the series after Baum died and wrote another nineteen volumes.

But back there in India, there were no other Oz books available. The local library did, however, have some rather antique British children's books, including the Doctor Doolittle series. So I went from flash cards to Oz to Puddleby-on-the-Marsh, and I spent that year in India doing the Doctor Doolittle series. And by then I already knew how to describe books with the peculiar indefinite article of the series book: *a* Doctor Doolittle book. *A* new Oz book. *A* Betsy-Tacy book I haven't read yet.

I spent my childhood reading one series after another. Laura Ingalls Wilder, Maud Hart Lovelace, Lucy Maud Montgomery, C. S. Lewis. Oh, and the Bobbsey Twins, I was very involved with the Bobbsey Twins for a couple of years there. But I never really connected with Nancy Drew, that queen of the juvenile series. And maybe that was because Nancy Drew novels, though there are many of them, exist somewhat independently of one another, without any obvious progression from one to the next. You can read them in any order; she's not growing up or changing, or not in any way I remember. She's just solving mysteries as they come along.

But the girls in the Little House books grow up and change. Anne goes from her first appearance at the age of ten in *Anne of Green Gables* through adolescence and adulthood; by *Rilla of Ingleside,* she's a mother of six, with two sons fighting in the First World War. And even in the Oz books, though the characters don't age, thanks to various magic properties, things change from book to book; Ozma becomes queen in one book and stays queen in the books that follow; Dorothy moves to Oz; other characters appear and join the standing cast.

And there's something both soothing and compelling about the sense of a series, about that awareness of change mixed with continuity. You come to the end of a book, deeply enmeshed with the characters, still involved in their lives—and you know you will eventually find out what happens next. It isn't like reading a singleton novel, which starts and ends at carefully chosen artistically suitable moments. Series books are days in the life, years in the life, parts of the life. There is a peculiar gluttonous delight in starting a new volume, and a remarkable sybaritic joy in going back over and rereading the ones you have read before. Yes, all fiction offers alternate worlds, but series fiction offered me more complete deeper alternate worlds, worlds which could be visited and revisited at will.

So all through elementary school I was a devoted reader, and my range was fairly wide. I was fortunate in going to a school which valued books and reading, and which operated on progressive principles; once you got your work done, you were entitled to spend the rest of your time doing anything you wanted to do. Ironically, I only landed in that school because of Dorothy and Dr. Doolittle and Dick and Jane; when we got back from India, my parents tried to enroll me in the local "regular" school, only to discover that I was going to have to be taught to read all over again, along with all the other six-year-olds. Years of Dick and Jane stretched ahead of me; there was no provision made for those who had other things to read.

So instead, my parents sent me to a school where I could and did spend large parts of every day on a brown vinyl couch in the library. There was a wonderful school librarian who pushed books at me, one after another, and there were wonderful teachers who read real books aloud to their classrooms. A couple of years ago my fourth-grade teacher saw my name on a book I had written and called me up. Did I remember her, she asked. "Miss Marecek!" I said. "The reading candle! *A Wrinkle in Time!*"

Now she's a professor of education and I'm a pediatrician.

Recently she reminded me of what she used to say, every day, when reading aloud was over, and we all blew out the reading candle. "There go your wishes, up in the smoke," she would say. "May they all come true."

And then, when I was in sixth grade, my parents moved to the suburbs, so the children could grow up with a yard and without the various dangers of the city. And in that good safe suburban school system, I found myself for the first time in a situation in which reading in school was generally a crime. You were supposed to sit and listen, even if you knew the lesson, even if you were bored past all boredom. You were supposed to read only at reading time, and then you were supposed to read what your group was reading. Dick and Jane had gotten me after all.

I was in every way a weird and out-of-place child in that school, and though I tried desperately to fit in for a year or two, chopping off my braids and searching the mall for clothes that looked like what the other kids were wearing, and circulating slam books, I got nowhere. I suddenly discovered that I was a strange ugly gross misfit. I hated myself, I hated my classmates, and I hated my teachers. This did not do anything particularly good for my character, but I will spare you the rather elaborate Pirate Jenny style mass murder fantasies which became my schooltime entertainment. When I was not actively involved in imagining the doom of my contemporaries, though, I retreated into story lines borrowed from books, usually from those same series. I would walk home from school at lunchtime, narrating my walk home inside my head—largely to spare myself the awareness that in fact I was a weird-looking child walking home alone because no one wanted to walk with me. Instead, I would tell myself every detail of my walk—in the third person.

"She paused at the corner, hesitating, watching every moment to see if the German soldiers were nearby. Then she slipped across the street, moving swiftly but silently." There was one block where I could walk on a little grassy rise instead of on the sidewalk: "Her skillful feet clung to the mountain path as she hurried towards the hut. . . ." Everything interesting in my brain started to happen in the third person. I narrated my meals to myself as I ate them, narrated my own gestures as I brushed my teeth in the morning or lay down in bed at night.

And so I grew up to be a writer, not much to my surprise. Many of the heroines I cared most about in fiction wanted to be writers—probably because that was part of what the authors remembered from their own girlhoods. Jo in *Little Women,* Betsy in the Betsy-Tacy books, Lucy Maud Montgomery's *Anne of Green Gables* and *Emily of New Moon* both, not to mention Harriet in *Harriet the Spy,* and Laura in the Little House books, who never becomes a writer in the books, but grew up to be the author, Laura Ingalls Wilder. And every single one of those girls I mentioned exists in at least three books.

So what was the message of all those books? Why did they grab me so, from the very moment I could read? What did they mean to me when I felt myself alone and misunderstood? Perhaps by their very nature series books assure us that life is made up of many different parts, that growth and change are possible, that there is another episode to look forward to. And that life is more interesting when it is narrated, and that little girls who tell stories inside their heads can grow up to be writers and tell stories on the printed page. And, of course, that she who writes the story is finally and completely in charge of what happens next.

 WAYNE KOESTENBAUM

First Books

SOME OF THE FIRST BOOKS I remember reading: a biography of Harriet Tubman; Signet paperbacks about witchcraft (how-to manuals); *Tituba of Salem Village;* endless encyclopedia entries about the movies. I remember spending recesses, in elementary school, at the library, reading *World Book* and *Collier* encyclopedia capsule histories of the cinema, which always included references to *Nanook of the North,* which I've still never seen. Also I read a book by Lita Grey, Chaplin's child bride, about her scandalous relationship with Charlie (somewhere in that book I remember she said that the star "corrupted" her by exposing her to such erotica as *Fanny Hill*). And I read books about childbirth: again, how-to manuals. This was in the days of *Childbirth Without Fear.* I guess I also read novels, and boy-child crap like *Encyclopedia Brown,* and a wonderful book called *Black and Blue Magic,* and the classic *Half Magic* (by Edward Eager?): I'd go for *anything* about magic. But mostly I read for illicit information: I sought arcane knowledge about how to mesmerize enemies and friends (a favorite spell concerned burying a mirror at the crossroads, and I remember puzzling about how to bury a mirror beneath a paved sidewalk), how to give birth, how to have sex, how to make movies. . . . Also I was fond of books about amateur photography, even though I wasn't particularly interested in photography.

I started reading poems in junior high: my eighth grade teacher, a world traveler named Mrs. Clarke, had us read

Emily Dickinson and go out to the field and eat daisies and then write a poem about the experience. (Or so I recall.) Another assignment was to memorize one hundred lines of poetry. For no good reason I chose "The Raven," in which my favorite phrase was, indubitably, "balm in Gilead," because I didn't know what it meant. Also there was a lovely Sara Teasdale poem I found in my mother's copy of an Oscar Williams anthology—I think the poem was about loss, and September, and something about trees in a park? I memorized it. Also I memorized Richard Wilbur's poem about the dead dog. And "Mending Wall." And an Elizabeth Barrett Browning sonnet. I thought of poems as an elaborate, beautiful, spidery type of homework, but not at all akin to reading, which meant the pursuit of forbidden knowledge, mostly about magic and sex and movies.

Then I went into a reading coma: or my reading went underground, became vaguely unconscious. I read for thrills, at this point, but didn't call it "reading"; I'd look for the dirty passages in great books. My favorites were *Myra Breckenridge, Our Lady of the Flowers, Lady Chatterley's Lover.* Those books I never read cover to cover; I just knew the sexual bits. Myra's rape of Rusty! Other, trashy books I took seriously and read cover to cover: *Valley of the Dolls, The Carpetbaggers. . . .* I was quite haunted by *Valley of the Dolls:* I read it while in a hotel room in Mexico City. My glasses were broken, and I couldn't see the tourist sights.

This isn't very highbrow!

The first book of poetry I actually bought and tried to read (as opposed to poems I was assigned to memorize) was by Herman Hesse, whom I thought was a great thinker, a European eminence right up there with Freud and Jung.

The poems were terrible but I loved the novels: I read *Steppenwolf* and thought it was like a Fellini film, though I'd never seen one.

I read *Gone With the Wind* in fifth grade; I wanted to read it in fourth, but my mother told me it was "trash," and wouldn't let me check it out from the library. Somehow by fifth grade she'd changed her mind about its merits, and I bought a blue paperback copy of it at Macy's. (Remember when Macy's sold books?) Certainly I identified with Wade, Scarlett O'Hara's son, whose refrain was "Wade hungwy." Then in sixth grade I wanted to give a book report on *Gone With the Wind,* but my teacher had a rule: we couldn't report on a book if we'd seen the movie version. I was crushed. I remember telling my father that my life was over, I was horribly depressed, because the one book with which I'd formed a passionate attachment was forbidden as subject for a "book report" (that supreme genre of vindication! chance to prove and demonstrate a plot to a captive audience of schoolchild peers!), so he recommended, as compensation, *Crime and Punishment.* I didn't take him up on the offer.

I also remember a formative encounter with *Doctor Zhivago,* which I wanted to read because I was in love with the ads for the movie. I went to the public library to check out the book, and looked under "Doctor" in the card catalogue, and a librarian came up to me and asked if she could help, and I said I was looking for books about doctors, and I had one in mind especially—*Doctor Zhivago*—and she said, "That's in the adult section," and guided me instead to medical books in the juvenile area. On a different day, when another librarian was on duty, I went back and checked out the oddly numinous *Zhivago,* which I didn't read, though I enjoyed the dust jacket.

I loved Andrew Lang fairy tale books. Especially yellow, blue, and red, as I recall. They came in colors. And Grimm's fairy tales. I remember one about a wheel of cheese rolling down a hill. A simpleton chases the wheel, which runs through village after village. I can still picture that wandering, out-of-control cheese.

I forgot to mention the all-important autobiography of Helen Keller, and a children's novel about a boy blinded by a firecracker, and a biography of Annie Sullivan.

Then came adulthood, and I read T. S. Eliot's essay about dissociation of sensibility, and the notion that a poet was the type of soul for whom the smell of cooking and the philosophy of Spinoza were united—ideas felt on the pulses—made "poet" seem an ideal identity, and I fell in love with poems: O'Hara, Rich, Sexton among contemporaries, and Yeats, Pound, Eliot, Keats, Wordsworth among the oldsters. In college, a dear friend read "Tintern Abbey" to me on the lawn. Already I felt quite ancient.

I forgot to mention: in high school I loved inspirational autobiographies of musicians and performers. Books by Wanda Landowska and Pablo Casals. (Many mornings still I remember Casals saying that he began every day by playing a Bach Prelude and Fugue.) And Elie Wiesel's *Night*. And *Marjorie Morningstar*. And Mel Tormé's *The Other Side of the Rainbow*.

I remember going on Friday evenings—right after supper—to the public library with my whole family. I was in love with the public library. How vividly I still can see the specific corridor where the books about film were shelved: *The Cutting Room Floor,* the history of screen censorship. . . . And the fairy tale region: I remember the books leaning against each other, because there weren't enough to fill out the shelf. One summer I participated in a program where you had to read twenty books to earn a certificate on which fake pearls (one per book?) were pasted. I lived for certificates. I associated books, too, with boxiness, with squareness and size. Chunkily a book—its deckle edges blurred and soiled—could close on its secrets.

My parents had miles of books, and I spent a long time exploring their shelves, without really reading the books—just sounding them out. But certain volumes seemed premonitory beacons: *Saint Genet*, by Sartre. I was fascinated by it. I don't know why. Because it was so fat, its cover so beige and bland? *The Second Sex*, by Simone de Beauvoir—a cheesy paperback edition with a nude woman (soft-focus) on the cover. These two were on my father's shelves. From my mother's shelves I remember the especial luminousness of a paperback *From Here to Eternity* (I think it was a reversible book: you could turn it upside down and a second novel—a bargain!—was nestled, a spectral twin, beside it), and of an early Joyce Carol Oates novel, *With Shuddering Fall*. I loved the word "shuddering," and the photo of Oates on the back cover of *them*. Also Nabokov's *Ada*. Nice fat book with a short short title, written by a man, but named after a woman. And *The Duino Elegies*, on my mother's shelf: the weird non-word "Duino." And the paperback Modern Library editions of Victorian novels, leftovers from her college years, with maternal handwritten marginalia. I was fascinated by the idea, new to me, that one could write comments in a book. The books that excited me the most were those my mother had signed with her maiden name: they seemed glamorously bygone.

Magazines. *Newsweek, Time, The New Yorker.* I cut out movie reviews and saved them in a clippings file. I knew that history was happening: the debut of Barbra Streisand, for example. I remember a cover story about her rise to fame. This, too, was reading.

Ted Kooser

King: A Dog of the North

When I was a freshman in college, when I was beginning to take myself seriously as a poet, I came down with pneumonia following a drunken tobaggoning party. I was very ill, hospitalized for ten days and out of my head with fever for all of the first week. The walls and ceiling of my room took on a strange, softly undulating life that terrified me. Once I saw glossy wet fur growing out of the grain of the wooden door. I later recalled having well-wishing visitors—friends and relatives—who in fact had never been to see me.

As my fever fluctuated, I experienced brief periods of clarity, and would lie with my sweaty bedding twisted about me, reading a book that someone had left by my bed. It was the only reading material in the room, a boy's novel about a German shepherd named King. Time and again, King came to the rescue of his blundering master. I knew that it was a book my intellectual college friends and teachers would sneer at, but my illness had reduced me to childishness, and as a child I fell for this simple, engrossing story. I was twenty years old, but because I was sick I had regressed to half that age. I was completely dependent upon the loving care of adults—my parents, my doctor and nurses. Near the end of my hospital stay, when my sweetheart of four years came to my hospital room to tell me that she had found another boyfriend, I let her go without an argument, having been beaten back into a bemused, passive, prepubescent state.

The story of the noble dog, King, sustained me against the billowy craziness upon which my bed floated and bobbed like a raft. His story was richly detailed and absorbing. He made his way through snowdrifts; up and down the sheer faces of mountains; through flooded, ice-choked streams. King's adventures were breathtaking, marvelous, and like the faithful dog he was, he was always within calling range whenever his master needed him.

When my temperature finally went down and stayed down, I began looking about the room for the book, but it was nowhere to be found. My nurses told me that I'd been given no books because I'd been much too ill to read. When my parents came to visit I asked them what had happened to it and they said that they couldn't recall ever seeing such a book. No one could account for the missing *King.*

But the book was vividly impressed upon my memory. I could still feel it in my hands and see its print in front of my eyes. It had to be there somewhere. I described it in detail: it had no dust jacket and was bound in red cloth frayed by wear; the binding was slightly sticky after holding it for a while; it was a little over an inch thick, and had a comfortable, serious-feeling heft to it; the pages were of good pre-war rag paper and had deckled edges; it had the good, glue-and-ink smell of a book; the spine was stamped with the title in gold foil: *King: A Dog of the North.*

There were, of course, many such books in print at the time, the dog story being a staple of juvenile reading, and I had possibly read one or two of them when I'd been younger. But what I came to believe is that in my delirium I wrote, printed, bound and published *King: A Dog of the North.* I made it all up. Just as King, the dog, was always there when his master fell into the arms of a bear, *King,* the book, had snatched me from the jaws of pneumonia.

I have been a writer ever since. Oh, I'd written some poems before I got pneumonia, but it took pneumonia to make me serious about writing. The creation of *King: A Dog of the North,* a solid accomplishment of the imagination, may have given me the confidence to try my hand at letting my imagination carry me forward, toward other stories, and poems, and essays like this one. And whatever success I've had as a writer I may owe in some part to that magnificent silver-haired German shepherd who vanished into the frozen wasteland once he had finally seen me back to health. Writing late at night, sometimes I think I hear his great paws padding through the snow.

In the Company of Books

IN THE BEGINNING was the Word. I was a lonely little girl growing up in suburban Waltham, Massachusetts, and the mystery of reading was my means to an end, my seemingly surefire way to be close to the people who were the most distant to me. When I was three, reading was the one way I could have a relationship with Ellie, a six-year-old deaf girl who lived down the block, whose raw guttural speech baffled me, and who nevertheless used to read the funny pages out loud to me every Sunday at my house. I never understood a single word that Ellie said, but I loved her and was desperate for her company. I lay on the rug and watched her face and her gestures. I gazed deep into the pictures she was pointing out, until I half-figured out what must be happening, and half-made it up. I cherished those Sundays with Ellie, right up until Ellie was sent off to a special school in California a year later. In homage to her, I kept the home fires burning, continuing to pretend to read the funnies on my own, working with surprising joy, until, gradually, with a little help from my book-loving mother, I unlocked the secrets and learned to read.

If reading gained me time with a friend, it gained me something even more astonishing: the company of my silent, distant father. My father lived for his books, which were scattered in every room of the house, and as soon as he noticed I could read, he noticed me as well, and he began taking me to the library with him, where I was encouraged to take out as many books as I could carry.

My father and I read together for hours in companionable

silence, sitting in the backyard on a lawn chair, sprawled on the beach or on a train, and although we never even exchanged smiles, or had a real conversation, in a way, we didn't have to. My father told me things through the books he gave me, choices that showed me a world I might like and the world that he loved. When I was nine, he plunked a dozen copies of his *Weird Tales* magazines casually into my lap. I read about holes in the universe causing people to disappear and monsters appearing in the dark and my imagination began to awaken and then to soar far beyond our scrubby backyard. When he saw how avidly I was devouring the magazines, he brought me books by H. G. Wells and Ray Bradbury. He introduced me to Raymond Chandler and Dashiell Hammett and Edgar Cayce.

And I did my part for our relationship, often with unexpected results. I picked up a book about ants called (I believe) *The City Under The Back Steps,* wanting to dazzle my father with my taste for the esoteric. In the book, two children shrink to ant size and spend a year living among a colony, but this book, intended to impress, instead hit me like an electric current, and began, all on its own, my lifelong fascination with the crawling world. I requested *1984* only because I thought reading it might somehow make me as pretty and stylish and acceptable to my father as Holly, the *Seventeen* magazine model who had touted it as a favorite, but as soon as I began to read, the model's looks suffered in comparison with her book—and I never thought of her in the same way again.

My father and I never once discussed a book the whole time he was alive (the few times I tried were greeted with monosyllabic replies) but I cannot remember my father without remembering the worlds he opened up to me with books—his acts and expression of love—and their glimpses into the man he was.

But if reading brought me closer to the people I loved,

it also helped me separate from and gain solace against the people I feared and a life I was unhappy with. At sixteen, I was a loner in my working-class high school, smart and offbeat looking and belonging nowhere. I was threatened with being beaten up, ridiculed for my good grades. In defense, I began carrying something to read with me everywhere. With a book in my hand, I was somewhere else, where extraordinary possibilities—and different lives—could be mine with just a turn of the page. I wasn't in a sour-smelling cafeteria dodging slurs and flying pats of butter, but I was a dancer in Spain. I was in love in a Paris café. I read about other writers and because their struggles seemed close to mine, because they seemed to love and need words as much as I did, I began to think I could be a writer, too, creating new worlds as well as experiencing them. Books—and writing—became my mood elevator, my comforter, my escape, my ammunition. I read voraciously through three years of high school, so enthralled I didn't hear the taunts or feel the scorn. People talk about virtual reality, but to me, reading is *actual* reality—a step across the threshold into a world as vivid and indelible as life itself.

Books helped me find my way. They began as a way to get close to others and ended up letting me discover myself. I'm not the lonely, scrappy little girl anymore. I became a writer. And my need for reading is still an addiction I want to push rather than cure. I am always sending books to friends. I write books with a need that borders on insanity. And now I'm pregnant with a son, and my husband and I read to him through my belly, giving him his prenatal word vitamins, so he, too, knows there are miraculous possibilities beyond the womb and that he can begin to experience them—and himself—through books. Because in the beginning is the Word—and it's holy, holy, holy, now and always, most wonderfully holy.

Elinor Lipman

Orphans, Stalwarts, and Plucky Girls

One of the best and least pretentious ideas I ever heard from a podium was novelist Robert Stone's comment that the purpose of a novel was to make the reader feel less lonely. When he said it to a Texas size book-and-author luncheon audience, a corroborating murmur passed though the room. I was waiting my turn to speak, considering my upcoming remarks more than I was listening to Mr. Stone's, but his quiet declaration flew into my ears and lodged itself in my heart.

Not that it applied to me, I thought at the time. "Loneliness" was not the noun that explained why I read so much. Months later I changed my mind when I pictured myself as a child reading and rereading my favorite books with a peculiar devotion that had to be the flip side of loneliness.

I wasn't by definition lonely: I had two doting parents, an older sister who sometimes played with me and shared a room, plus friends, cousins, aunts and uncles. But I wasn't great at being a child; I preferred the company of adults, was happier indoors than out, didn't consider myself fun or adventurous. The neighborhood kids were either younger or older and they traveled in packs. I felt they were doing me a favor when they called.

So I read whenever I could find a loophole in the law that children should play outside after school. I was the baby, mama's girl, a mouse. My favorite books, the ones I reread obsessively, were about orphans or semi-orphans, girls who were stalwart: *Daddy-Long-Legs* by Jean Webster, my all-time favorite; *Anne of Green Gables, Pollyanna, The Secret Garden,*

The Wizard of Oz, and all the novels made into Shirley Temple movies: *The Littlest Colonel, Rebecca of Sunnybrook Farm, The Little Princess, Heidi.*

I liked tragedy, but only what I could manage. Because I had a safe home and a nuclear family, I think I found missing parents to be an imaginable dilemma, my ten-year-old version of living on the edge.

I wanted my heroines to talk back—I could hardly open my mouth in class until fourth grade, and when I did, my teachers couldn't hear what I was saying. (*Anne of Green Gables* was the ultimate assertive role model.) Both Anne and Pollyanna were the way I wanted to be: good, but no pushover, spirited, funny, clever, and brave. I was afraid of horror and monsters and the dark, so a confident heroine who yelled back was all the daring I required.

Pippi Longstocking didn't work for me. She lived alone (I knew there were laws against this), so there was a magical element to her coping that I didn't trust. I liked structure; I liked my orphans to have guardians or orphanage trustees or kindly servants *(The Secret Garden)* around them. Or best of all, strong, silent, bearded grandfather types like those in *Heidi* and *The Littlest Colonel.*

Back in real life, I was closely monitored. The children in my favorite books had autonomy and the freedom to solve mysteries and go on adventures. I loved girls who outwitted adults, pushed boys around figuratively (Nancy Drew, Jo March, Pollyanna), and led groups of other plucky citizens on adventures (*The Wizard of Oz, Our Hearts Were Young and Gay* by Cornelia Otis Skinner and Emily Kimbrough; *Two Little Women on a Holiday* by Carolyn Wells).

When I ran out of orphan stories, there were resilient children from single-parent families to love: Nancy Drew, my hero along with Jerusha Abbott, orphan turned college student of *Daddy-Long-Legs,* and the siblings of the *Five Little Peppers and How They Grew* (plus sequels)—a saintly mother, brave, hungry children, all managing on potatoes, thrilled to have a tiny cake of brown flour with raisins on a birthday. ("The father had died when Phronsie was a baby, and since then Mrs. Pepper had had to work to scrape together money enough to put bread into her children's mouths and to pay the rent of the Little Brown House.") I loved the hovel part and I loved when they moved into the mansion of a rich but exceedingly nice family.

I didn't mind boy characters, as long as they were non-interfering and not the heroes of these books. (We had no boys in my family.) Polly Pepper had brothers, but she was the family brick. I liked the fact that Nancy Drew's boyfriend, Ned, was something of a schlemiel, and that Nancy had her driver's license (my mother never drove, so that skill seemed Amelia Earhart-ish to me). And *Jane Eyre*! Orphan turns governess—ah, heaven.

Little Women, of course, had much to recommend it: one parent off fighting in a war, a distracted mother, an all-girl family, an author-hopeful as its heroine, and a boy neighbor who was, let's face it, no macho threat.

I liked novels where the heroines wanted to write (*Daddy-Long-Legs* again), which appeared to be a career with the comforts of reading—solitary, indoors, under the eaves of a garret room. It seemed so civilized: you wrote by the fire then sent stories away to magazines in big cities where a kindly editor in a cutaway invited you to tea. I liked their quills and inkpots and I liked the way these young writers saved their pennies for sheaves of paper. To prepare myself for a similar future, I didn't write, but I chose a pen name (never used): Malcolm Brody.

The Little Princess was a tad too tragic for my taste—no mother, a reluctantly absent then heroically dead father, a cruel headmistress who got what she had coming, so I read it only twice. And *The Little Match Girl*—what a betrayal, death. For a long time, I steered away from male authors.

It seems my loneliness was treatable: I found friends on the page who were constant and true no matter how many times I called on them. They were always home. We never fought. Their worlds were small and accessible, and I was happy there.

These stories about orphans and poor families were, in a sense, romances that a little girl could digest. They promised happy endings, reunions, windfalls. They said to me, *Children who are alone can be safe and secure and happy, so you don't have to worry.*

I inferred from the lives of Anne, Pollyanna, Jerusha, Heidi, Dorothy, Mary, and all the Peppers that for every act of cruelty there is an equal and opposite act of kindness and generosity. The rude and mean get punished. The poor get comfortable. The orphaned get adopted. These familiar stories were my private society of reliable friends, and all I had to do to belong was to read them.

Susan Lowell

Reading Up

I STAND ALONE on stage before an audience of five hundred faces, and nightmarish panic seizes me.

"But you don't have to sing or dance," I comfort myself. "You just have to read to them."

To read! To breathe! Nothing could be easier, no pleasure more vital. So I step forward and face not a many-headed monster but a group of children. They are the students of Lincoln Elementary School in the town of Prescott, Arizona, where on a fall morning nearly forty years ago, with a missing tooth, a skinned knee, and perpetually unravelling pigtails, I first breathlessly opened a primer: "See Dick. See Dick run. Run, Dick, run!"

In all my life, I've never wanted anything more than I wanted to learn to read, and reading has never disappointed me. Poor Dick, it is true, ran and ran and never got anywhere, but luckily I already knew that the world was full of other books, not textbooks but real books, and they were full of power. My brother and I had listened while my mother read nursery rhymes, Pooh stories, and *Charlotte's Web* (we all wept). I watched enviously while my mother read to herself; I watched while my father doggedly studied. We were nomads in those days—Lincoln was the second of six elementary schools that I attended—and my parents owned almost nothing, but we did carry along with us several boxes of books (mostly old and used, including the tooth-marked survivors of an attack by rats while in storage), and one of these books particularly obsessed me.

In it, Hansel and Gretel had glassy pink skin and fixed

goggle-eyed stares, but their spilled milk looked real, and it probably was, since this strange board book was illustrated with photographs of a puppet show. The tempting gingerbread house was also probably edible. Oddest of all was the fact that the front cover of *Hansel and Gretel* was also a 45 rpm record that squawked out a little tune about a mousie nibbling on a housie, which I was startled to recognize in the Engelbert Humperdinck opera twenty years later. The summer before I went to first grade, a visiting first-grade graduate read *Hansel and Gretel* over and over to me, and I deeply, darkly craved her magical skill.

But reading is pure. It has the thrill of skiing and the primal satisfaction of food, but you don't fall down, and you don't get fat. I do know a girl who broke her arm reading, but that was because she tried to ride her bicycle at the same time. Readers have friends, freedom, equality, and control over their destinies, although their experiences may not be pure or sweet. *Hansel and Gretel* is, after all, a story about starvation, child abuse, and cannibalism, but it leaves a young reader, and especially a girl, with a glorious sense of triumph over evil. Returning with my children to the old tales, I found them richer than ever, and a source for my own writing.

Miraculously, the furnished house that my parents rented in Prescott came with full bookshelves, including a children's collection arranged in ascending order of difficulty, so I lay on my stomach and read my way up the wall until we had to move again. I mainly remember some preachy stories about a family of squirrels who wisely never drank cold water when they were hot. Neither at home nor in school nor in the subterranean children's room of the old Prescott Library was there any book even remotely resembling the life I knew as a Western child of the 1950s. But I was no longer a child, no small weak mortal female stuck in a particular place and time, but a shape-changer of infinite range.

Throughout all our moves, my written universe held steady. Or rather, it steadily expanded.

I see now that my own story is part of a larger pattern, and certain books tell the tale: my great-great-great-grandmother's Yorkshire cookbook, my great-great-grandfather's guidebook to Italy, my great-grandfather's copy of a Western novel that inspired him to leave England and become a cowboy, my grandmother's Latin dictionary, and my other grandmother's dusty paperbacks with lurid covers. After Uncle Bill, her golden boy, her favorite child, was killed at Iwo Jima she was able to do nothing for a long time but read murder mysteries, in which death was a conundrum to be solved in 250 pages. Then at last she packed the whodunits away, and she went on. These ancestors suffered tragedies, died young, and never had any money, but they did have books, and books do not exist apart from life; books are life. Nobody ever once told me to read, but they told me stories. Selling magazines, my mother's cousin once got the brush-off: "Go away, little boy, I don't have time to sit down and read." To which he retorted: "*My* mama reads standing up!"

At first Lincoln School seems unchanged: the same shabby red brick building, the same paved playground that permanently scarred my knees. But my first-grade classroom has become a computer lab, and Lincoln students now have new and terrible problems as well as opportunities unimaginable in 1956. In general, children's books are vastly improved since the 1950s, and primary school is probably better taught, but I worry about older children, and especially boys, who tend to stop reading when they outgrow picture books. Yet literacy is still the key to basic survival, as well as to computers, mathematics, and books. Without it, hope fades . . . for all of us. Once, at a school less promising than Lincoln, a rumpled, tired woman came up to me, dragging her embarrassed son behind her. "I want you to know," she said with vehemence, “that yours is the first book he’s ever taken any interest in!”

This is why I have to put aside my other work, trample down my stage fright, and read standing up.

GREGORY MAGUIRE

Apologies of a Bookworm

WHAT IF AN ADULT had lumbered along the crazy pavement of my childhood, thirty years ago, and looked down at me squatting with a book at the bottom of my grandmother's stoop, and asked me the question of the hour? "Why are you reading, little boy? Why?" Here's what I would have thought.

◇ This is an adult seriously short of spare change in the smarts department. Adults already *know* better than anyone else why to read. They tell you all the time. It is virtually the only thing you and adults can agree on. Reading is fun. Other reasons follow.

◇ Reading indicates supreme indifference to the world at large, including the three Wolf brothers next door. They like to beat up any kids who demonstrate terror. Kids who are reading only demonstrate nonchalance to such threats. Especially kids who are reading THE CARE AND FEEDING OF ATTACK TIGERS.

◇ Reading gives you things to sniff, taste, touch, think about, care about, remember. The world does this too, but sometimes the world gives you things you don't want to remember (let alone sniff). Reading also provides distraction from such.

◇ Grandma may give you a nickel if you finish the book. She may not, either, but you're ahead either way. Grandma is fickle. Books are not.

◇ Your parents are the strictest pair of fiends in the known universe and won't let you do anything, anything. (You can't have a two-wheeler bicycle. You can watch TV only an hour a week, on Sunday nights. You have to baby-sit your younger four siblings, and if you're not kind to them your parents will have more, in revenge, and you'll be babysitting until you're thirty.) Reading is the only thing you're *allowed* to do. Luckily, you love it. You even pretend not to love it so much so that they won't take away your reading time as punishment for some very bad thing you might by accident do someday. Maybe to the Wolf brothers, if you could just think of something good.

◇ Reading can give you the creeps, in a good way, especially when you scrunch down at the end of the bed to keep reading by the hall light ninety minutes past your bedtime. Getting the creeps is good, if you manage your tolerance correctly.

◇ Reading gives you ideas for plays, drawings, and stories of your own. You're already up to Chapter Six on your latest effort: THE SLOW PAINFUL TORTURE OF THE WOLF BROTHERS.

◇ The librarian is the most beautiful adult you ever saw. She has red hair and wears kneesocks and turtlenecks, and she likes the Narnia books too, but it took her all summer to read the series—it took you only two weeks.

◇ When you walk home from the library with four books, you can balance them on your head to develop your posture. You might get to be a movie star one day, and then you can give interviews and say, "I owe it all to the library!"

◇ Reading helps develop binocularity: the ability to look at something from two points of view so that it becomes three-dimensional. How a book makes you feel and how living with a grandmother and four siblings and two parents makes you feel can be two different things, but by considering them together you have a larger sense of the validity of both.

- Reading is free.
- Reading is the mark of a brainy kid. You might draw the line at being called "Four Eyes" or "Einstein," but all kids like to feel smart. When the Wolf brothers lean over the fence and call you names, reading provides you with snappy and withering rejoinders like "Supercilious vagrants!" *That'll* cow them into silence.

That was thirty years ago. Now that I can afford to travel, to spend hours surfing the Internet, to stare at rented movies until my eyes glaze over, why do I *still* read?

- Reading is still free.
- Reading is private. Every time I travel, I notice that TV screens are more and more intrusive—not only in airplanes, but in airplane lounges and sometimes even in the van that brings you to the airport. I cherish private time. Reading is the second most intimate thing to do that I can think of.
- Reading is refreshing. Frankly, adult life can wear you down. Politics, health, the environment, the decay of a sense of community—we try to fight for what we believe in where and when we can, but all soldiers require rest and restoration. Reading works. Reading is great R and R.
- Reading reminds you that you don't yet know everything about everything. Occasionally, remembering this can provide a novel *frisson*.
- Reading keeps Grandma busy. She's halfway through the latest Anne Tyler novel, and has even taken to quoting little snippets to the Wolf brothers next door, who are back living next door to her again, after their stint in prison. Grandma visited them there once a week, and read to them, whether they liked it or not. They liked it, which was part of their rehabilitation.

◇ Reading will ensure a literate citizenry, which is required for the survival of a healthy and democratic and fair society.

◇ Reading is a ritual by which you recall that events have significance, that words matter, that what is said and done makes a difference.

◇ Reading brings you outside of the *here* and *now*, the *me* and *mine*. It is spiritual Velcro. Everything is caught up with everything else. Sometimes you can lose yourself in books, even now. Sometimes, mercifully, you can find yourself, too.

J. D. McClatchy

Myself Reading

Because I was the eldest child, and because my father was off fighting in the Pacific, my mother kept an elaborate Baby Book, recording my earliest this and latest that. A few years ago, in a forgotten attic box, she discovered the book and sent it to me. I have it open in front of me now. When I reached age three, she was asked to list my Favorite Outdoor Activities. She's put a line through "Outdoor" (from the start, I was all for the inner, or at least the indoor life), and written: "Books. Records. Puzzles." They are still my favorites.

One puzzle to record here, a half century later, is my abiding interest in books. I was read to, but my family was not literary. The gilded bindings of their sets of Dickens and Twain gleamed on high shelves. *Time* and *Life* are what I remember on their laps. What am I saying? I was there too! To this day, I like most to read in bed, and I suspect that's because it recalls snuggling into my father's lap, propped on his arm, warm, the book close to my nose, the sound of a man's voice telling me a story I already knew by heart.

But it's not myself I want to talk about. It's books. It's the difference between "reading" and *reading*. I offer three memories, three morals. And a motto.

First, the motto. It's from Goethe: "All great excellence in life or art, at its first recognition, brings with it a certain pain arising from the strongly felt inferiority of the spectator; only at a later period, when we take it into our own culture, and appropriate as much of it as our capacities allow, do we learn to love and esteem it. Mediocrity, on the other hand, may often give us unqualified pleasure; it does not disturb our self-satisfaction, but encourages us with the thought that we are as good as another. . . . Properly speaking, we learn only from those books we cannot judge."

It was not until prep school that I discovered how to read properly, and I owe the discovery to a madman. At fourteen I started in on the classics. The Jesuits who ran the school are renowned as taskmasters, and that first year we were drilled in declensions and conjugations. By the following year we were considered ready for Homer, and were turned over to the old priest who was to be our guide through *The Odyssey.* As it turned out, several years later he was retired to a mental hospital, but I remain indebted to what were still then merely called his "eccentricities." Each night's homework consisted of a long episode to be read, parsed, translated, and *understood.* And our teacher did not think we could truly understand Homer, or his hero's trials, unless we duplicated the circumstances of the poem. To that end, we were told each night to go to the basement of our homes, with a lighted candle and a bowl of applesauce—and, between gulped spoonfuls, declaim the Greek, pretending we were in the hold of a storm-tossed ship. I was never, before or since, so enthralled to a text. I now realize that what excited me then was not just the story or the theatrics. It was the words themselves. Because the Greek words were strange, I had to *think* about them, about their sound and etymology, their meanings and overtones, how they were combined into sentences and metaphors. The mad old priest was right: *reading* Homer finally involved the same struggle and search, adventures and homecoming Odysseus himself was driven to.

After my sophomore year at Georgetown, I stayed on in Washington for the summer and enrolled, by special permission, in a graduate seminar on Elizabethan literature. Our textbook was the old Hebel and Hudson *Tudor Poetry and Prose,* a massive, closely printed compendium as stuffy as our professor with his wedge of white hair, steel-rimmed spectacles, and stack of file cards that, having drily relayed the fact or "idea" on each, he would snap like playing cards to the back of the pile. I was intimidated, not by being over my academic head or by the lackluster recital (actually, for reasons I can now neither recall nor imagine, he inspired me to a love of Hooker's *Of the Laws of Ecclesiastical Polity),* but by the enormity and grandeur of the subject. Perhaps in imitation of my younger self, I made of my apartment that summer a context for my study: curling Hilliard and Holbein prints on the wall, Julian Bream plucking Dowland on the stereo set. Still, I was playing at it, accumulating rather than concentrating. Then one day the assignment was Marlowe's "Hero and Leander" . . .

> On Hellespont, guilty of true love's blood,
> In view, and opposite, two cities stood,
> Sea-borderers, disjoined by Neptune's might;
> The one Abydos, the other Sestos hight.

So the poem begins, and goes on to trace the heavenly path that runs along Leander's back and the pearl-strewn seabed where, stripped to the ivory skin, his body comes to rest. I was literally overwhelmed. It rarely matters who precisely initiates you—the old whore in a walkup, a teenager in the locker room, the telephone lineman picked up at a bar. The experience is decisive. So was this one. It was the first time I had felt the erotic power of a poem. In retrospect, that seems a crucial moment in anyone's reading life: to fall in love with a text, to feel its sexual heat, to sense it unbuttoning your shirt.

Some years later I was in graduate school at Yale, a class on American poetry with Harold Bloom. We were reading Emily Dickinson. At last I was under the spell of a great teacher, and what he taught me was this: the highest form of reading is asking hard questions of the text, as one should of a teacher. Bloom had—probably still has—a classroom manner that is deliberately provocative, at once gripping and infuriating. Like all great teachers, he merely brooded aloud. His questions of a poem—"What exactly, my dears, does Miss Dickinson *mean* by 'circumference'?"—were nearly always uncanny and unanswerable, but prompted endless discussion (abruptly cut off by another oracular question on a different matter). The effect of these lessons was only felt hours later, at home, in bed with the book. It was then that I *read* Dickinson, and listened—because I had been taught to challenge her—as she took the traditional language of belief, emptied it of any reassurance, then charged it anew with a startling force. In their own way, her methods mirrored my teacher's . . . and became my teacher. *Reading,* I'd been taught, means questioning, sensing that what you read is unfinished until completed in the self. The first text is the soul. And the last.

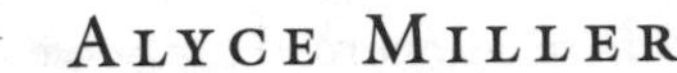

Alyce Miller

Up in the Back Room

Some of my earliest memories are those of being read to. When I was four, it dawned on me that if I knew how to do it myself, I could read whenever and whatever I wanted. I could hold the book, and I could turn the pages as I chose. I was filled with a sense of power and encouraged by a bargain my mother made with me. If I could successfully read aloud a short chapter in a small children's book with very large print, I would earn a potted cactus from the Blue Front in Ann Arbor, Michigan. And I did.

Cactus aside, why did I want so badly to read? From early on, I loved stories, and words and word play. My mother, finding herself alone with two small children while my father, an opera singer who was busy with his career, began to read to us. Sometimes two or three hours at a stretch. We had no television, something of an anomaly in the late 1950s, so we naturally turned to books for entertainment. It didn't take long for us to shed our Little Golden Books on how to help Mommy. We read poems from T. S. Eliot's *Old 'Possum's Book of Practical Cats* and a little green book of poems called *Silver Pennies,* which contained my favorite poem that began, "The moon is the North Wind's cookie. . . ." Another favorite was a rather brutal collection of vignettes *(Strewelpeter)* written in German about dire consequences for children who deliberately violated parental and societal interdictions, replete with graphic pictures of the awful consequences. My mother had brought the book from Switzerland, which is where she and my father lived for five years, and my first brother and I were born. My favorite vignette featured a little girl who played with matches and caught herself on fire and burned up. Serves her right, I thought, as I happily flipped to the next story, perversely enjoying the girl's transgression, and then comfortably perched on higher moral ground, relishing her fatal punishment. I think it was Graham Greene who observed that the psychology for such stories differs greatly between children and adults. Children, unlike adults who know they are guilty and seek forgiveness, presume themselves innocent and are relieved to see wrong punished.

Our first real novel, I think, was an English translation of the un-Disneyized *Pinocchio* by Colladi, when I was no more than five. It is actually a cruel book, with mean tricks and twists of fate framed as moral lessons. The Blue Fairy is sadistic and unforgiving, the Cricket overly self-righteous. In many ways *Pinocchio* is not a child's book. Each night after we read I went to bed haunted by the relentless procession of marionette mishaps, and Pinocchio's unfulfilled yearnings to be a real boy. The book was both frustrating and anxiety producing.

We went on to *Wind in the Willows,* then "dog books" like *Beautiful Joe,* and a lot of Johanna Spyri, including *Gritli's Children* and *Heidi*. There were the Alcott books, *Little Women* and *Little Men* and *Jo's Boys,* not to mention *Hurlburt's Story of the Bible,* which reminded me of opera plots, full of passions, plagues, betrayals, and violent deaths, and then on to another book of myths, these being Greek and Roman. There was *Tom Sawyer* and *The Little Lame Prince*. In the first seven or eight years of my life, my mother read to my brother and me well over a hundred and fifty books.

My mother was a practical, no-nonsense reader. We were expected to sit still and listen. If we fooled around, she would quit, and we were off to bed. Our routine was to pester her until she'd washed the dinner dishes and cleaned the kitchen, and then we'd meet upstairs in what we called "The Back Room" in our house in Ann Arbor. My brother and I would have arranged ourselves on the old sofa when she arrived with whatever we were reading. She laid the book face down, rubbed Jergen's lotion on her hands, dry from washing dishes and changing diapers and scrubbing floors. The sweet, moist aroma of Jergen's was a prelude to reading, like the rising of a curtain on a stage play. Then she gently pressed open the pages of the book, which emitted its own unique paper scents, and recapped, "You remember we ended with David Balfour on his way to see Uncle Ebeneezer," or, with a new book, announced, "Chapter One." It was thrilling to hear her say that, the world opening up and arranged in neat succession, a beautiful tension, the enigmatic code ignited. What would chapters two and three and four bring?

She didn't stop when she read and we didn't interrupt much. Occasionally she would pause to clarify a word or expression, or to identify a geographical location, but her readings were seamless and elegant. There was something about the inflections in her voice, the rises and falls and pauses, that paved the way to understanding, that made sense of what we might not otherwise have known. Through her voice, the words turned to images and pictures. I never thought of alphabet letters or single words, lined up in rows on a page. Words were pure image, like music, like color, and as she read, the boundaries between myself and the page dissolved, and all physicality vanished. Avid readers often speak of being "transported," and I think that is a fit description of what took place in our Back Room. We proceeded with *Downright Dencey, The Princess and Curdie, A Girl of the Limberlost,* selected not for period or location or theme, but from curiosity and appetite, in the way that John Ciardi says we learn poetry: "one poem at a time."

Even after we learned to read on our own, we still begged to be read to. *A Tale of Two Cities* was one of those books. But as more children arrived, my mother's time was consumed with babies, and our reading sessions were shorter and farther apart. By then, my brother and I were independent and omnivorous readers on our own.

Because my mother's voice implied a confidence with words and ideas, I was undaunted by books well beyond my abilities, and frequently assaulted my parents' own shelves for books I could make little sense out of. In first grade I checked out *Huckleberry Finn,* much to the amusement of the school librarian. I brought it home to show my mother. She agreed it might be tough going, but encouraged me to try to read aloud. It was a painful struggle. I made it through a few pages with her help before deciding it was "too old" for me. But there is an intimate connection in holding a book and opening its pages. I remember this one as a red hardback, somewhat battered along the binding. The print was small, by my standards.

I was not giving up on *Huckleberry Finn,* I was simply waiting. When I came back to it, years later, the voice in those opening pages was familiar. Even though I was reading it for the first time, it felt as if it were a book I already knew.

By fourth grade, after we moved from Michigan to Ohio, I spent large amounts of time reading on my own. I devoured books during the long, dark crawl through midwestern winters when the weather was too inclement to play outside, and all I wanted to do was lie on my bed, eat apples, and read books. I took whatever came my way. There was the collected works of Poe I discovered after falling in love with my mother's reading of "The Cask of Amontillado" from an anthology of classic horror stories. I became obsessed with gruesome excess. But I would as easily turn my attention to the Hardy Boys and Nancy Drew, sometimes two books in an afternoon. I also read a lot of book club books featuring teenage protagonists, with titles like *The Kid Who Batted a Thousand,* and all the Beverly Cleary books. There was *To Kill a Mockingbird* and *Island of the Blue Dolphins.* Someone suggested *Gone With the Wind.* In fifth grade I came across a volume of Shakespeare and read *Macbeth* in a fever of excitement, relishing mostly the three witches, though I was kind of partial to the unmitigated torment of Lady Macbeth, and then tried *The Rape of Lucrece* (drawn to the accompanying illustration of a man flinging himself on a helpless damsel), though I missed the whole point because I didn't know what "rape" meant. When I asked my mother, she looked at me dubiously and said, "Mustard seed." I kept trying to discern what Lucrece's mustard seed had to do with the story. Umberto Eco says that every reading is a misreading, and I must confess to some serious misreading during my early years, but even those misreadings ironically taught me how to read. When I later came back to *Macbeth* and other Shakespeare plays, the language and memory were there, and I built rapidly on the echo of familiarity. At nine, I had memorized the third witch's "Where hast thou been, sister?" speech, rejoicing when I came across the phrase "rump-fed runyon." I didn't know what a runyon was, but I fell in love with the alliteration, the cadences, the rhythms, the language play. More importantly, I didn't know enough to be afraid of Shakespeare because no one had told me I should be. I wasn't a very discriminating reader. Lady Macbeth was every bit as interesting in my mind as Henry and Ribsy, or Poe's narrator from "The Tell-Tale Heart," or Alice in Wonderland herself. In my mind they all resided in a world every bit as real and perhaps even more truthful than the one I inhabited.

In sixth grade, when my mother was in the hospital giving birth to my youngest brother, I discovered *Lady Chatterley's Lover* tucked away in the bureau drawer of the woman who came to care for us in our mother's absence. I didn't always get the point, but I couldn't stop reading it, compelled by the language of sexual passion I didn't understand. The reading planted the seeds for my late adolescent love affair with Lawrence. I read *Rebecca* shortly thereafter, which launched my love of gothic, and Victoria Holt and the Brontës followed closely on its heels. Strange, brooding men and anguished women. Excellent stuff.

The summer going into eighth grade I came across *Crime and Punishment* and *Brothers Karamazov* on the shelf in our house, and the titles deeply intrigued me. I took them along to Cape Cod that summer where my father was directing a whole summer of Gilbert and Sullivan. I remember an adult, a stranger, laughing at me when she saw what I was reading. "But do you understand any of it?" she asked with thinly veiled condescension. Offended, I said I did, and she eyed me with an adult's mild disbelief. But I spoke the truth. I wasn't lying, because I did understand. I understood enough to want to keep reading. Because when I read anything, I heard my mother's voice: patient, exacting, sorting out the clauses, teaching me to hear, and situating unfamiliar words in a context that made them come clear. I wasn't afraid of what I didn't understand. That was how I learned to read. Naturally, when I reread *The Brothers Karamazov* years later, I discovered what I had missed earlier, but I was just as surprised by how much I'd managed to extract and how much I remembered.

Reading is a very cheap education if you live near a library. Growing up, my parents had lots of books, but we didn't often buy new books, and most of the books I read came from the library. I generally checked out more books than I could really read in a week, and I was reading myself into double vision by age ten with a flashlight stashed under my pillow at night.

I sneaked books to my classes and read when I was supposed to be doing other things: *A Tree Grows in Brooklyn, Member of the Wedding* (which my father had given me). My junior high and high school report cards were therefore mostly checkered. And if I wasn't reading I was scribbling in a notebook or staring out the window. Math is a mystery to me to this day because while my classmates labored over fractions and percentages and teachers reviewed apothegms and theorems, my mind often was, as Joan Didion calls it, "on the periphery," or clandestinely engrossed in a novel, tucked inside my textbook.

I had been seduced by magic: the assistant cut in half, the four balls that unexplainably become eight, the dove that appears from nowhere and flaps off into space. I was inspired to discover how to perform such tricks myself, motivated by the mystery from which such desire springs. I began writing little stories when I was six, and never stopped, though it took me thirty-five years to decide I wanted to be a writer. If I had been simply taught the mechanics of language, it would have been just like showing someone the tedious manipulation of the magician's balls and strings and scarves (or in this case, the awful rote memorizations of alphabet and phonics and exposure only to the utilitarian benefits of reading), without having ever been drawn into the enchantment of the act itself. If I'd been left to English classes, I probably would have, like many of my schoolmates, despised reading and, by extension, writing, for their collective tedium and pointlessness. Imagine being given a page of musical notation then questioned sharply why you don't like music. Hearing language is every bit as important as hearing music and seeing pictures. Words offer a wonderful synthetic experience, and if I'd come across Baudelaire's "Correspondences," for example, before I'd experienced language through reading, I think I would have been baffled. But from the time I was a child, words had color and texture and scent.

At fourteen I read, among other things, *The Bell Jar, The Catcher in the Rye, A Separate Peace, Lisa, Bright and Dark,* and *I Never Promised You a Rose Garden*. These were all appropriately depressing, and were passed around with adolescent zeal in my ninth grade, along with *Valley of the Dolls,* which didn't interest me simply because the cover was "wrong." Meaning that the drawing on the front seemed to answer, instead of raise, all the questions with which I usually entered a narrative. And I wasn't all that interested in the slick lives of the women taking all those pills.

The summer I was fifteen I discovered Faulkner through *Light in August* on my aunt's farmhouse bathroom bookshelf in Maryland, and went on a Faulkner binge. More southern writers burst into my field of vision, and I couldn't stop. Next came Black American writers, beginning with Ellison's *Invisible Man,* and Baldwin's short fiction.

When later, my formal education demanded a more systematic approach to reading (by period, by writer, by form, by content) I didn't object, but sometimes I missed the randomness of grabbing Baldwin after Dickens, and Plath after Baldwin, and Austen after Plath. Nothing at stake. Nothing to lose. Powered simply by my own desire for what was on the page. Being an undergraduate English literature major, after forays into such horrors as "pre-law" and "education," struck me as an awfully sneaky way to have fun and get college credit at the same time. I emerged from my undergraduate studies generally scattered but reasonably literate.

Graduate school had its pleasures, but reading began to feel like work, and my arbitrary habits of the past were not a promising foundation for academic success. I did well only if I liked a course. James Joyce was almost ruined for me by a professor teaching a highly prescriptive version of a class precariously titled "Literature and Psychoanalysis." I never fully recovered from his decimation of *Portrait of the Artist,* but fortunately someone thrust *Dubliners* into my hands, before he could butcher it, and I recovered.

Oddly, after graduate school in my early twenties, I read very little, and worked, returned briefly to school, and then traveled instead. My adult life was often punctuated by nonreading periods, when I was teaching a lot or too busy with life. By nonreading, I don't mean that I never read, I only mean that I read in smaller spurts, and instead of reading several books a week, I was lucky to finish one.

I no longer had or took the time to lounge in my bed for hours, eating apples and finishing off books at my leisure. The demands of adult life militated against such luxury. Besides which, I chose to be out in the world more, abandoning the solitude of reading for more social activities. Were my reading days over?

In my late twenties, I began to follow a habit my father, who is also a reader, taught me: reading in the spaces between other activities: fifteen minutes while waiting for a phone call, ten minutes before I dropped off to sleep, five minutes here, twenty there. In this way I read a lot of poetry, nonfiction, and fiction, trading back and forth on whim.

Now that I teach creative writing and literature at a university, a great deal of my reading centers on student papers and stories, as well as the readings I assign my students in my dutiful effort to expand their horizons. And since the mid-1980s, I've read a lot of theory, throwing into question the "text as manufactured pleasure and commodity" and my own presumed innocence as a reader. Certainly I am aware that most of the aforementioned children's books in this essay fit into the preordained canon of classic children's literature, full of readerly, not writerly, texts, and that I have been guilty in this piece of waxing nostalgic for a kind of "old-fashioned reader values" that would most likely meet with William Bennett's approval.

The point I'm trying to make is that I rarely read "strictly for pleasure" any more, by which I mean that it is harder for me to pick up a book and "get lost" in it. What I do now for a living requires that I read extensively in the voluminous field of contemporary fiction and I often find myself skimming and hurrying along to get through so I can pick up the next book. An occupational hazard. My critical eye and ear sharpened, I'm always taking the book apart piece by piece, analyzing it, passing judgment, even if it's in the form of praise. I'm afraid I've become, in some ways, an impossible reader.

When my own students ask me about what to do to become writers, I stop and think back to the Back Room where my mother and my brother and I convened for our nightly reads. I always give my students the same advice they assuredly hear from everyone: "Read." Read, read, read. Read aloud. Read silently. But read. I'm afraid to tell them the truth, that I can jot down lists, and require books on my syllabi that we discuss and write about, but it is difficult to duplicate in class the joy of discovery, of browsing along a library or bookstore shelf and landing on a book that demands to be read. It is a glorious kind of urgency that when I was a child ordered me to forego all other responsibilities, and abandon myself to the page. Therein lies the pleasure of reading.

SUSAN MITCHELL

Confessions of a Child Reader

ACTUALLY, there are two stories of how I learned to read. Like the two versions of Creation in *Genesis.* No, correct that, there are three stories, maybe even five. Since reading is the first thing I do in the morning, the book held in my left hand as I manage a slice of toast with my right, and the last thing I do before I fall asleep, the book gently placed on the floor beside my bed, there need to be at least a dozen stories to account for such a prodigious appetite.

STORY NO. 1: Shortly after my fifth birthday, I had my tonsils taken out. There is a photo of me looking wan and in need of sunshine as I hug an enormous yellow plush duck nearly three times my size, so this must have been why my parents brought me to Florida. We stayed in the area now known as South Beach—at that time, Miami Beach. Nights in Florida were romantic, exciting, and sexual even for—maybe especially for—a child. I am thinking of sexual excitement not as genital arousal, but as arousal of the total being. At night we would drive down an avenue of hotels, huge signs throbbing out their names—Seville, Bal Moral, Atlantis, Sea Isle, Fontainbleau—in parroty yellows and greens and screeches of flamingo. Nearly every hotel had its own logo—a palm tree, a sea horse, a dolphin—that waved or shimmied or leaped as the lights that spelled it out rippled on, then off. I wanted to know the name of each hotel, so each and every name had to be read to me night after night by my mother or my father. To know the hotel names was to enter an adult world where women in sequined dresses, where mermaids with long blond hair and bright red mouths, where the rumba and the samba from every club and passing radio, where cars of boys slowed and cried out to and pleaded with groups of girls, where I got mixed up with a wedding party one night at our hotel and was finally found on the dance floor. Reading was my first sexual experience, my rite of passage into glitter and dazzle and pizzazz.

STORY NO. 2: I grew up in New York City where it rained a lot in the winter and was gray and cold. On cold, raw days I went to museums because by the age of five or six I had already fallen in love with the ancient Egyptians. Somehow I had acquired a book of hieroglyphics which I committed to memory—to visual memory, that is, since the stylized drawings of beetles and lotus flowers and eyes rimmed with kohl had no sound for me. I learned to read them the way the deaf learn signs. So my earliest forays into reading were soundless, mute. First, the unheard melodies, later the heard.

STORY NO. 3: My mother read to me all the time—*Winnie-the-Pooh, The Jungle Books, Babar, The Secret Garden, Mary Poppins, The Water Babies.* We traced the tracks of Pooh and Piglet with our fingers, we dreamed over the illustrations, we went places together inside our heads, which at that time was one head. My mother read me stories from a book that is still in my bookcase, *Tales from the Silver Lands.* I loved the story of El Enano, an ogre with a magical arm that could suddenly stretch to enormous lengths whenever he wanted to grab someone by the ankle. I never tired of grabbing my mother by the ankle, my aunts, my grandmothers. I never tired of saying Mowgli, Bagheera, Shere Khan, Baloo. Baloo was a name that poured slowly like honey. To say Bagheera was to press my mouth into fur.

STORY NO. 4: My father told me stories that all began *East of the sun and west of the moon.* He made them up as he sat in his chair and I sat on the floor. My father's father told me stories about a magic pencil. My mother's father told me stories, and my two grandmothers. There was lots of snow in their stories and also, food—huge peaches that glowed like the balls on our Christmas tree. In a story my mother's mother told, a bear ate up a brother and sister. When the heart-broken parents killed the bear, they pulled out its guts, stretching them into a city made of gold, a city with golden fountains and golden park benches. What happened to the children? This question of mine always annoyed my grand-mother. Was it because she understood that art is made out of tragedy and loss?

STORY NO. 5: Every week my mother bought fish from a man who loved to sing opera. In his store I kept to the fringes of things, patting the hard dead eyes of snapper, grazing the silvery scales of salmon with the edge of my hand. All at once, Mr. Miele would notice me. He would place his hands on his enormous stomach that pushed out his bloody apron and sing the bass arias from *Aida* or *Rigoletto.* I would look way into his mouth as he sang, and afterward, I would watch him whack the heads and tails off fish. He knew that I took piano lessons, and each time we bought fish, he would ask me if I was ready to accompany him. I was terrified he would turn up in our living room, with his bloody hands and bloody apron, his enormous voice erupting from the huge belly which seemed to grow bigger as he sang. Nevertheless, I practiced the arias. Which came first, reading music or reading words?

STORY NO. 6: Every book I received at Christmas was individually wrapped in taffetas and silks and bound with plush red ribbons. One Christmas I got *The Brothers Karamazov,*

The Conquest of Mexico and the Conquest of Peru, Moby-Dick, and *Great Expectations.* To a not quite twelve-year-old, these books looked very grown-up, especially the colossal Dostoyevsky and Prescott in their Modern Library jackets which came off to reveal on the reverse side lists of books I had never heard of, each with its Modern Library order number. The Melville was illustrated by James Hanley, and I lingered over the illustrations even longer than I lingered over passages in the story. My favorite chapter was the one that describes Ishmael and Queequeg in bed together—perhaps because they reminded me of something I had almost forgotten, my mother and me in bed together reading a book. *Then there you lie like the one warm spark in the heart of an arctic crystal.*

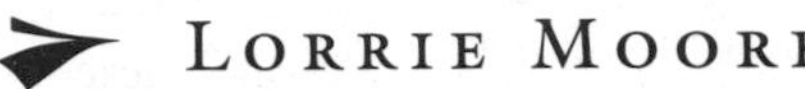

Lorrie Moore

The Fireside Book of Fire

The first book I fell in love with was a songbook. Sitting on the piano bench and flipping through the Provensen-illustrated pages, or listening to my father sing one or two selections of our choosing, I was flown off to other worlds: the *Fireside Book of Folk Songs* set my imagination ablaze like little else available to me. Where else would a four-year-old hear of a cabin boy tricked, betrayed, and left cruelly to drown by a ruthless British sea captain ("The Golden Vanity") or two lovers ("Lord Lovel") whose doom was also a kind of heaven, dying for love as they did and, in the graveyard, sprouting flowery intertwining vines from their respective skeletons (a common destiny in folk ballads). Such a fateful mix of flora and fauna left me, a small child, breathless and stunned. I loved the songbook for its blood and gore: the Minstrel Boy going off to war; the Three Ravens checking out the corpse of a slain knight (one verse includes the birds' discussion of breakfast); John Henry dying with the hammer in his hand; Casey Jones smashing up his train. Even Clementine tripping over her painful herring box shoes and drowning in the brine. I loved the book for its naked calls of love: Oh Shenandoah, I love your daughter; or that mournful girl on Buttermilk Hill bemoaning her Johnny who has gone for a soldier. I loved it for its bawdiness—Betsy from Pike getting drunk and flashing the whole wagon train—for its pirates ("Coast of Barbary") and dissolute sailors ("What Shall We Do with the Drunken Sailor?") and for its seemingly forbidden vocabulary, for this was a time when even "bosom" was a dirty word and could prompt fits of giggling from my brother and me. "Oh, Rock-a My Soul in the Bosom of Abraham" often had us doubled over.

The *Fireside Book of Folk Songs* was spicy stuff. Such adult material, such pessimism and sorrow about the human condition, seldom made it into conventional children's literature, and when it did it was usually in fairy tales, which my mother read to us in a highly regulated way, suspecting their troublesome content. Though I begged, she would no longer read "The Little Match Girl," with its class rage and unrelenting heartbreak, because I cried every time. "Hansel and Gretel," because it was about parents abandoning their children, quickly became off-limits, as did "Bluebeard," since, in a fugue-state of political incorrectness, I totally identified with the bad guy. ("What did the wives expect? He told them not to open the door.") The songbook, however, escaped my mother's censorship—perhaps because it was mostly my father who sang from it. Here, with impunity, I could puzzle over Barbara Allen: her virginity and awkward independence condemned in a ballad that deems them a hazard to malekind, though the final verse gussies her up with deathbed remorse. *Wait a minute!* Clueless, I studied the illustration for a clue, which I decided might just lie with the red ribbons on her dress. A few pages away, thank God, I could think about the Arkansas Traveler, not fixing his roof in good weather because in good weather it didn't leak. Now *that* made sense to me.

Probably my mother thought all these were mere tunes, only songs—not stories, with a story's power to haunt and inform and disturb. Which is, obviously, where she was wrong.

And so, because my father seemed to care less about protecting us from the tragedies western culture was eager to point out, we often preferred our evening song-and-story time to be spent with him. If possible. While my mother

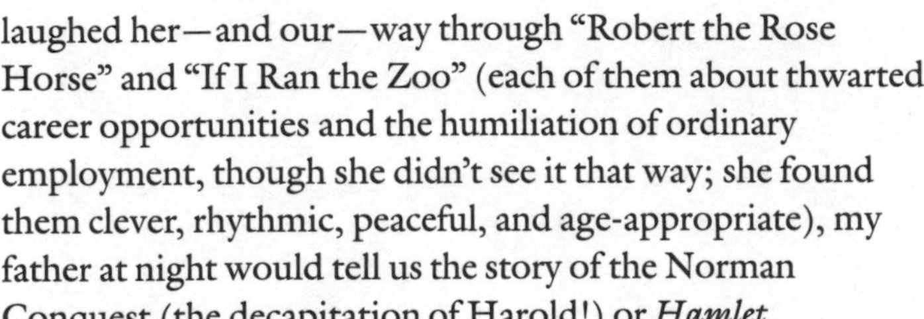

laughed her—and our—way through "Robert the Rose Horse" and "If I Ran the Zoo" (each of them about thwarted career opportunities and the humiliation of ordinary employment, though she didn't see it that way; she found them clever, rhythmic, peaceful, and age-appropriate), my father at night would tell us the story of the Norman Conquest (the decapitation of Harold!) or *Hamlet*.

"Your father told you the story of *Hamlet* when you were four years old?" someone said to me recently, a bit astonished.

"But it's a great story," I said. And, of course, it is. Leave out the soliloquies, and you've got a ghost, a queen, a drowning, a sword fight, and a glass of poison—my four-year-old self was mesmerized. It was as good as a song.

That was the beginning of my literary life.

DAVID MURA

Goodbye, Columbus

THE FIRST WORK OF LITERATURE I fell in love with—that is, in the way you love a book whose protagonist you identify with—was Philip Roth's *Goodbye, Columbus.* In the opening of this novella, the protagonist, Neil Klugman, is sunning himself poolside at the country club of his cousin Doris, when a girl approaches and asks him to hold her glasses. A few minutes later, Brenda Patimkin rises from the pool, takes back her glasses, and as she walks away, pulls the bottom of her bathing suit back down. Although Neil quickly notes this *frisson,* it's clear that Brenda's appeal is not just her good looks and marvelous body. A daughter of a wealthy sink manufacturer, Brenda is at home in the suburb of Short Hills and its country club life in a way that Neil, who works in a library and lives in Newark with his aunt Gladys's family, is not. Later, when Neil first kisses Brenda, she is sweaty from a bout of tennis, and beneath the wet spots on her shoulder blades, he feels "a faint fluttering," as if there were somehow tiny wings hidden within her: "The smallness of the wings did not bother me—it would not take an eagle to carry me up those lousy hundred and eighty feet that make summer nights so much cooler in Short Hills than they are in Newark."

As the summer progresses, so does Neil's affair with Brenda, and he is both amazed at his success and at the same time, resentful of Brenda's status, the ease at which the goods of life seem to have fallen at her feet: from the sports equipment permanently scattered across her lawn to her air-conditioned house to the quantities of fruit that fill the basement refrigeraor which Neil and Brenda raid after making love in secret on the basement couch. Behind this resentment lies his sense that he is an interloper in her house, that her parents eye him with suspicion, that her friends look down on him, despite the fact that he finds them artificial and silly. He fears he bears with him the stink of Newark, his Aunt Glady's garrulous working-class ways. With the self-righteousness of youth, he tells Brenda that unlike her friends, he does not have plans, he does not want to go around acting as if making a buck were the most pressing question of his life.

The situation of this story is an ancient one, and its American roots go back to that classic American romantic novel, *The Great Gatsby:* Neil seems to combine within himself both the dreams of Gatsby and the skeptical moral sense of Nick Carroway. But none of this explains why I am citing *Goodbye, Columbus* in an essay on the situation of the Asian-American writer. What could this tale of a young Newark Jew have to do with the life of a sansei, a third generation Japanese-American?

Well, for one thing, I grew up in a Jewish suburb. And because I was obviously a member of a minority, I grew up feeling like an outsider among suburban Jews: if Neil Klugman was an interloper, I was even more so. This became clear when I reached high school and tried to go out with the Brenda Patimkins of my high school. The girls were forbidden go out with *goyim,* and they could not disguise me as a Jew as some did with their Caucasian Christian boyfriends. Other barriers were less obvious, more elusive: being of Japanese racial ancestry, I also felt somehow more socially inept, less good-looking, than my Jewish counterparts from Lincolnwood and Skokie.

And so, I had even more reason than Neil to look down on the middle-class Jews around me, to buttress my self-righteousness with a self-conscious concern for civil rights and political issues, and later, as the sixties progressed, with a distrust of materialism and our military machinery. During one of the first phone calls I ever made to a girl—she was Jewish, of course—I spent much of the time talking about the condition of blacks in the South. It was hardly a way of wooing, and when the phone call was done, she remarked that she was impressed but still was not interested in going out with me.

Perhaps, in my own confused way, I sensed that the question of race was somehow essential to my situation, and perhaps this sense also spurred my love for Roth's novella. In the middle of the novella, Neil befriends a young African-American boy, who has taken to looking at the art books in the library at which Neil works. Coming upon the young boy one day, Neil sees that the boy is looking at the works of Gauguin; at first the boy feels that Neil is checking up on him, but after a while, when Neil wins the boy's trust, the boy points to one of Gauguin's Tahiti pictures and remarks, "Ain't that the fuckin' life?" Not surprisingly, Neil comes to identify with both the boy's sense of being an outsider and the boy's desire for a richer, more luxurious life, a desire which in part means: I want a new self (isn't this, ironically, the dream of all American literature?).

As someone who had only six dates in all of high school, who never went to prom or homecoming, who felt inside that women were always destined to run from me, I was burdened with adolescent ressentiment, and I readily identified with Neil and the young African-American boy, since both were outcasts from the world of Brenda Patimkins. Still, I did not understand where my sense of sexual inadequacy came from; nor did I understancd why it was I so desired the Brenda Patimkins, why I found my own Brenda in a beautiful young Jewish girl named Gail Golman, who, in four years of high school, never acknowledged my existence.

But beneath these questions lay a deeper ignorance. What I did not understand, and what I am still trying to figure out, is how, despite my love of *Goodbye, Columbus,* I differed not only from the young Jewish man from Newark, but also from the young African-American boy from Newark. Which is to say my most difficult task was in identifying with myself: an adolescent Japanese-American boy from a Jewish suburb in Chicago.

Cornelia Nixon

Dolls Alive

THE FIRST TIME I was electrified by a book, it was a volume called *Dolls Alive,* which I made my mother read to me every night, skipping not a single syllable, since I had them memorized. I remember it as a book with no pictures and lots of text, set in some nineteenth-century nursery, in which a miracle occurred one night when the children were asleep: the dolls came to life. The difficulties of this proposition were not glossed over: the dolls were hungry, but the dollhouse food was fake and painted, glued down to the plate, the dollhouse forks flimsy, and one doll had a missing arm, her head on backwards, half of her hair pulled out—painful problems when she came to life.

I must have fallen asleep routinely in the middle of this situation, since I have no memory of how it ends; but the next night I wanted to start again. It wasn't that I found the real world boring or too limited in possibilities. At the time, I had what I considered a red-hot kid's life, especially weekends and summers on my grandmother's farm, where I was allowed to help milk fifty dairy cows (monstrous creatures that terrified and fascinated me in every way), caught fireflies and tadpoles, and rode a pony every now and then.

But I had room for other universes too, the live dolls in their nursery, and *Black Beauty,* and later Marie Antoinette and Anne Boleyn, especially Anne Boleyn, in whose honor I learned the whole succession of English kings and queens, though most of the rest were not so interesting. I also had room for a family of real dolls, which my sister and I deployed secretly long past the time when it would be acceptable to anyone we knew, making up tales for them to live, which I then reported in *The Dollyland Star,* a newspaper issued to my mother and grandmother. (When my Alice-in-Wonderland doll became engaged to my sister's rabbit, and later left him for my teddy bear, this was headline news.)

I have never read an adequate theory of doll-playing; my sister and I were not *practicing for motherhood,* pretending to be the dolls' mothers. Sometimes we took a role in the tale ourselves, but more often we were simply offstage authors, readers of each other's stories, in a grandly interactive fiction that had its own history and consequences from one year to the next. ("Off Dollyland," we would say, switching off that universe, when we wanted to stop playing or began to argue over some event.) We were practicing to read and write, Alice and Teddy and Gentleman Flophopper to be replaced in a few years by Stephen Daedalus and Lily Briscoe and Humbert Humbert, Los and Urizen, and the "I" of every lyric poem, as I moved through serial obsessions with William Blake, Gerard Manley Hopkins, Sigmund Freud, Albert Camus, Virginia Woolf, and other great poets, crackpots and visionaries of the past and present, whose thoughts are available to anyone through the magic of squiggles on a page.

I think we read because we can, and because it's beautiful to leap through the double remove of words and print into another world. A person shovelling a walk can also be in nineteenth-century Paris or the Garden of Eden, or lit up with some radioactive image made by a poet seven hundred years ago. Anything said well is exhilarating, no matter what awful thing it is about. We read because we can see so much more behind our eyes.

 HOWARD NORMAN

Bus Problems

IN GRAND RAPIDS, MICHIGAN, summer of 1959, the six or seven hours a day I spent in the bookmobile were a reprieve from the unbearable heat, and the rising anxieties of a dilapidated home life. I was ten. My library district's driver (and mobile librarian) was named Pinnie Oler. Mr. Oler was in his late forties, to my recollection. He had a Dutch accent—he wasn't Dutch, but, orphaned at age eleven, was raised by Dutch Reformed parents. And that was all of his biography I ever got—for some reason, he had the need to explain his accent, even to me. His physical self was rather slight; he was about five feet six, thin, his black hair slicked back tight to his scalp, and he was almost comically fastidious, in his driving, as well as his upkeep of the entire interior of the bookmobile, the blue school bus fitted with shelves and two black leather reading benches, both mended with masking tape. Mr. Oler had a transistor radio dangling from the rearview mirror. He had a small electric fan screwed to the dashboard. A floor fan circulated air throughout the rest of the bookmobile, and I knew all the angles at which to sit, in order to stay cooled by the fan, but not let the pages of my book flutter and distract. Mr. Oler had a gray ice chest filled with bottles of NeHi Orange, which he didn't share—never offered me a NeHi once that summer. But he said if I brought a bottle of soda, I could keep it in his ice chest. Parked in the parking lot in front of Bethany Church, or in front of Hillcrest School, or near the Mississippi Steamer Ride at Reeds Lake—or any of eight daily stops—Mr. Oler seldom left the bus. He listened to the radio turned very low, drank orange soda, nodded off. He always wore long-sleeve shirts. After I stayed on the bus a total of about twenty hours over three days, he said, "I'm not going to ask why. As far as I'm concerned, it's between you and whoever's at home. You don't bother me, I won't bother you. And you can consider this bus like a café in Paris; stay as long as you like. You should pack a lunch. You'll have to eat it outside, though." I didn't know from cafés, but I took the "as long as you want" part as literally as anyone could.

But Mr. Oler was a reader, too. He read expansively of a single author, as far as I observed that summer. Behind his seat, he had bracketed to the wall a special shelf which held the novels of the historical melodramatist, Rafael Sabatini. On the leather spines the titles were *emblazoned*—and I mean that more often than not, their individual letters were in a cursive script shaped like flickering flames: *Scaramouch, Captain Blood, Captain Blood Returns, The Sea Hawk, Master at Arms, The Black Swan, The Sword of Islam.*

He said, "Sabatini is the real thing."

Otherwise, I never heard Mr. Oler offer any literary judgment, general opinion, advice, nor suggestion about a book to adult, teenager, or child.

He would not let kids on if they were dripping wet from the public swimming pool near Hillcrest School. That was a hard and fast rule. I can still recall a girl, perhaps she was thirteen or fourteen, sitting across from me, intently reading a novel; her hair wet, her face flushed from the bike ride, the damp press of her swimsuit beneath her shorts and blouse, which she had taken from her saddle bag and slipped on right there on the sidewalk before stepping into the bookmobile.

Thirty-seven years later, I can still smell the moldy book smell, could get out a piece of paper and sketch the interior configuration, the location of book categories. Standing next to the driver's seat, facing the back: along the right side wall, on the top three shelves, were SCIENCE (zoology, geology, astronomy, medicine); the bottom three shelves contained GOVERNMENT/SOCIAL SCIENCE. The wall of shelves along the back held SPORTS/RECREATION/HOBBIES. Along the left wall, on the top three shelves was FICTION/POETRY. The bottom three shelves held JUVENILE. The card catalogue was at the back left. There was a slotted ballot box for BOOK REQUESTS. Mr. Oler would try to have a requested book within a week.

What I want to say most, is that the bookmobile offered me virtually a private library—some days maybe only two or three children, and four or five adults used it. Compared to my schoolmates, I didn't consider myself much of a reader; "an average reader," one report card read. But I never thought I chose "average" books to read. When you don't know much about anything, there's wide opportunity for revelation. And I had a number of subjects I was very personally interested in, such as reptiles and amphibians, weather, the arctic, and painters such as Picasso. I loved the privacy of reading in the bookmobile. I think it is accurate to say that at first I read because I was on a bus full of books all day—reading was what there was to do. Yet by summer's end, I got on the bus because I wanted so badly to read, and read *there*, as opposed to anywhere else. And the whole enterprise had enough resemblance to being in a summer school, that my mother didn't much question it. When asked early on what I did when I left the house, I answered directly, "I ride the bookmobile. I read books." I know that she consequently made a phone call to Mr. Oler at his house. But in the end, I suppose she was mainly relieved that I had chosen anything at all.

Of course, like any ten-year-old, I killed time, either with my only best pal, Paul Amundson, or by myself. I went swimming, as well. I rode my bicycle. I fished for crappies at

Reeds Lake, and stayed away from the "polio pond," which was near the furniture factory. (That was the summer a rotund boy named Gary Van Eerden scooped up five polly-wogs from the polio-pond with a jar, then swallowed them, thereby winning ten dollars in change from a circle of boys—later, he got sick at the thought of what he'd done, more than anything. But it wasn't polio.) But at least three days a week, I was on the bookmobile all day.

Engine-wise, the bookmobile had a lot of problems. Stalled out at a corner, blue hood raised, radiator geysering steam, friction smell and grind of metal, fan belt sliced by its own fan, oil spill—"Bus problem," Mr. Oler would announce, most often to an audience of one. He would shrug philosophically. Then he found a telephone booth and called his wife, Martha Oler, who was a bus mechanic for the Grand Rapids School System. Looking back at it, a woman bus mechanic in the 1950s was no doubt a rare occurrence, and perhaps still is today. Mrs. Oler was an absolutely beautiful woman, and at least ten—maybe fifteen—years younger than Mr. Oler. I thought she looked savvy and confident and unusual and pretty in an *interesting* way in her smudged mechanic's smock. He was always so happy to see her, too. Like it was a big surprise to see his wife in the middle of the working day, even though he had phoned her and she had driven right on over. She would carry her toolbox to the bookmobile. Before she worked on the engine, though, she always kissed Mr. Oler; I mean, they took a long moment to hold and kiss each other, and this was not something I saw much of in public, nor at home. That summer, there were at least a dozen bus problems, so I saw Mrs. Oler quite a bit. She was taller than Pinnie; she had dark red hair and a quick smile, and always acknowledged me—"Hey, fancy seeing you here!" Which was of course an understatement; I was a fixture on that bookmobile, and Mr. Oler must have commented on this at home. Or at least I hoped he had. I needed an identity in *somebody's* house. Sometimes Mrs. Oler could fix the bus problem, sometimes she called in a tow truck. Waiting for the tow, they would hold hands, lean against her car and talk. He would pop open a NeHi for her. It was very hot that summer—record heat, the radio kept saying. I wore shorts and T-shirts, tennis shoes, no socks.

One late summer day, I got on the bus at about nine o'clock at my usual spot, the corner of Giddings and Fremont. I had my lunch box. I put a root beer in the ice chest. I had the "pointer" finger of my left hand in a splint and thickly bandaged. "What's that mummy on your finger, there?" Mr. Oler said, pointing to the layered white bandage. "What the hell happened to you?"

"I don't wanna talk about it, okay?"

"Suit yourself," he said.

I went to the back, got out a book on planets, I think, and sat down, brooding and paging through.

I saw Mr. Oler adjust the rearview, catching me in it.

He let a few moments go by, then said, "You know by now, I don't open up my Sabatini collection to just anybody. But you've put your hours in this summer, haven't you, so if you want to read one of them—I'd suggest *Captain Blood* first. Are your hands clean? I don't want fingerprints. Don't tell anybody I gave you this special treatment, got it?"

"I won't." I was pretty much taken aback by his offer.

Captain Blood was a little advanced for me, but I slowly worked through it. We were parked near the Fulton Pharmacy. After an hour or so, Mr. Oler said, "Pretty good, don't you think?" I just nodded and went back to reading, which I meant as a way to show that I was entranced. I struggled with the vocabulary, but the story was great, a real exotic adventure. "It's called a swashbuckler," Mr. Oler said. "It's an old-fashioned word, but there's still use for it." Then Mr. Oler took a nap.

It was a novel replete with vivid incidents of revenge, the

emotional dimensions of a great Italian opera, uncanny heroics, highly inventive despicable cowardice—and I applied every page of it to my own life. I read deeply, hoping not only to get lost in the story, but to locate some ethical strategy, some instruction as to how to revenge my father for his extended, unexplained absences, his ambushing temper, his "accidental" breaking of my finger, his—yet again—new set of luggage. But by page two hundred, I forgot all about that, and was fully resident in the novel itself. The new qualities and possibilities of life I cared about were being played out in an earlier century, and nobody was in a rush to beckon or force me out of it. It was only about twelve-thirty. I did not want a lunch break. The pharmacist walked in, browsed a moment, picked a book, signed it out, and left, not waking Mr. Oler. I had till maybe four o'clock. Time was opening as slowly as I chose to turn the pages. That summer on the bookmobile I became a reader because of what I read to flee from, and what I read to enter into.

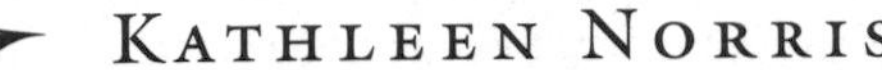

Kathleen Norris

In My Mother's Lap

It is refreshing to be asked not "Why do you write?" but "Why do you read?" Many readers are not writers, but I doubt that the reverse is true. My first memories of reading are inseparable from my memories of music. From the time I was an infant, I would sit on my mother's lap while she played the piano, and watch her fingers on the keys as I listened to her humming. I happily shared the music's vibrations in her belly, being enclosed in the rhythmic movement of her arms. By the time I was two, I wanted to sing with her and so my mother began to teach me songs—hymns, folk songs, Christmas carols. I was probably in kindergarten by the time I realized that the black marks on the page were connected to the letters I was learning in school. That they were "words."

That shock came all at once, an epiphany that excited me greatly but also plunged me into a panicky sadness. The world had opened wide; it seemed much larger than I had understood it to be, and I wondered how I would ever come to comprehend letters and words in all the dazzling combinations that now seemed possible. The curly-haired angels in my children's hymnal seemed a part of this conspiracy of words, still welcome if newly dangerous. But being on my mother's lap helped to ground me, so that I did not lose my bearings entirely (although that seemed altogether possible to me at the time). My mother, a schoolteacher, knew what reassuring words to say when I began to recognize words for the keys they were, and are. Our daily singing lessons became my first reading lessons. I suspect that this early binding of music to language is what made me a poet.

I read indiscriminately as a child. Dr. Seuss. Fairy tales (my mother's childhood book of the Grimm's stories, lavishly illustrated, was a favorite). Dog stories. Horse stories. *National Geographic.* The public library in Lemmon, South Dakota, where I spent childhood summers visiting my grandparents, provided both a wealth of comic books and hundreds of books in series old and new: not only the Bobbsey Twins and Nancy Drew, but Tarzan, Tom Swift, the Campfire Girls, and the Little Colonel. Even though I went swimming at the WPA pool very chance I got (sometimes three times a day), and pestered my siblings mightily, as I got older I also found time to read a book a day. Encouraged by my parents, I began, precociously, to explore the classics, unabridged—*Alice in Wonderland, Treasure Island, Jane Eyre.* (Once I comprehended how it worked, I haven't read a Gothic romance since, unless you count *Rebecca*.)

The first "adult" book I read (considering the word in its sleaziest connotation) was *Peyton Place.* I was eleven years old when it became a best-seller, and also a national scandal. I was slightly curious about sex, much more interested to learn how a book could cause such a fuss as to be denounced from pulpits. My indulgent parents checked the book out of a public library so that I could read it. Maybe they figured that it was time to counteract the dubious sex education that I was getting from my peers on the school bus and playground—much of it hilarious in retrospect, though it seemed solemn enough at the time. The book did raise questions about sex that my parents answered as best they could. Because I read it when I was still very young, protoplasm in Mary Janes, if you will, the book reinforced my notion that sexual intercourse was for grown-ups, and not for me. At least, not for a long while.

But it was as literature that *Peyton Place* stunned me. It was by far the worst-written book I had ever encountered, and I marveled that people would pay good money for such a thing. Even at my tender age, I was an experienced enough reader to find the writing so dreadful, often laughably so, that I soon lost interest in finishing the novel. I had not yet heard the word "editor," but I recognized in my bones that editing was what the prose of Grace Metalious desperately needed.

I suppose I read now for the reasons I've always read—because it takes me out of myself, it enlarges me and pushes me into new relationships with other people, other stories, and the human imagination itself. Reading is a transformative activity. I think of the young African-American and Hispanic "latchkey" children I met in the South Bronx in the early 1970s, when I worked with the Academy of American Poets to establish poetry workshops in the Carnegie Libraries—places that stood like beacons of sanity in neighborhoods that then consisted mainly of burned-out buildings, garbage, and rubble. I think of the ranch children in one-room schoolhouses in western North Dakota, their shelves full of books next to snakebite kits. And I wonder where their reading will take them.

I marvel that my reading of late has led me to the fourth-century monastic deserts of Egypt and Syria, and that the ancient men and women have become companions to me in my middle age, in late twentieth-century South Dakota. I am grateful to other readers, the scholars who have made these ancient Greek and Syriac texts available in English. But mostly I read for the human joy of it, to hear Amma (mother) Syncletica say, "Imitate the publican, and you will not be condemned with the Pharisee. Choose the meekness of Moses and you will find your heart, which is a rock, changed into a spring of water." I am only too happy to listen to her, to contemplate how rich life might be were I to attain the holy simplicity of Abba Pior, about whom Abba Poeman once said, "every day he made a new beginning."

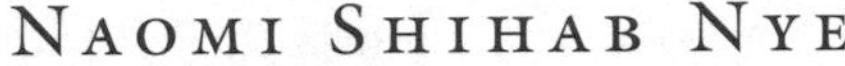

Naomi Shihab Nye

Wealthy with Words

Our parents pressed careful language into the air around us. *Mint, nutritious, patient, sky, remember, exactly.* . . . Mommy's voice sounded musical, emotional, intelligent. She loved accuracy, honesty, and crossword puzzles—games where proper words crisscrossed like weavings in a fine blanket. Later we would play Scrabble together with an old blue dictionary warm beside us.

Daddy's genial voice sometimes traveled slowly through sentences, shaping each syllable correctly. He was polishing the skin of a second language. He would come to speak it much more eloquently than most people who grew up speaking only English. Sometimes he slipped Arabic words into our days like secret gift coins into a pocket, but we didn't learn his first language because we were too busy learning our own. I regret that now.

When someone else who spoke Arabic came to visit us, their language ignited the air of our living room, dancing, dipping and whirling. I would realize: all those sounds had been waiting inside our father! He carried a whole different world of sounds—only now did they get to come out!

Because of words pressed into the air around us from our parents' mouths, my brother and I grew up understanding them as crucial tools and precious bounty from the beginning, before we could read, before we could even speak. *Adults must give children the gift of words, through real, accurate talk, from baby days onward, if children are to feel the power of language. Teachers and friends may help where parents fail. It is our blessing and our responsibility!*

Sometimes I imagine now how it might be for children growing up in rooms of grunts and mumbles, TV trickling its endless trivial talk, gnawing away at the air.

Where will they learn that a verb has teeth and a noun is round? How could they feel the shadings between *possibly* and *probably* if no one told them?

We weren't rich but we were wealthy with words.

How astonishing the day individual letters lined up to become *messages!* Billboards unleashed their mysteries high above us. Signs on barbershops welcomed us to step inside. Lists at the laundromat instructed us about dyeing and lint. When I read the words "cream puff" for myself on the menu at the tea room where my grandma had taken me for a grown-up ladies lunch, tears rose in my eyes! The code was now mine!

I wrote my first poem on the back of a white laundry bag at a Chicago hotel. Each rounded humpy letter felt like a separate animal for a long time. Slowly, slowly, the family of animals grew. Right away I saw how writing made things feel more real somehow than just *thinking*. You could stand back and look at them. You could almost live twice!

Our parents took turns by our beds, where our father added new installments of funny old-country folktales each evening. He had trouble remembering what he'd told the night before, but we could remind him. *("The little pan inside the big pan! The goat that couldn't find his friend!")* Our mother read to us, and sang. I closed my eyes with the words of Margaret Wise Brown or E. B. White floating around me.

At the library each Saturday I stacked my bounty of books, arranging their spines, feeling exhilarated! Bindings smelled delicious. I felt nervous when we visited people whose living rooms were bare of reading matter. Books were the getaway car, idling at the edge of every scene. I learned never to go anywhere without one. Once my mother came out of a pharmacy and found me in the car reading the auto manual from the glove compartment. She raised her eyebrows, but must have known she'd done something right.

When the television set full of black-and-white pictures came to live in our house, we didn't pay it much attention. One of my earliest and only TV memories is the radiant white head of Carl Sandburg, the poet, reciting his musical verses about city streets, and people and cash register clerks and evening skies and "the peace of great books." I felt electrified, transfigured! This was the person I wanted to be! He resounded, "Sayings, sentences, what of them/Flashes, lullabies, are they worth remembering?"

Everything inside me sang out, Yes! Yes! Yes!

I went from *seeing* and *hearing* Carl Sandburg (what a lucky flip of the dial that was) to reading and reveling in him. I love his words to this day. And always that sense of his physical presence, his voice from inside them, feels very close.

Expose our children to the *heard word,* then they will feel more like pilgrims to the page!

Our elegant, elderly second grade teacher, Harriett B. Lane, believed in memorization (Emily Dickinson, William Blake), weekly writing, and constant poring through anthologies to *find works that spoke to us.* If we didn't understand something, she said we could turn it over and over in our heads like a lemon drop. She taught us to copy and stitch together our own poetry collections. She taught us never to be afraid of a word we didn't know. It was a challenge! A delicious mystery! We could track its meaning down! All of us were writers and editors by the time we left her class. She spiked our belief for life—*there are words out there that are meant for me.*

In books I could wander for hours. I sat in the stairwell at my grandmother's ancestral home, sunken deep into *Little Women.* I was Jo for three whole years and no one knew. If you knew how to read, you could never be lonely.

Being an addicted reader didn't make me oblivious to the world around me—on the contrary, my appetite for detail seemed to grow according to the expansion of my mind. The dog that bit me under the eye, the vine wrapped around our porch, the cat that froze in the snow, whom we tried to thaw out in the oven, the blood-red stain of a strawberry on my fingertips—all were MATERIAL, parts of the story that was already my life. Reading was not a give-and-take experience. It was give and give and give. It took nothing away.

I was always thinking how everything could be *described*.

Now this reminds me of writers who say we need to develop a story-sense about our lives, so when hard times come to us, we can trust they will ease up again, swooping down and moving forward—that sense of a turning page offering solace in times anxious for change.

Reading is, simply, the best thing I ever do in my life. My son and I curl up together each evening, hungry for "our book," our story, our private world. He goes nowhere without a satchel of books. He can "amuse himself" anywhere. We pass it on.

As he falls asleep, I retreat back to my bedside table with its precarious skyscraper of reading matter, treasures waiting to be held.

Because of Libraries We Can Say These Things

She is holding the book close to her body,
carrying it home on the cracked sidewalk,
down the tangled hill.
If a dog runs at her again, she will use the book as a shield.

She looked hard among the long lines
of books to find this one.
When they start talking about money,
when the day contains such long and hot places,
she will go inside.
Soft shadows are waiting.

Orange bed, story without corners.
She will have two families.
They will eat at different hours.

She is carrying a book past the fire station
and the five-and-dime.
What this town has not given her
the books will provide; a sheep,
a wilderness of new solutions.
The book has already lived through its troubles.
The book has a calm cover, a straight spine.

When the step returns to itself
as the best place for sitting,
and the old men up and down the street
are latching their clippers,

she will not be alone.
She will have a book to open
and open and open.
Her life starts here.

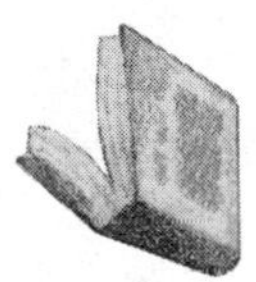

Robert Olmstead

On the Way to Books

The fire. On the way to books there was fire. Like this: Me and my friend Billy, we rode our bikes to the library every Saturday. On the way we'd collect bottles and turn them in for deposit, two cents and five cents, to buy soda and ice cream. We'd dally along the backroads, sometimes ride down by the County Farm and see the prisoners hoeing the vegetable gardens, one trouser leg bleached white so they wouldn't run off, the old folks reclining on the long front porch, somnambulant in the long days of summer heat. Sometimes ride to the Connecticut River and wet a line and speculate as to where they buried the elephant that came to town on a night in 1820 and fell through the wooden bridge that spanned the river to wreck itself on the rocks fifty feet below. Or over to Spofford Lake and watch the sailboats and wish we were rich enough to own such marvelous things.

But one day was a brush fire we came upon. It was snapping and crackling, licking the air and threatening a house. Seems something had gotten out of control that shoudn't even have been set in motion and the man who'd done it was in a panic. He was beating at the flames with a wet blanket, but the hillside where he'd laid up his brushy litter was ledgy and leaf-strewn from clutches of dry sumac, clumps of straw grass, brittle ferns, dusty bracken, and poison ivy, and the breeze was at his back and every time he came down with the blanket it fanned the fire to burst from another crevice, to course roots the way electricity runs a wire. His wife was watching him, the back of her hand up to her mouth. In a moment she was realizing how what is small can get big, how what is in hand can get out of hand, how intentions and consummations are not the same. And he was afraid too and didn't look used to it.

We dropped our bikes and went to help and she ran for the house to call the general store and from there the call went out and shortly the siren blew in town and the volunteers came and we strapped into water tanks and fought the fire that afternoon alongside the men who were the fathers of kids we went to school with. It gave me to understand later in life the strangeness of firefighters setting fires so to be able to put them out. A fire inspires reverence and dread, not unlike our regard for God. Not a wonder that Prometheus was to endure such suffering for the bringing down of fire from the sun for the comfort of man. We put out the fire that day and rode on to the library and filled our steel baskets with books on the Panama Canal, the Pyramids, the Revolution, the life of George Washington, the adventures of Richard Byrd, Roald Amundsen, James Cook, *Kidnapped, The Count of Monte Cristo, The Northwest Passage, Johnny Tremain.* Books by Francis Parkman, James Fenimore Cooper, Rudyard Kipling, Stephen Crane, Jack London, John Steinbeck and Franklin W. Dixon.

It was not the last fire I'd be around in my own life. I have attended barn fires, house fires, chimney fires, forest fires, mine fires, and when I was a kid the town would burn the dump. There have been campfires and bonfires and fires we'd set to burn away grass at the edge of the lawn, to burn leaves we'd raked and brush we'd cut. Attended all what warms the body and what burns within and can't be held. So to hold a book was always a way to arrest time, a way to stay the world. To hold a book was to hold steady what I could not.

Katherine Paterson

Why Do I Read?

Like most readers, I began reading because I was read to. There were five children in the family in which we grew up. We lived in China in a large city where there were no English bookshops or libraries, but we had parents who read to us every day from the books in our small family library. Even today when I read *When We Were Very Young* I still recall that thrill of delighted fear that I got as a three-year-old pressing against my mother's shoulder as she read about James James Morrison Morrison Weatherby George Dupree whose delinquent parent went off without asking his permission and has never been heard of since.

On Sundays the only permissible reading in our missionary household, besides the King James Bible and the fat Egermieier's Bible story book, was the bland-as-saltless-porridge children's story in the weekly denominational magazine which, since it took about six months to arrive by slow boat, was never in season. Our poor mother would stretch out for a Sunday afternoon nap, but we'd pester her until she'd finally agree to read us the dismal weekly tale. Invariably she'd fall asleep in the middle and have to be poked awake to finish. Which proves, no doubt, that children will listen to nearly anything read by a loving adult.

I cannot remember when I first began to read for myself. It happened naturally well before I started school. I read anything that had print on it. I read the Bobbsey Twins and Elsie Dinsmore but I moved on to *The Secret Garden* and *The Wind in the Willows.*

When war forced us to leave China I ultimately landed in Winston-Salem, North Carolina at a school with a wonderful library, packed with books I had never read. For me, a weird and lonely nine-year-old, it was like entering Paradise. I was the favorite target of the playground bullies, so you can imagine my joy when I was allowed into the sanctuary of that library where I could find so many friends who never sneered at my castoff clothes or cruelly imitated my peculiar accent.

When I was about eleven, my mother went off on a trip and brought me back a book. I didn't own books in those days. The books in our house belonged to all of us, so it was a rare treat to be given a book that I could put my own name in. Even more than that, the book my mother gave me was a book written for adults. It had won the Pulitzer Prize for fiction a few years before, so I felt honored that my mother thought, not only that I would understand the book, but that I would love it.

I still have that copy of *The Yearling* that my mother brought me more than fifty years ago. It is stained and buckled, having survived a typhoon when I lived in Japan. Still I treasure not only that faded green binding and the story it contains, but also the special language it gave me. As the middle child of five who often felt lost in the crowd, I could simply mention Fodderwing or Flag or Jody, and see my mother smile and know that she understood what it was I was trying to say.

In college I was introduced to all the greats of English literature, but the writer I cherish most from those days is the poet Gerard Manley Hopkins. I met him in a seminar on nineteenth-century literature. Each of us was to sign up to give a report on a writer of the period and I couldn't think of anyone I really wanted to write about, so I said Kipling, remembering from childhood his *Just So Stories*. But my professor said, "You don't want to do Kipling, Katherine, you want to do Gerard Manley Hopkins."

How could I want to do Gerard Manley Hopkins? I'd never heard of him until that moment, but Dr. Winship had yet to steer me wrong. If he thought I would like Hopkins, I was sure that I would. At first I was baffled by the poet's sprung rhythm and exotic use of words, many of which were beyond the limits of my vocabulary. I couldn't understand the poems at all, and I would have given up, except that Dr. Winship had said that I would want to do Hopkins. Finally, in desperation, I began to try to read Hopkins aloud, and gradually the alien lines began to make sense, first to my ear, and then to my heart. Hopkins is still my favorite poet, though I have learned to love many others, ancient and modern, since that time.

Nowadays I read for fun, for vicarious travel or adventure, for spiritual and intellectual nourishment, and sometimes simply to fill a lonely space.

I read because unless I read, how can I know what to write? It was the letters of nineteenth-century factory girls, excited about their new lives in the city and desperately homesick for the rocky Vermont farms they had left behind that made me know I wanted to write a novel about them.

Fiction remains my favorite. I love to be able to eavesdrop on someone else's thoughts. I love the sweep and power of story and the sweet pain of sharing deeply in someone else's suffering.

In the movie *Shadowlands,* C. S. Lewis's most troublesome student says to him, "We read to know that we are not alone." I certainly read that way as a child, but even now when I have a loving family, an abundance of friends, and a full rich life, I keep reading. I read, of course, for information. I want to know more about almost everything—science, religion, philosophy, geography, history, human nature. But I also want to know more about myself. And I have always felt that when it comes to exploring the geography of my inner life, great books are my most effective guide.

Reading makes me want to write, and writing makes me want to read. And both reading and writing make me joy to be a part of the great human adventure we call life.

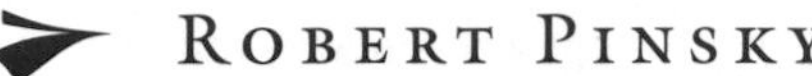

Robert Pinsky

Some Notes on Reading

I LONG SOMETIMES for that early, ardent perception when all narrative provided one engulfing reality. In that Eden I saw little or no distinction between movies and stories in books. Neither was there any essential difference of kind distinguishing dreams from daydreams, or daydreams from conscious fantasies, or separating all those private narratives from the collectively composed dramas of kids playing Robbers or War or Cowboys: "Say, we got our guns back, and you don't see us coming." "Okay. And then say, I see you from the roof." And so forth.

This doesn't mean that I was stupid or innocent. I recognized the different levels of expertise, vividness, plausibility among such different kinds of made-up story. But underneath such qualities was a single unquestionable essence: a populated, imitative reality, as seamless and coherent as the world itself. Available when the real world grew tedious or oppressive, or merely at whim, there was a reality of imagination. Genre and form did not come into it. Though one collaborated in those clumsy, derivative dramas of shootouts and pursuits, slapping a thigh while running to simulate horseback riding, the idea had not emerged that this was a particular kind of making, with an essential character different from that of Errol Flynn in *Robin Hood,* which was in turn different in nature from a book about Robin Hood.

I know a woman who as a child used to be afraid to begin a new book. In the inert little object, in the squared-off ranks of black sentences, lay a terrible power she had not elected: within a few pages she would become subject to that power. She might start to care about the fate of a character the author could thwart, humiliate, even kill, the character a hostage not even to fortune but to the authorial need to create just that caring my friend dreaded while also craving it.

Reading at this stage is as ecstatic and unfathomably vivid as the movie screen and as inward as dreams. The film technologies of projection, synthesized sound, and so forth, if I was aware of them at all, were theoretical, like an older boy's explanation of special effects, the collapsible arrow that exploded backwards out of an actor's shirt simultaneously with a bursting sack of ketchup. Despite the explanation, I flinched at the movie. And I think I was even more innocent, once, of the technology of narrative in words. The creation of the stories I experienced had a density I did not see through.

My favorite reading for many years was the *Alice* books. The sentences had the same sombre, drugged conviction as Sir John Tenniel's illustrations, an inexplicable, shadowy dignity that reminded me of the portraits and symbols engraved on paper money. The books were not made of words and sentences but of that smokey assurance, the insistent solidity of folded, textured, Victorian interiors elaborately barricaded against the doubt and ennui of a dreadfully godforsaken vision. The drama of resisting some corrosive, enervating loss, some menacing boredom, made itself clear in the matter-of-fact reality of the story. Behind the drawings I felt not merely a tissue of words and sentences, but an unquestioned, definite reality.

I read the books over and over. Inevitably, at some point, I began trying to see how it was done, to unravel the making—to read the words as words, to peek behind the reality. The loss entailed by such knowledge is immense: is the romance of "being a writer"—a romance perhaps even created to compensate for this catastrophic loss—worth the price?

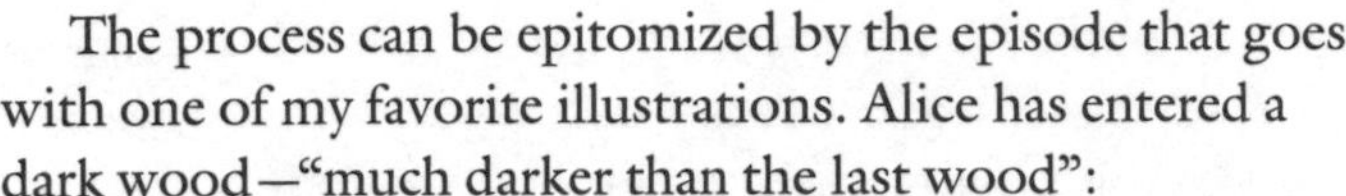

The process can be epitomized by the episode that goes with one of my favorite illustrations. Alice has entered a dark wood—"much darker than the last wood":

> she reached the wood: it looked very cool and shady. "Well, at any rate it's a great comfort," she said as she stepped under the trees, "after being so hot, to get into the—into the—into *what?*" she went on, rather surprised at not being able to think of the word. "I mean to get under the—under the—under *this,* you know!" putting her hand on the trunk of the tree. "What *does* it call itself, I wonder? I do believe it's got no name—why to be sure it hasn't!"

This is the wood where things have no names, which Alice has been warned about. As she tries to remember her own name ("I *know* it begins with L!"), a Fawn comes wandering by. In its soft, sweet voice, the Fawn asks Alice, "What do you call yourself?" Alice returns the question, the creature replies, "I'll tell you, if you'll come a little further on . . . I can't remember *here.*"

The Tenniel picture that I still find affecting illustrates the first part of the next sentence:

> So they walked on together through the wood, Alice with her arms clasped lovingly round the soft neck of the Fawn, till they came out into another open field, and here the Fawn gave a sudden bound into the air, and shook itself free from Alice's arm. "I'm a Fawn!" it cried out in a voice of delight. "And dear me! you're a human child!" A sudden look of alarm came into its beautiful brown eyes, and in another moment it had darted away at full speed.

In the illustration, the little girl and the animal walk together with a slightly awkward intimacy, Alice's right arm circled over the Fawn's neck and back so that the fingers of her two hands meet in front of her waist, barely close enough to mesh a little, a space between the thumbs. They both look forward, and the affecting clumsiness of the pose suggests that they are nearly tripping one another. The great-eyed Fawn's legs are breathtakingly thin. Alice's expression is calm, a little melancholy or spaced-out.

What an allegory of the fall into language. To imagine a child crossing over from the jubilant, passive experience of such a passage in its physical reality, over into the phrase-by-phrase, conscious analysis of how it is done—all that movement and reversal and feeling and texture in a handful of sentences—is somewhat like imagining a parallel masking of life itself, as if I were to discover, on reflection, that this room where I am writing, the keyboard, the jar of pens, the lamp, the rain outside, were all made out of words.

That may seem an exaggeration, but Alice's loss, which reflects the loss of that Edenic illusion, has behind it a whole Romantic authority: the Fawn bounding away is also Keats's nightingale, fading into the dim forest. Artfully capitalizing every reference to the Fawn—its *name*—Dodgson makes it by that much more a specific, unique reality. When it fades far away, what is left behind is the surrogate of language—the categories and rhetorical choices of writing:

> Alice stood looking after it, almost ready to cry with vexation at having lost her dear little fellow-traveler so suddenly. "However, I know my name now," she said: "that's *some* comfort. Alice—Alice—I won't forget it again. And now, which of these finger-posts ought I to follow, I wonder?"

The brisk cheerfulness that takes up the next narrative move is another joke on the scenic effect of verbal causes. The omnivorous pressure of Story moves on.

Was there the specific moment or occasion I imagine, unmasking the happy illusion of words as read dramas, discovering that those panoramic densities were a series of propositions? Possibly not. My passionate childhood escape into reading, perhaps driven by the fearful prospect of my mother's mental illness, may have been doomed to drive itself behind the seamless, frail screen of the surface and in among the gears, the grease, and wheezing pumps of sentence and paragraph, the capital "F" of Fawn.

I still find the miracle of narrative prose almost unattainable. I marvel at the ability of even the humblest genre writer to assert the existence of a world: *A man came into the room.* I read it and I behold a man, and a room; but if I write it, I feel a kind of embarrassment, even shame: there is no man, no room, only my own voice. In a poem, which is my own voice, relying on the physical presence of consonants and vowels formed by my body, I feel as if I can talk about anything, include anything. But fiction asserts that a world exists. In a couple of published stories, in unpublished strivings and hopes, I try to take up that proposition, but unlike speech it does not come easily to me.

My mother was a passionate escape reader; sometimes even in the midst of her worst episodes she would read thousands of words of science fiction a day. She and I traded volumes and magazines from the boxfuls she traded with another devotee she found somehow, a soldier at Ft. Monmouth. Even at her worst, even when I was in deepest retreat, we maintained a decorum of taking turns with a given volume, a tacit courtesy maybe resembling that of drug addicts.

She had a withering doubt of the actual world, and I suppose that magazines like *If* and *Galaxy* were her Lewis Carroll—and mine, too, and I would say my successor to Carroll except that I have never abandoned him. In the grave, formal strangeness and practicality of his books, in his actual poems and in his ability to suggest always an ineluctable meaning in words that is behind or under the words, he conducted me toward poetry. Poetry for me is possibly a route to the real world, a way of respecting the actual—and all the more vital a route for twists, obliquities, compressions, and shadowy implications. Possibly, it is after all the form that brings me closest to that old, blessed belief in Creation.

Mark Rudman

Disorder, Sorrow, and Early Reading

1

Why do I read? Who knows—but I can make certain conjectures from my preferences, from the way I lean toward work which is autobiographically based, yet concerned with the connection between memory, imagination, and truth; to writers like Villon, Rousseau, Wordsworth, Tolstoy, Apollinaire, Proust, Lowell. Psychologists might offer that all our utterances, however distanced from the actual circumstances of our lives, are rooted in an inescapable grid, that all our creations are ultimately projections. Have I chosen to "explore identity" in what I choose to read or in my own writing, or has the subject chosen me?

2

I keep coming back to the *circumstances* in which I encountered books. The iguanas (the bellows of their underbellies) breathing beside me under the yellow sun in Mexico where I spent July mornings reading Proust until I was soaked in sweat. Proust asks us to use his book as an optical instrument to help us find out more about ourselves, to help us realize, through his vegetal metaphors, that if we are astonished to note the transformations in people as they become seemingly unrecognizable over time, the seeds were there if we looked back and beyond their youth, and the styles of the time.

3

One night, when I was perhaps ten, we were the guests at a lawyer's house in a small town fifty miles south of Chicago. They were a cosmopolitan couple (he was becoming prominent in Illinois politics). I felt calmer than usual in their house amidst the absence of clutter, the tasteful gray carpets, off-white walls, blue velvet sofas, wing chairs and wooden furniture, a mixture of Dansk and antique. My mother has told me repeatedly that I searched the house "like some kind of detective" and then announced there were "no darts," which everyone found amusing. ("Darts" was a word I had picked up in summer camp in the east. "Tough darts" meant "tough shit," but "darts" used by itself also meant "tough.") That night the couple gave me a book as a present. My heart thrilled to it. White cover, spare Giacometti-like sketch of a young boy on his way somewhere, with an anxious yet expectant expression. I can't remember the title of the book, but the boy leaves home, joins a traveling circus, quits, drifts, becomes adept at staying alive. The boy wanders, he's often hungry and lonely, but holds out hope in his heart that he can get through this trial. He's not concerned with returning home, so much as living in a way that has meaning to him. I read the book over and over again, each time filled with gratitude toward the couple who gave it to me and curious as to why I could never lay my hands on another copy or another book quite like it.

4

I had encounters with books filtered through a complex system of signs.

My mother claims she read to me all the time, but from the *Book of Knowledge,* not fairy tales, *Winnie-the-Pooh,* or fiction.

There were the books my rabbi stepfather had on his shelves, the Everyman editions of *Minor Seventeenth Century Poets* (Crashaw, Lovelace), but even then that "minor" seemed presumptuous and condescending; Donne and Spinoza with the rough faded green covers, books I grazed in at a very young age, fascinated by the stanzaic designs, the numbered sentences on the page and the blessed absence of any story.

There were the books I obtained, never in the abridged edition if I could help it, after I read the Classic Comics. In third and fourth grade I read the first eighty or so pages of *The Count of Monte Cristo* and *The Man in the Iron Mask*. I think I read all of *The Three Musketeers* and while I "identified" with D'Artagnan I was obsessed with the darker figures, exiled from themselves, burdened with disturbing secrets. I held myself responsible for not being able to read every word of these books even though the type was small and the stories themselves top-heavy and overwrought. I made up for this in fantasizing endlessly about their fates. Something must have stuck or this would not have resonated for me while composing a poem called "Chrome" about riding motorcycles in the Sonoran desert:

> Once I rode toward it [the cliff's edge]
> hearing only the hush of the tires,
> the pure elation of it taking my head off as I took
> a horseshoe curve at 50 and approached
> an even sharper one—the slender cycle shaking apart—;
> and I wondered what to do, like Porthos
> going back to the bomb he'd planted to make sure
> he'd lit the fuse . . . when—BOOM!—;

I was thankful to discover Poe and his exquisite (I can hear Fortunato's bells jangling as I write this sentence) "The Cask of Amontillado," "The Purloined Letter," and other more atmospheric and always blessedly brief tales. (Rereading is still where the pure pleasure begins.) When things were turning out too badly in stories, I wanted to intervene, as Buster Keaton's projectionist in *Sherlock Jr.* does when he dreams himself into the film he's showing.

5

Reading is above all active. The first book I read whose majesty and solemnity and mystery overpowered me (the way hallucinogenic drugs did so many of my generation) was *Great Expectations.* It was an assignment sophomore year at Highland High School in Salt Lake City and when my teacher handed back my paper she said, "I've given you a B+ because it's so much better than anything else you've done in this class, I'm not convinced you wrote it. Otherwise, you deserved an A." Later I handed in a paper on *Lord of the Flies* which she treated similarly, this time marking it A-/F, which she evened out to a C. When I stormed to her desk for an explanation she said "you knew very well that you weren't allowed to choose *Lord of the Flies, Brave New World,* or *Catcher in the Rye.*" There was a certain irony to these encounters since she was right about me in general and wrong in particular. There had been no "ghostwriter" and I simply (and typically) had been absent or lost in some reverie when she announced her ban on those three popular books.

I gradually discovered that literature legitimized the dark emotions; the characters were suffering from inner divisions which I knew only too well and which had served to isolate me.

6

Like many teenagers in the late 1960s, I reveled in entertainments (in Graham Greene's sense of that word) like William Goldman's *Boys and Girls Together* and Romain

Gary's *The Ski Bum*. And we encountered many of these wonderful books, along with stories by Evan Hunter and Irwin Shaw, in glossy magazines like *Esquire* and *Playboy*.

7

My father talked a lot about certain writers whom I gathered, from the tone of these utterances, expressed some secret of his inner self. So in my late teens I spent some time as a psyche-detective, using reading as a way of divining the mystery that was my father. His favorite book was Romain Rolland's *Jean Christophe* and when I was nineteen (and had become very serious about what I read) I got through about one-third of its two thousand and some pages before deciding I was too susceptible to the very kind of thinking it engendered: in his *roman à clef* Beethoven is portrayed as misunderstood and almost too sensitive to live. Even though my father had abandoned music for business he was still an idealist and an "outcast of the islands." On my visits east he liked to obliquely deride my life two thousand miles away from his influence by saying "What! You haven't read *Lord Jim*." But when I scanned his bookshelves, I could not locate a single work by Joseph Conrad.

8 *Before proceeding further, see chapter three of* Walden, *where Henry David Thoreau writes about reading*

I have been reluctant to own up to a certain fanaticism about sources and mystery. And listening to Emmy Lou Harris talk-chant-sing her way through "Jerusalem Tomorrow," especially her hard-edged rendition of the line—"Well I'm in this desert town and it's hot as hell"—over and over and over again, has made me remember a crucial adult experience with another *Jerusalem*. Before I dared taking myself seriously as a poet, I felt I had to study (as well as the books I've already mentioned) Blake's *Jerusalem,* which, for all of its renowned difficulty, seemed as necessary a part of the task at hand as the standard "masterpieces of the canon," including Blake's own songs and shorter poems. I had to give myself over entirely to reading these long, demanding books in which the stones are pity and the bricks are religion and he tries to warn the reader of the limits of technology. Every globule of his blood opens into eternity "of which this vegetable earth is but a shadow," and "The Microscope . . . and the Telescope . . . alter/The ratio of the Spectator's Organs but leave the Objects untouched." He was more urban than the later Romantics and railed against "natural religion"—a point which some of those who claim to admire him seem to forget.

A culture which allots us time to read and make love as our final acts of a draining ordinary day is perpetrating an insidious lie. As with Proust, I gave my mornings over to reading *Jerusalem,* but even approached fresh it made my temples throb, my brain ache, and I resented the academic notion that you were meant to consult secondary sources, concordances. Therefore, I approached several friends in the creative writing program at Columbia, to accompany me on this journey during our final semester and to get credit for the course. (Where was Kathleen Raine, the poet and author of an encyclopedic, personal, and inspired study of Blake when I needed her? And why do certain great poets and not others inspire inspired criticism?) There was only one problem: the four of us needed a professor to sponsor us. We all thought of the famous poet who lived in New York and portrayed himself as a Blakean, but he couldn't help because he claimed not to have read any of the prophetic books! And the genteel nineteenth-century scholars simply "hadn't the time," and Blake fell in between the cracks. Somehow I was directed toward the biographer (of Hart Crane), critic (of Yeats), and blossoming poet, John Unterecker, who was going through immense changes in his life (divorce, heart surgery, a new post in Hawaii beginning the next fall), and was delighted to do what he could to help, and while he hadn't yet read *Jerusalem* either, he knew how to read a poem by taking it on its own terms. "Professor Jack" could spontaneously conjure up the most convincing interpretations of Blake's most private-seeming passages.

9

I've always loved genre writing, and just as I read *all* of the Hardy Boys and Chip Hilton, the Nordoff-Hall trilogy, Ian Fleming, I still (until recently) read all of writers Ross MacDonald, Elmore Leonard, Maj Sjowall and Per Wahloo, etc. I read Jim Thompson to remind myself how twisted and desperate and confused American life is. I read Pascal, whose "wager" derives from his own obsession with gambling, to remind myself of the necessity of remaining human.

I am drawn to the philosophical aphorists, Heraclitus, Chamfort, Joubert. Pascal lives (spine broken, spirit whole) next to my bedside—beside Blake's "A Marriage of Heaven and Hell." I was recently lamenting to a distinguished psychoanalyst that I sometimes got too tired to go on writing just when I reached a point where a push was necessary. "Try throwing some cold water on your face," was his response, and I remembered that Keats used to do the same. A few sentences by Pascal can have the same rejuvenating effect: "We run heedlessly into the abyss after putting something in front of us to stop us seeing it."

MARJORIE SANDOR

You with Your Nose in a Book

I DON'T REMEMBER reading my first book so much as smelling it. This was a folktale collection called *Under the Green Umbrella,* and by the time it got to me—I was the youngest of four—its green covers were spotted with pungent mold and the spine was rubbed bald at the tips, all the little threads exposed. The pages, like the pages of my father's ancient army pocket-books of Steinbeck and O'Hara, were a pale pale brown with yellowed edges. These had their own separate bouquet, dry and infinitely more delicate: one you had to really put your nose into for full effect. Of these pages, the most pleasurable was the supremely beautiful sheet of tissue paper over the frontispiece, which I riffled lightly, ceremonially, between my fingertips before each reading.

Once inside the stories, the pleasures grew deeper-hued, glossy, indestructible: pen-and-ink drawings every four pages, and every fifteen, a shiny page illustrating a dramatic moment, in colors to long for afterwards, and never find. A certain chalky blue-going-white, a dusky duck-egg green, a sealing-wax red, and goldy-yellow for the magical apples rolling away from the princess on the glass hill, her hair the same brightness, with lines radiating out.

I recently rescued this book from my oldest brother's bookshelf: his children are long since grown, and my daughter is five now, exactly the age I was when my father first began reading it to me. The first story, in the manner of an overture, introduces Old Lokoie the Sandman, who blows sleep-dust in little children's eyes as they sit before the fire on their quaint three-legged stools. If you are bad, he holds over your head a plain umbrella, and no dreams visit you that night. But if you are good, ah, the green umbrella turns and turns all night, bringing scene after vivid scene your way.

It strikes me that the books I love best now, in adulthood, have precisely this kaleidoscopic effect: that of a constantly changing group of saturated colors and interesting scenes. I still long for the unexpected turns of old folktales, for imprisonments and escapes, foolish mistakes and last minute changes of heart; I confess to a particular weakness for tales of unrequited love and interminable delays. I am afraid of nothing more than the possibility of the umbrella turning plain and worse—not turning. I love those writers who play with the nuances of color and voice, and especially those whose voices sing like the old storytellers and who walk a tightrope between the real world and the fantastic one of dreams: E. T. A. Hoffmann, Franz Kafka, William Faulkner, Christina Stead, Gabriel García Márquez. Best of all is Eudora Welty, who holds time still in ordinary towns and ordinary lives by shading them with pagan and Biblical mythologies—stories read aloud to her by her mother in deepest childhood. In these writers there is a touch of the vaudeville and the circus, an imaginative abundance that never wears you out, because beneath it lies a perfect pitch for detail and drama, until finally a truth is briefly caught—gracefully, barely, exactly in the way of a circus performer in midair, catching the swinging trapeze.

The smell of that first book is mixed up for me now with the smell of my father, long since passed away, so there is something of yearning and loss mixed up in my love of reading. I remember the smell of him as he read: a peppery odor that came off his black hair and his red cardigan, even his leather chair. With that father-smell came the voice I'm always looking for in books: the singsong leftovers of

Yiddish with a velvety rumbling underneath, like that of some sleeping volcano, a rough music to lull and worry the listener all at once. It was always after dinner that he read to me, and his big stomach sang harmony: while he read, I listened to that, too, from my place smashed close up against his side in the leather chair, my arm going numb in the brief paradise of his attention before he yawned hugely and sent me to bed.

My father, like all fathers, had his favorite tale in *Under the Green Umbrella*. This was "The Three Billy Goats Gruff," which must have displayed most beautifully his fearsome and gravelly bass, his pleasure in exaggerating the musical scale and volume of everyday speech. I knew he was tired when he called me to the chair for my nightly story; that soon enough, he would be closing the book and giving me a little push, "to bed now, before Old Lukoie the Sandman gets you," the little aggravations of grown-up life creeping back into his voice, turning it ordinary again. But he always saved his strength, his biggest effort, for the last and biggest Billy Goat Gruff. *Who's that walking on my bridge?* he'd rumble. *It is I, the third billy goat gruff.* I trembled, the other arm going stiff, knowing the finale was close. We'd be nearly there, right at the penultimate moment, reaching for the crisis, and my mother would appear in the doorway, waving her dishtowel at him.

"You're scaring her," she'd say.

And he: "Poo—she loves it!"

They were both right, of course, my mother and my father, these two people forever in disagreement, between whom there must have hovered some faint truth, some right answer. Maybe that's the moment that made me grow up loving literature, sniffing and feasting and terrified all at once, suspended in that moment just before the story ends and I am sent to bed to dream my own.

 GREG SARRIS

My Back Pages

I WAS NEVER a *natural* reader, if there is such a thing. As a kid, I didn't go to libraries. I didn't read late into the night, hiding under the covers with a flashlight devouring adventure stories, comics, or Boy Scout manuals. Aside from vague memories of *Dick and Jane,* which I had to read in school, I can't think of anything I read until my freshman year in high school when I was forced to read *The Old Man and the Sea* in my remedial English class. I felt sorry for the fish.

At the time, when I was about fifteen, I was still a street kid, living with American Indian families and others in and around South Park, a poor section of Santa Rosa, California, where the "minorities" lived, the Blacks, Mexicans, Indians, poor Anglos. I am mixed, American Indian (Kashaya Pomo/Coast Miwok) and Filipino on my father's side, Jewish and German on my mother's.

What I knew best were the stories people *told.* On front porches, at the dinner table, in front of the corner grocery, I *listened* to stories. . . . Stories about Old Uncle, an Indian doctor, how he once took a woodpecker's bones out of Grandma's eyes, how he could turn into a hummingbird and make it from our front porch to the Old Courthouse Square uptown fast as you could blink an eye; stories about Crazy Ida, a black woman who sold smack until she fell in love with Delfino, the Filipino farmworker who played harmonica each Sunday morning in front of the corner grocery; stories about Manuel and Robert, the Portuguese guys who taught me how to box, about the fights, their women, their run-ins with the law. Stories, stories, stories, stories. . . . And I was a pretty good storyteller, too. With wide eyes and a way with words, embellishment and flair, I told others the stories I had heard as well as those I had just plain made up. "You're going to come back in the next life a gossipy old Indian woman," a friend once told me.

I started reading seriously during my junior year in high school, not because I wanted to. I was forced to. I wanted to get rich, the Horatio Alger thing, so I began studying, pulling myself out of remedial classes. In a college prep English class I read short stories by Hemingway, Steinbeck, Fitzgerald. I particularly remember Faulkner's "A Rose for Emily," and it would be Faulkner's stories (and eventually his novels) that made the most sense to me, that seemed most familiar—Yoknapatawpha County with its myriad storytellers, those folks on front porches telling tales about themselves and one another, endlessly.

Eventually when I began to enjoy reading (and finally changed my major in college to English), I knew why. I had been lonesome. Studying night after night alone in my room, I was separated from the life I knew, the voices of people talking in Santa Rosa, the stories. Reading filled the void. Good books became for me good gossip. I read to hear people talking about one another. And it's no wonder that to this day I like best those books about particular communities, those novels, large and small, filled with different characters, different voices crisscrossing in one place.

If I am going to mention some of my favorite "community novels," I must start with a couple by Faulkner, since he is the one who hooked me first. I just finished rereading *As I Lay Dying*, a wondrous novel about the death and long burial of Addie Bundren, a poor country wife and mother. Hearing the story from over a dozen different narrators, some of whom are members of the Bundren family while others are not, the reader can experience the characters and the events as they take place from multiple points of view. You are truly there, in that place and time, experiencing a particular people in the various and complex interactions and interrelationships that make them particular. You get to go back and forth between families and even people within the same family. Albeit with different people and different situations, I get to do what I always did as a kid—hear a whole community talking.

Another of Faulkner's novels that appeals to me in the same way is *Light in August*. Again, we are taken into a particular community, this time by a runaway girl, and by the time we come out of that community with the girl, we have witnessed, among other things, the murder of a white woman by a biracial (African-American/white) young man that illuminates the underpinnings and consequences of racism in this place. The runaway girl takes us into the town, but by the time we are out, we have been inside the heads of many of its members, including the victim and the murderer.

More contemporary "community novels" that pop into mind are those by Toni Morrison and Louise Erdrich. Two I especially like by Morrison are *The Bluest Eye* and *Beloved*. In the former, a relatively short novel, we watch through the eyes of two young girls the effects of poverty and internalized oppression as a community of African-Americans from the south attempts to assimilate in a northern town. In *Beloved*, Morrison exquisitely portrays a group of African-Americans shortly after slavery who are trying to start their lives over (again in a northern town) in a house that is haunted. The ghost, who eventually appears in flesh and blood, is none other than these peoples' past, the past that was and *is* slavery.

Louise Erdrich's novel, *Love Medicine*, about two extended Chippewa Indian families on and around a North Dakota reservation, feels very familiar to me, not just because its characters are Indian, but also because of the particular things Erdrich chooses to reveal about this American Indian community. The death of June Kapshaw, a leggy Chippewa prostitute, is the catalyst for seven different narrators, all of whom are related to June somehow, to tell their stories. In their stories we see family rivalries, bickering, and alcoholism as well as humor and the community's unimaginable strength against all odds to survive.

The stuff of *Love Medicine*—bickering, gossip, unbelievable strength—made me take a look at my own Indian community. I recognized not only these similarities as well as some differences, but something more profound, personal. It brought me close to home; so close that I saw reading was no longer enough to cut the mustard, to fill the void of my people talking to me, telling stories. Yes, perhaps I was hearing stories, especially in the novels I enjoyed, but I wasn't talking back, telling mine. I needed to talk now, if only to keep my people alive, so I started to write.

Before I read *Love Medicine* I dabbled here and there with fiction; I'd even been in an M.F.A. program. But I had to get the lead out, as folks say. I had to hear Grandma talking, see Old Uncle flying faster than you can wink an eye, know the woman Manuel and Robert nearly killed themselves over. And where did Delfino who loved Crazy Ida come from? What did he see in her, and her in him? No one knew, but the answers make for a good story.

 GEORGE SHANNON

A Platypus in the Garden

WHY DO I READ? I'm lucky. Books and family stories filled my childhood home for years before a television arrived. I'm still surprised to see living rooms that don't include a wall of books. Economics dictated that buying books was for special occasions, but going to the library was as common as going to the grocery store. I was read to frequently—both picture books and anthologies—and, as soon as I began to read, I read to my youngest brother, an ideal audience captured inside his big playpen. Clearly, I was encouraged by word and action to read. But what I got from the act of reading and from the books that became my favorites was what kept me reading. Both brought to life the Asian proverb: A book is a garden carried in the pocket.

From the beginning, reading brought me the garden's sense of solitude and privacy. Lost in a book, I was (for the moment) far from brothers, school, chores, and insecurities. Being able to read also let me explore changing dreams without fear of those dreams being exposed or judged. Each new wish, like that of becoming a famous ventriloquist, remained my secret as I delighted in books and possibilities until a different fantasy took its place.

Reading also brought the pastoral garden's sense of music and play. Having been read to by others I not only knew the books *I* read had emotion and sound, I knew they needed *me* to bring out that sound. I got to help make the story's excitement and laughter, whispers and tears. Later, when I traded picture books for novels, I happily added private movie-making to my creative role as reader.

My creative role also extended to trying on different lives as I read—playing to discover who I was and could be. Not only characters that seemed like me, but those I viewed as strange or apart till I'd lived their joys and sorrows and learned how much we shared. Other discoveries were as basic as blue and yellow make green, but all revealed that the world was wider than the life I knew in my small prairie town.

The range of books that passed through my hands and home was as vital to this sense of discovery as variety is to a gardener's joy. Three of my favorite books as a child weren't published for children, but intrigued me more than many that were. Two were filled with art. I had favorite images by van Gogh, Matisse, and Klee before I knew the world approached them any differently than the images I loved by Rackham, Gág, and Shepard in my three anthologies for children. The third volume was *The New Yorker Twenty-Fifth Anniversary Album, 1925–50* (Harper, 1951) of cartoons, though I didn't know the magazine for years to come. There were many cartoons I didn't initially understand, but more that I did, with their humor that reached across ages.

My three favorite children's books brought the heart of the pastoral garden—friends to celebrate the world, reminding me I was not alone. I was no more aware of fame or critical acclaim when it came to these books than I was with van Gogh. What mattered was a sense of kinship, sharing feelings and concerns I couldn't put into words.

All three books shared themes of honoring one's true self as exemplified by Platypus in Richard Scarry's *Rabbit and His Friends* (Golden Press, 1953). After hatching alone in the woods, bewildered Platypus is inspected and questioned by Rabbit and his judgmental friends. Once they've decided Platypus is not *enough* like any of them to claim, they abandon him. By story's end Platypus has triumphed as a star in the circus *and* gained their admiration by being exactly whom they'd rejected—a unique combination of traits.

The specifics of my kindred books and how they mattered to me as a child (or how they inform my writing now) is of little importance to anyone else. But my experience of finding and loving them *is* and one I wish for everyone, whatever each reader's kindred titles may be. Finding these books brought reading to its most intimate and satisfying level. To be sure, reading still had its difficult times and mispronounced words in front of the class, but these books assured me that more such friends were there to be found.

Of the kindred books I've found since then, *Goldie the Dollmaker* by M. B. Goffstein (Farrar, 1969) holds a special place, for it brought words and shape to feelings I always had for the authors of books I love. After buying a Chinese lamp she passionately loves, a lonely Goldie falls asleep worried she's foolishly spent too much money for a lamp that gives little light. But the lamp's creator speaks to her in a dream: "we are friends. . . . You know me better than the people I see every day." When Goldie argues that he doesn't know her, he replies, "Yes I do. I made the lamp for you—whoever you are."

Why do I read? To savor and nurture my garden—my private, intangible place to which I can always return to renew and affirm as I make my way through the daily world. My garden of gifts from unseen friends.

BAPSI SIDHWA

A Private Addiction

WE WERE ALONE TOGETHER one afternoon in Lahore when, in a fit of remorse, my mother suddenly unburdened herself of an old anguish. This was about fifteen years ago, when I was going through a spell of undiagnosed illnesses. Averting her penitent-schoolgirl's face and displaying a chiseled profile, she solemnly said: "It's my fault. I was young. When your *ayah* said she wanted to go to her village for a month, I panicked. I told her she could go only if she took you. . . . A few days after she returned, you got your polio."

It must have cost her to confess. So far as I knew no other living soul was aware of this indiscretion: or at least no one had told me. To think of the pall cast over her already troubled life by such a deep well of guilt. On consideration, though, my father must have known. And, even if he had tried to shield my feckless parent from the wrath and ridicule of his austere mother and her principled daughters, they surely must have noticed my prolonged absence.

My mother's family belonged to Karachi. Since it is customary for the first child to be delivered in the maternal household, and since my grandmother was dead, my mother went to her eldest sister Dhunmai's house in Karachi.

Dhunmai Kanga's husband was a doctor. I was born when the European vogue to keep the environment around babies antiseptic and germ-free was all the rage even in Karachi. As behooved an up-to-date doctor's wife, my conscientious aunt boiled and sterilized everything that mattered, and tied a white surgical mask over her mouth when she attended to me. Instructed to do the same, my mother nursed me with her nose and mouth tucked away in the mask's pristine purity.

The onslaught of the horde of germs from the buffalo-infested ponds and dung-plastered adobe walls to which I was so abruptly exposed in my *ayah*'s village was more than my fastidiously nurtured constitution could withstand—and the feisty polio virus got me.

I was about two. My distraught mother promptly hauled me off to Karachi, and delivered me to my aunt's surgically masked and tireless care. Dhunmai's almond oil massages and wakeful nights must have served me well because a decade later I was not only able to climb lofty mountains but to run down them too—and with such fleet balance that I thought I flew.

However, before I could achieve this fleet-footed surety, I underwent a series of procedures involving manipulation, heavy plaster-of-paris casts, and steel calipers—all of which culminated in an operation to straighten the steep ballet-dancer's poise of my right foot.

Up to then I'd had no problems with my self-esteem; having polio as a child was like a benediction. The precipitate angle of my fallen arch set me up for favor and attention. Although I cannot vouch that I felt sorry for the herd of normal-footed children, I did, because of the kindness shown me, feel especially endowed. The prosaic accomplishments of other children were transformed into sensational feats of dexterity and intelligence when performed by me. And, it helped also, that I could contort my body in extraordinary ways. Another favor bestowed on me by my disease.

Limping audaciously and teetering on my toes, I held my own as I ran with the other children in nursery games. Gregarious by nature and trusting too—life had not yet taught me to be wary—I was blissfully content attending school.

As the consuming regime of ultraviolet rays, casts, and massages to stretch my retracted tendons got under way, a doctor—I don't remember now if it was Colonel Bharucha or Colonel Mirajkar—counseled my parents not to send me to school. In my novel *Cracking India,* I transmute some of this into fiction thus:

> Father sniffs and clears his throat. "What about her schooling?" he asks, masking his emotion. I can't tell if he is inordinately pleased by the condition of my leg or inordinately disappointed.
>
> "She's doing fine without school, isn't she?" says the doctor. "Don't pressure her. . . . She doesn't need to become a professor." He turns to me. "Do you want to become a professor?"
>
> I shake my head in a firm negative. "She'll marry—have children—lead a carefree life. No need to strain her with studies and exams," he advises, thereby sealing my fate.

And seal my fate he did.

In retrospect the creeping encroachment of my isolation, the arbitrary withdrawal of my right to be among other children, caused an increasing bafflement and disarray in my mind. Inevitably this led to an erosion of my self-regard. The psyche that was left intact by my polio, and in fact had waxed robust as its consequence, was destroyed, unwittingly perhaps, by the doctor.

My happy interlude at school brought to an end, I was handed over to Mrs. Penherow's gentle tutoring. This middle-aged Anglo-Indian woman sat me down at a small table beneath shady trees, and tutored me for two or three hours a day. I remember the solitary tedium of those hours. But, as I have concluded from the unfolding history of my particular providence, almost every apparent misfortune has eventually turned out to be its opposite.

When on my tenth birthday Mrs. Penherow gave me

Louisa May Alcott's *Little Women,* some favorable star, I'm sure, must have kicked in. The novel sent me reeling into a blissful orgy of reading from which I have still to recover.

Isn't it odd that a Paki child languishing in Lahore should have her senses awakened to literature by a book that constitutes a rite of passage for American girls half a world away? As an orphan of the British Raj in India, English was as much my legacy as my family language Gujrati was, and, by happenstance, I belonged to that minority which still forms the privileged English-speaking crust in the subcontinent.

Besides instilling in me a passion for reading, this beguiling book also alerted me to amorous possibility. The delicately evoked romantic encounters between Jo and her male teacher friend were as erotically charged for me then as the headier tumult later provoked by the emotionally complex and sexually driven passions of Anna and Vronski in *Anna Karenina.*

My initial tumble into romantic fantasy was soon augmented by the other books I devoured. Tears streaming, curled up like a tiny shrimp in the canvass hammock of my grandfather's armchair, fingertips and embryonic breasts tingling, I read *Jane Eyre* on a visit to Karachi when I was eleven. Daphne du Maurier's *Rebecca,* with its dark motif of jealousy and revenge, held me in a vice as palpably fraught as the stormy brooding of Heathcliff in Brontë's *Wuthering Heights,* and, by the time my twelfth birthday rolled along, the incipient amorous bent triggered by *Little Women* had burgeoned into a naïve, hormone-driven yearning that saturated every wakeful moment of my bewildered existence, and filled me with torment and shame.

But my reading provided diverse dimensions. Simultaneous, and as seductive, was the vigorous world of adventure to which *Sinbad, The Swiss Family Robinson,* and *Robinson Crusoe* introduced me. And, before them, Enid Blyton's daring "gang of five"—who aged as I aged—and afforded me the thrill that the Power Rangers pack for today's tots. Banished to a dull existence, more or less confined to the house, distanced by edgy, preoccupied parents, and abandoned to loneliness, I had discovered an alternate existence to nourish the demands of my evolving emotions and intellect. Mind and body surrendered to the turning pages of books, I lay snug in their embrace, in the heady intensity of their printed spell.

My books became not only my surrogate parents and my family, friends, role models, and teachers, but they also unveiled the almost mystic quality that shimmers in beautiful language, and the subtle labyrinth of meaning words lead one to explore.

By the time I was thirteen the world of books and magazines held me in thrall. So much reading upset my mother, it would ruin my eyes: I had also lost my ability to communicate with my parents. Since she could offer no alternatives, I read lurking in corners, sneaking off to the roof, with a flashlight beneath my quilt, and in the bathroom till the commode's wooden rim engraved welts in my bottom and, cutting off the flow of blood to my legs, numbed them. Even though I still cannot be deprived of reading without experiencing the disorientation of withdrawal, it is as nothing compared to my obsessive and desperate dependence on books and magazines during my teens. They educated me, befriended me, and saved me from a desolation bordering on lunacy.

My reading was indiscriminate. Since I did not have access to a library I read whatever came my way, and much of what came my way—besides magazines and comics—were classics: French, Russian, German, English, and American. These books, capriciously dusted, sat mustily on four recessed shelves in the sitting room, which constituted our household library. Although my business-oriented family was not given to reading (I doubt if either of my parents ever read fiction) they looked upon books as repositories of wisdom. And authors such as Tolstoy, Scott, Forster, Henry James, Melville, Balzac, Mann, Waugh, Maugham, Graham Greene, found a place on our shelves because their names were recognizable, and their work considered estimable enough to have been bestowed upon us as gifts.

Having shed Mrs. Penherow by the time I was twelve, I read only what I could assimilate. Shakespeare, and all the major poets in English and other European languages, were out of the reach of my unaided comprehension. I regret this lack. There are many holes in my education I have yet to fill. . . . If I ever can. . . .

Tom Sawyer's dialogue and Huck Finn's audacity are as much responsible for my incurable addiction to humor as are James Thurber's short stories, and a book called *Mame*. Our four-shelf library had the obligatory Dickens, most of which (with the exception of *A Tale of Two Cities)* I abandoned because of tedium, until I came upon *Pickwick Papers*. I read it so often that it wore familiar grooves in my brain. The mention of Sam Weller or Mr. Pickwick even now charges circuits that flood my psyche with laughter. A family friend once caught me laughing while I was reading. He gave me my first P. G. Wodehouse: I think it was *Lord Emsworth's Pig*. It was a landmark occasion: tap anyone versed in English from the Indian subcontinent, and you will discover a Wodehouse devotee.

I have many favorite authors, and an entire galaxy of favorite books. Some of them I have named in the context of my youthful reading; but to name them is to neglect other books by other authors I have delighted in and savored as much—and to list them all, especially the poets I cherish (among them are the romantic Urdu poets), in this short piece is impossible.

When I ruminate on the books I've read, I feel like

congratulating myself on the good luck that brought them my way, and there is little doubt in my mind that my earlier, polio-stricken reading fashioned me not only into a writer, but also into the almost functional woman that I think I am.

 MONA SIMPSON

Learning to Read

CAN I BE the only child in America who learned my ABCs from Campbell's Alphabet soup? We collected letters on the rim of the bowl, first my name. My grandmother taught and it was so easy, like a blink or a swallow and then you saw it, the whole word. Once I knew a word, my grandmother would write it in different places. With her fingertip, on condensation over the night window. "What does it say here?" On the back scrap of paper with her pencil no bigger than a pinkie.

It said "boat," on paper, "boat" on the window, "boat" on my hand.

With my parents, nothing was like that. It wasn't that I couldn't get the answer—I saw it, but it looked too obvious, a trick. The real one had to be hidden, harder. I became a good test taker only years later when I stopped looking for the hidden secrets inside questions.

I remember learning to read. It was another day in school, during the endless granularly boring minutes of afternoon in our classroom, and the nun asked whether anyone knew how already. Some pupils' hands shot up, the ones who had older sisters or ambitious mothers.

Then she ambled to the board slowly and wrote three words. "What does this say?" she asked, of the odd-looking little truck.

I had simply no idea. I guessed to myself, thinking of moss on trees, soup in my bowl, noise.

But the know-everythings already had their hands up, antsy, wiggling.

"I love God," one boy said, and as I began to smile, knowing he was wrong and I still had a chance, the nun nodded profoundly, and then turned around to write another set of words, this time slanting up, like a train to the corner.

"What is it over here?" she asked, "Class?"

"I love God," everyone said in unison, me too, because why would it be different just because it was in a different place?

Our elementary readers were the usual ones, much criticized in the seventies and eighties and now sought after, expensive, in urban flea markets, *See Spot Run, Daddy Comes Home;* they made me happy.

The advance from three words to reading is like the leap from wobbling practice, two or three revolutions of the wheel and then a wipe-out, to really riding a bike, and has more to do with hurling courage than intelligence.

In our attic, I found four of my mother's old Bobbsey Twin books, long missing their jackets. Soon, I was craving more. We'd go to the department store and I'd get to pick one out. As soon as I got it home, I'd lay on the bed until it was finished, nine or ten hours later.

The plots were remarkably similar, even when I went through all the Bobbseys that existed and had to graduate to Nancy Drew. But I wasn't reading for the mysteries. I was reading for the life. In the evenings, Nancy Drew's father read with the windows open in the kind of house you see in the better parts of Palo Alto or Cambridge. Baroque music leaked out into the sidewalks. I remember the blinking unhappiness with which I reawoke at the end of them, back.

Children's classics. I never read them until my twenties, and I'm not sure I would have liked the odd-shaped, escapist fantasies of *Peter Pan* or even the *Alice* books. What our teachers and librarians steered us to were horse books. Girls were known to like to read about horses. Books were a station in the hobby shop, between other productive—i.e. harmless—pursuits. Basket making. Pot holder weaving. Knitting. Making Christmas trees out of folded *Reader's Digests.* These homegrown American occupations for girls now seem so different from those obscure attempts toward art in Jane Austen novels: wool-work pictures, paintings on glass, or even musical performances.

To us, reading was something you did, like Baton.

The Bobbsey Twins and Nancy Drew were smooth mysteries, soothing. I later read that they were all created by one man who farmed them out to generations of Vassar girls to rewrite and update, all according to formula. I think it was the formulas I read for. I wanted to try on convention, feel what it felt like, the same way I looked inside department store windows and wanted to sit on that furniture, wearing those clothes.

I remember the first real book. It was called *Seventeenth Summer.* Although it was set in Wisconsin where I lived, it was about teenagers and included sex and smoking and a textural sense of class difference. I read it when I was twelve. It had no message, that I could say. Most of the books my friends and I read then had messages. A typical book of the message sort was called *Sixteen*. In it, a nice girl gets asked out by the best boy, the one everyone likes. She and her mom save up money and spend all afternoon making a special dessert. But he comes late and isn't particularly grateful. She ends up happier with the boy who was just a friend and a little chubby. What I remember from that story is the dessert, a loaf made with alternating chocolate wafers and whipped cream.

In *Seventeenth Summer,* the girl feels strange when her boyfriend eats over at her house and his spoon clinks on his teeth. Her parents notice. But then, at a jazz club, he is the leader again and she follows him to the woods at night, into something farther and deeper than I understood.

I finished the book disturbed, feeling something like complication, which made me go back and back again, as if I'd missed some crucial part. Rereading the book and the ending never solved the question or alleviated the emotion, particular yet unnamed.

Of course, the way childhood love is the template and medium, the passage to other loves, books are the ladders to other books. Before I knew it, I'd begun.

Debra Spark

In Bed with a Book

Last week, I was traveling down a North Carolina highway with a bunch of writers. Because I'd said, "Boys in the front, girls in the back," as I'd tucked myself into the car's backseat, I had an urge to say something that might make me seem, however vaguely, like an adult. So I asked my companions what made them readers, and they all had the same answer: "My mother."

Rick, the driver, said that when he was young, his father abandoned the family, so his mother had to work all day. His grandmother served dinner at five o'clock, the hour when his grandfather returned from work. "She would not," Rick said, clearly still amazed, "wait on dinner. She *would not wait* on dinner." When Rick's mother came home, she had to cook her own dinner, clean up, wash the family's clothes (by hand) and tend to her son. Apparently the last thing she did each day was climb into bed and read for an hour. "It gave me the idea," Rick said, "that reading was something to look forward to. A pleasure."

My mother tells me that when my twin sister, Laura, and I were little, we would go to the library and each pick out ten books. Back home, flanking her on the living room couch, we'd make her read through all twenty at a sitting.

I trust my mother's memory. I've seen photographs of just this scene, but I don't remember experiencing reading as a pleasure till I was older. As soon as reading was something I could do (as opposed to something that was done for me), reading became a matter of ambition. In first grade,

I felt humiliated by my place in the intermediate-level reading group. In third grade, when we were given a reading wheel to fill out—you colored in a square for each book you read—I gave myself headaches trying to read one hundred books in a week. I hunkered down with Shakespeare's *As You Like It* in fourth grade (not that I understood a word) and took—what can I say, it's true—*Crime and Punishment* to camp.

All this embarrasses me now, for none of these memories involve the pleasure of reading. In the car in North Carolina, when I started to rant and rave about my own impure motives for reading, another passenger politely quieted me with a "But look where it got you." And he was right, right mostly to shut me up, since it wasn't *really* ambition that made me a lover of books but, as with my companions in the car, my mother and, as with Rick, an image of my mother reading in bed.

A family joke:

"Do you know him?" someone asks.

"Know him?" my father responds with the kind of mock glee that seems to say, *Hell, yes.* "Why we went to different schools at different times together!"

I should write, "A family cliché," for we've all repeated the line so many times, that it's not really a joke but a verbal tic, one of the things we always say. Like: "Girls in the front, boys in the back," when we get into a car. Or: "All out, Brooklyn Bridge," when we get out.

But the line strikes me now because when I think about my reading life, when I try to recall moments that seem not merely significant but potentially different from the norm, I have one strong memory, a memory connected to the fact that my mother and I went to different schools at the same time together, that when I was in elementary school, she returned to school to get her M.A.T. in elementary education.

As a result, for a chunk of my childhood, we were often reading the same books.

My mother had always been a reader. Newly married in Cleveland, she worked for the Department of Welfare, but when that proved too depressing—she remembers sitting on couches and having rats escape from under them—she became a children's librarian. Not long after, my mother abandoned her career for motherhood, which involved, among other things, introducing her first two children, the twins, to the classics—*Madeline, Winnie-the-Pooh*—and to some of her own discoveries—*Zeralda's Ogre* and *Lyle, Lyle Crocodile.* Just when her children's librarian knowledge might have run out, just when there might have been a gap between her knowledge of kiddie books and her extensive knowledge of adult literature, she went back to school. Which was lucky for me, since I was starting to bristle at the young adult classics—*Black Beauty* and *Treasure Island,* books in which everything was divorced from what was beginning to strike me as the most interesting thing in the world: me. Or, to be fair, girls like me, which meant, as far as I was concerned, deep, soulful, social cripples.

I loved books like *Anne of Green Gables* where a girl triumphs over her awkwardness, where female intelligence counts. Indeed, I loved that book so well that today I would have no trouble marching to the exact spot in the hometown library where the "Anne" books used to be shelved. And I would have no problem recounting the pleasurable shock of finding that a book in the series had *not* been checked out. I only once had such luck. At all other times, a waiting list for the "Anne" books rested on the librarian's desk. Each week I'd check it to monitor the slow trudge of my name to the top of the paper.

What I remember about my mother's education is that I was jealous of it, of the time it kept her away from me. The loose gray skin of our old lady baby-sitters, their dotty way of letting us eat all the cookies we wanted, terrified me. And yet, when she was home from classes, I didn't particularly want my mother's time, what I wanted, beyond her orderly presence, were the books she kept recommending. Between Laura, my mother, and me, there were friendly tussles about who got a book first. Often nobody would win, and we'd read the books simultaneously.

I remember combing the house one afternoon for Bette Greene's *Summer of My German Soldier.* I was halfway through that book's true story of a Southern Jewish girl hiding a German POW in her family's garage. The girl's family—particularly her father—was over-the-top abusive, even before he'd discovered what his daughter had done. Aside from the POW, the girl's only friend was the family's black maid. Something—perhaps the requirement of showing up for school—had made me put the book down, and now, maddeningly, I couldn't find it. Where could it be? I'd checked under the bed, on top of the laundry hamper. This left only my parents' room and, as was my habit, I barged in without knocking. There was my mother, in bed with my book, and she was weeping. "I'm almost done," she said, licking tears from her lips.

I'd seen my mother cry before, so the strength of the moment wasn't at seeing her overwrought but at realizing that this was what books could do for you: they could get you somewhere real.

When I was young, my home life struck me as suspiciously cushy. The outside world seemed to be comprised of large tragedies—plane crashes, classmates tripping down the stairs and dying, and the Holocaust—and small ones—the tortures of the playground, my own stumbling self. How was I ever going to resolve all this? By, I suspected, thinking and experiencing "important" things, and my mother helped me do that. Certainly what I read in school didn't. Nor did the Nancy Drews that my friends devoured. But the books my mother found for me did. What transformed me from a reader who was merely an overachieving student to a reader who loved books was realizing where books could take me and understanding, as perhaps all reading mothers do, that that journey, no matter how tired you are, no matter how heartbreaking the destination, is always a pleasure.

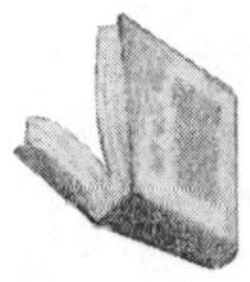

Scott Spencer

Janitor's Daughter

So it's come to this: we are now a band of devoted, isolated Readers recalling their first encounters with the Word, like parishioners in an underground Albanian church whispering of their sightings of the Blessed Virgin. I was raised by first-generation Americans who believed a child must learn to read, just as he learned to speak, or relieve himself without the benefit of a diaper. They had the right idea, even if the pacing was questionable. I had my first library card before I was two, could recite selected, highly dramatic passages from *Julius Caesar* not long after, and was reading comfortably by the time I was three. But let's face it: with the exception of the Shakespeare, which my parents admired for its practical take on politics, I was pretty much reading crap. In my family, you read for inspiration or instruction, or because the book was a classic and good for you—flights of fancy seemed to have little space in my parents' tightly packed bookshelves. We were far too poor to spend money on something so insignificant, so transitory and disposable as books about make-believe, much less books with pictures. Children's books were for dummies. And so I had to wait until I was eight years old and discovered the baseball novels of John R. Tunis to read books that spoke directly to the bright green and white, diamond-shaped paradise that constituted my secret life. The Tunis books, at least as I recall them, were written with fully adult, i.e., respectable diction, but they perfectly caught the hope and hubris with which boys like me dreamed of major league stardom. The other great reading experience of that year was Girls' Books. Our

Janitor's Daughter

South Chicago steel town branch of the public library was scantily stocked; I went through the books for boys in a few months. Idly, I borrowed a young adulteress novel called *Janitor's Daughter,* about a high school girl who is ashamed of her lowly status, her basement apartment. I was poked wild fun of for walking around with a book written for girls, but I had never read about Relationships before. The world of Girls' Books, in which feelings and even a bit of self-pity were not only allowed but were respectable, was exotic and thrilling to me. And so the seeds of romance and melodrama were sown within me, where they so fragrantly—or is it flagrantly?—flourish today.

Faith Sullivan

Babes in the Wood

In the time it took to flick her stubby tail, my first dog, Patsy, decided she really belonged to Mama. But my first book was faithful forever.

The Mammoth Book was so cheap that its pages were already yellowing when we bought it at the Ben Franklin Dime Store. But what a bargain! On the slick, hardboard cover five apple-cheeked boys and girls pored over a big green book. Inside were nursery rhymes, Bible stories, fairy tales, a condensation of *Black Beauty,* plus 365 bedtime stories!

About the same time, Mama was reading to me from the Lambs' *Tales from Shakespeare.* In the up-and-down-round-and-round of childhood, Charles and Mary Lamb went to live in the limbo of Forgotten But Not Gone till years later, when, reading Shakespeare's plays in high school, I was plagued by the notion that the Bard had stolen his plots from me. Not until I unearthed Mama's copy of Lamb in a box in Grandma's hay mow did I abandon the fancy that I was, by some cosmic fluke, responsible for Shakespeare's plays.

Though the Lambs lived for years in limbo, *The Mammoth Book* remained immediate to my life; at hand even as I ventured down the road to *Heidi* and *Nancy Drew* and *Tales from the Arabian Nights.*

Of all the selections in that first book, the poem "Poor Babes in the Wood" was my favorite.

My dear, do you know, how a long time ago,
Two poor little children, whose names I don't know,

Were stolen away on a fine summer's day
And left in a wood, as I've heard people say. . . .

Something about those brave, abandoned children spoke to me of the thousand abandonments, large or small, real or imagined, which even the most fortunate child endures; indeed, to be abandoned and to abandon seemed sadly integral to the process of growing up.

For better or worse, I believe that the babes in the wood have informed my adult writing. I recall as a child thinking that those few lines of poetry were not sufficient—some explanation was required! And I formulated elaborate and exotic prequels to the children's deaths, rife with betrayal and repentance. Much repentance.

Later, when I received a paperback of *Heidi,* with the tiny Pocket Book kangaroo symbol in the corner, I found, in a sense, another case of abandonment. But, unlike the babes in the wood, Heidi found a way to cope and even to triumph. As did Sarah Crewe still later, and Mary Lennox, and Anne Shirley. In literature I found reassurance, a sense of solutions, and of compromises struck with life.

When I was nine, Pearl Harbor was bombed; my parents separated; and Mama and I moved to California. *The Mammoth Book,* much yellowed, brittling, and smirched with Crayola, went along, remnant and proof of a life whose predictability had made it seem permanent.

The hastily erected housing project for defense workers in a beach suburb of San Diego seemed barren and alien after the tree-and-neighbor-lined streets of southern Minnesota. Angry, I clasped to me *The Mammoth Book;* toted home from a meager grade-school library all the other books the librarian would allow; begged for Nancy Drew volumes at birthday and Christmas; and scraped together dimes for *Wonder Woman, Fritzi Ritz,* and *Superman* comic books.

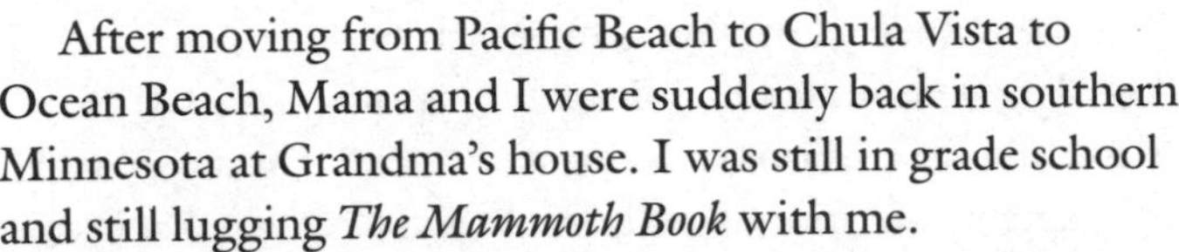

After moving from Pacific Beach to Chula Vista to Ocean Beach, Mama and I were suddenly back in southern Minnesota at Grandma's house. I was still in grade school and still lugging *The Mammoth Book* with me.

Immediately I began checking books out of the Pipestone Public Library, with its stained glass windows and air of permanence and good will. The old library liked me, in fact, liked me better than anyone else. Of course, it allowed others to borrow books. It was, after all, gracious and generous. But secretly it favored me.

The spines and covers of its books, clothed in dark green, deep red, marine blue, or leathery brown, and embossed with elegant gold lettering, seduced me. The titles, especially those not intended for grade-school children—*The Moon and Sixpence, To Have and Have Not, The Rains Came, A Tree Grows in Brooklyn*—called with irresistible voices. I was especially drawn to thick books, as if the affection and reassurance that books proffered could be measured by the pound.

I kept them too long. In hushed and serious tones Miss Studt, the school librarian, and Miss Earhart, the public librarian, reproved me for keeping *The Good Earth* or *Les Miserables* well past its due date. My fines were astronomical, eating up monies earned collecting pop bottles and, later, babysitting.

Usually I had finished reading the books. Yet I could not bring myself to part with them. To see them stacked on top of my bureau, witty and charming, dark and mysterious, daring and bold, friends waiting for me, especially for me; to pick one up and feel its purposeful heft; to let the pages fall open, revealing handsome print, felicitous words, transporting phrases, was a breathtaking seduction. Books were evidence of some sort of love. About that I was not wrong, for years later I found that I loved the unseen reader of my own writing.

Part with books? How did one do that?

At college the siren song of the bookstore promised Modern Library editions of Keats and Shelley, Aristotle and Plato. I spent food money on books, then lived weekends on coffee and Oreo cookies. I dated local boys whose mothers cooked dinners for me.

Now my house is cluttered and crammed with books. My husband looks askance and sighs. But for sixty years books have lighted my way through the wood. I cannot separate them out from my other friends, and I cannot sell a friend at the neighborhood yard sale.

On a low shelf in my office *The Mammoth Book* lies on its back, resting its spine. Now and then I take it out, delicately turning its crumbling pages until I find the babes in the wood.

> They sobbed, and they sighed, and they bitterly cried,
> And the poor little things, they lay down and died.
> And when they were dead, the robins so red
> Brought strawberry leaves; and over them spread. . . .

Some explanation is required!

JANE RESH THOMAS

Across the Marsh

IF YOU SET ME DOWN in the dark vestibule of the Washington Square Library in Kalamazoo, Michigan, a beautiful building with ivy-covered walls, I would recognize the holy place at once. The entry's unique aroma and the coolness of the slate floor and stone walls are still in my bones. Past the gothic door, I would sit beside the fireplace and stand again at the leaded windows, looking out across the golden marsh.

I know the place by heart, for every week when I was a child I tottered the mile home from the library under the beloved burden of as many books as I could carry. (I still know where the librarians shelved that purple book about a brownie who lived in a coal bin.) After I had read everything in the children's collection more than once, I begged for admission to the adult side of the library, but the authorities locked me out until I achieved the magic age of twelve.

When experts talk of cutting library services to children and moving all children's books into schools; or "media generalists" and "reading specialists" speak of "library skills" and "decoding," my heart trembles. For to treat reading as a bag of technical tricks is to devalue the sacred mystery at its heart. As Keats wrote in "Lamia," philosophy can clip an angel's wings and unweave the rainbow. Unless children *love* reading books, there's no payoff for learning how to do it. Who would struggle to unlock a heavy door if only drudgery lay on the other side? Which of us adults would read if, every time we finished a book, some autocrat tested our comprehension?

It is no exaggeration to say that books saved me, and the public library was the fount of books throughout my childhood, a haven, a refuge where adults never tried to teach me anything, but trusted me to teach myself what I needed to know. I grew up in the isolation of a troubled family with an abusive alcoholic father. Books taught me that life might be otherwise. They expanded my imaginative scope. They gave me hope. They displayed so vividly the world beyond Kalamazoo's city limits that I clearly remember literary trips I made fifty years ago to Hungary and China, Norway and Holland, an English manor house and the Oregon Trail. Showing me how other families lived differently from mine, books helped me begin to sort out what was valuable in my own days. Imagined life is not merely a substitute for reality, but is itself experience of a kind.

As an adult, however, I had forgotten the intensity of my reading until I stumbled on the book I had sought for years. I had remembered only the vaguest information about it—something about a doll, something about a wall, something about corn, and there was blue on the cover. Of course the librarians I asked had never been able to divine the title from these facts that were so viscerally suggestive to me. Now suddenly the book was in my hand, the most meaningful book of my childhood, *The Doll Who Came Alive,* set in Cornwall, with a girl and a doll and blue skies on the cover. Familiar feelings swept over me, sensations that I hadn't felt since I was ten, an intense physical response different in kind from my adult reaction to books. I nearly swooned. It was well that the fit lasted only a moment; to sustain the feelings I regularly felt when I was a child reading books might kill me now.

Nobody at the Washington Square Library knew how crucial the librarians' presence was to me or how healing their kindness, how transformative my reading, how intense my feelings, how eagerly I drank in every treasure that came my way. Reading enabled me to see through the mist across the marsh to the blue sky on the other side.

Children everywhere have looked from the library into the brave new world as I did. We should cut library services for children no sooner than we shrink the fire department. We should give new mothers library cards in the obstetrics wards and promote the delight of reading to babies. Only people who themselves love books should be permitted to become librarians and reading teachers, and they should wear laurel wreaths. We should read to every child every day from nursery school through high school, to transmit the pleasure in books, to motivate children to read for themselves. We should finance outreach programs from the library to homes. The libraries in our poorest neighborhoods should be the best in the city. Children who are reading are not in trouble, but are learning to read better. If they can read, they can learn anything.

The last time I visited Washington Square, the neighborhood had gone to seed. The drugstore and shoe shop, the hardware and dime stores had all closed, and new businesses selling liquor and pornographic movies had moved into the buildings. Administrators had lowered the high ceilings of the library and installed glaring fluorescent lights. But the gothic door and the cool vestibule were still there. The fireplace promised warmth, and the leaded windows still overlooked the marsh. And though that purple brownie book had worn out, or had been borrowed by some lucky child, others stood on its shelf. The place reminded me of a lighthouse on the edge of oblivion.

Thank God for the Washington Square Library and the people there who gave me the keys to the kingdom.

Rosanna Warren

Midi

We lived, the winter I was twelve years old, in a two-hundred-year-old, decrepit, manorial farmhouse in a village of the Alpes-Maritimes, in Southern France. The province is well named. The Alps there do pour down to the sea so steeply that all roads must zigzag, and the habitations barely maintain a toehold on their narrow terraces. The whole, large region, though, is called "le Midi," and as a child I thought that an even better name: it means "noon," and though the winter proved chill and gray enough, this was still the land of palms, cypresses, and flagrant meridional sunlight.

Our house, called a "mas" in local parlance, had stone walls about a meter thick, and was built into a cliff three storeys high. One entered the massive front door to the "salon" and downstairs bedroom from the front of the house, which faced the plunge down the valley with its terraced vineyards, gardens, and tile-roofed villas; but one could just as well enter the back way, through the olive groves, by clambering up steps cut in the cliff face, coming in at the kitchen on the third floor, through the broad old oak door at the back—and upper—storey of the house. The "mas," called "La Moutonne," was set in three hectares of ruined garden: half-tumbling terraces for olive trees, ivy cascading down stone walls, twisted fig and quince trees, tall swordbladed cacti, nettles, tufted ochre-colored grass. My ten-year-old brother and I roamed this wilderness with our white goat, Lily, who bounded ahead of us up walls and grizzled olive trees, then paused, and regarded with agate-yellow, unblinking eye our struggles to follow her. The eucalyptus trees soared over the house and driveway, with their dark, massy foliage, and their mottled bark which peeled off in parchment strips. Above "our" property, the olive groves straggled up the slope, past the road, into the high, thistly pasturelands for goats and sheep. At our gate, half a kilometer down the rutted driveway, the village of Magagnosc perched on a spur over the valley, a cluster of gray stone and apricot stucco culminating in the church of the same terracotta color as the very earth of the Midi. On clear days, we saw the Mediterranean below us, a streak of lapis lazuli, or turquoise, or sometimes a blade of pewter held at the throat of the horizon. It was here, in the ruined garden, that I began to memorize poetry. It was here that I learned my school French for the daily exercises at the Lycée de Jeunes Filles. It was here that I began to learn Latin conjugations and declensions, to catch up with my "lycée" class which had entered on its third year in those mysteries.

"Amo, amas, amat," "hic, haec, hoc," "ille, illa, illud," still evoke for me the scents of lavender, thyme, eucalyptus, cypress, dried goat turds: the sweet and acrid odors of the Midi. The Latin forms gave inward shape to this new world. "He, she, it," "this one, this one, this one,"—and most of all, though I knew it only obscurely at the time—"I love, you love, he/she/it loves," ordered that world for me. And how eagerly did I collect, savor, and compare its forms, whether drawing in India ink and watercolor the spiky leaf shapes of the garden, or copying and recopying Latin in my "lycée cahier," with its neat pages ruled, not in horizontal lines like American paper, but in tiny boxes in whose confines I struggled, with cartridge ink pen and blue-stained fingers, to shape the fat, squat script required of French schoolgirls.

If there was "Amor" at work in my hours of copying and memorizing, it sprang not only from the involuntary association of the discovery of Latin with the discovery of the wild garden and the latent, ruined, Mediterranean Latinitas that surrounded us. It must have come, as well, from my teacher. The good angel of pedagogy delivered me, that year, into the care of Mme. Péron for both my Latin and my French classes. In the harsh regime of the "lycée," with its daily humiliations and beratings and rankings, its "pions" (spies), concrete walls, and the smell of boiled lard in the refectory, she stood out in a radiance of generous wit. My other teachers, that year, all seemed angular. When I remember them, I see women with collapsed cheeks and lips pursed in permanent disapproval, and I hear the crack of rulers across desk tops. But Mme. Péron had a serene and stately largesse of figure which suited perfectly her fine Greek head, held always high, with her black hair coiled up behind.

My mother, when she had gotten to know Mme. Péron, asserted that it was the half-Greek lineage that accounted for her remarkable humanity within the "lycée" system. Of that, I could not judge. But on the first day of school, as I stood awkwardly before the class in my regulation blue "tablier" (not so much an "apron" as a long-sleeved, buttoned smock), trying to muster my unsteady summer French to respond to Mme. Péron's interrogation, I felt her amused sympathy, like sunlight across frost. "Alors," she concluded, with a hint of a smile and a tilt of her chin, "Vous allez vous débrouiller?" (meaning, roughly, in that wonderful French verb, that I would "manage"). "Oui, Madame," I replied, pulling myself together, "Je vais me débrouiller." "Bien," she said, and sent me back to my desk.

And so it was my fortune, on Thurday afternoons, when the other schoolchildren had been released from classes, to climb the steep, unevenly paved street from the Lycée de Jeunes Filles in Grasse to Avenue Fouques, an even steeper and narrower street leading to the Pérons' house. In spring, the walled gardens of Grasse send forth hazy bursts of yellow mimosa blossom and tumbling, starry veils of jasmine.

In autumn and winter, the first months of my tutorials, those gardens revealed, over their stone and stucco ramparts, only dark green foliage, occasionally the deeper green of cypress. But whatever the season, the ascent of Avenue Fouques was a progress past mysteries, with the glimpses of inner courtyards through iron grille gates, the ruddy roof tiles, the tawny walls (some studded with broken glass along the rim), the green shutters, all suggesting interiors ripe with domestic narrative. But it was in Mme. Péron's apartment—at the top of the street, up two flights of stairs—that the real mysteries began to unfold.

There, in the small rooms made somehow enormous by the balconied window giving over the swoop of the valley down to the sea, and by the entire interior wall space being given over, Pitti-Palace-fashion, to the watercolor scenes—Breton seascapes, Provençal landscapes—painted by her husband Yves, she lead me, step by step, into the chambers of Latin grammar. Looking back, I remember not so much toiling at home, back at La Moutonne with its drafty rooms in the early winter dusks, as those sessions over the smudged "cahiers" in Mme. Péron's eyrie. Night would fall and still I would be staggering through the imperfect tense—perhaps even in the subjunctive!—side by side with Mme. Péron at her oaken dining room table as she coaxed me forward into still stranger regions. The subjunctive mood, for instance: I think it must have been that winter that I found there were verbal forms reserved for purely hypothetical states of being or action. Finally, Mme. Péron's daughter Sylvie would come in—my age, but, I thought, infinitely sophisticated—and M. Péron would arrive with his shy, sweet grin, and my lesson would be over. Three or four years later, back in New England, when another teacher had opened for me the poems of Catullus, Horace, and Virgil, and in solitary, early morning hours I labored to make sense of First Asclepiadean meters and ablative absolutes, I could shut my eyes and call back the sensation of climbing the corrugations of Avenue Fouques toward Mme. Péron, and her window opening over the Mediterranean.

It didn't take a lot of imagination, in that landscape, to feel the Romans as a parent civilization only recently departed. We were, after all, on the Côte d'Azur, just above Nice and Cannes; a slide eastward down the coast would land us in Monaco, and another two steps would take us over the border into Italy. But one didn't need to cross a border to feel the Romans. In late spring, we left Lily for a long weekend with the local shepherd, and our parents took us off exploring the Roman sites of Provence. As my brother and I scampered in the ruins of Roman theaters in Nîmes, Oranges, and Arles, or teetered across the great aqueduct, le Pont du Gard, we felt—or I imagine now that we felt—those stones as an extension of the stone terraces in our garden at La Moutonne.

Latin, of course, went hand in hand (or hand to mouth?) with French: Mme. Péron taught both. French pedagogy in those days was based on memorization. We were expected, if called on, to be able to recite the lesson in any subject, every day, which was a little like playing Russian roulette, since it was impossible to be prepared in algebra, geometry, history, geography, Latin, French, and English, all of which we were learning. I remember standing in front of the class to recite, to the approval of the math teacher, the lesson involving fractions: "A fraction is a number composed of two numbers separated by a horizonal line." And I dutifully recited for the history and geography teacher what I knew from observation to be untrue: that "Vermont has an economy based on métallurgy and the cultivation of grain." For Mme. Péron, however, I memorized with love. Every lesson in French grammar—and with what beautiful precision did those chapters tease us with the behavior of dependent clauses and the agreements of tense and mood!—was linked to a literary passage. So it was, that as my classmates and I learned to hitch dependent clauses within main clauses, we filled our minds with the verse rhythms of La Fontaine and Leconte de Lisle, the prose rhythms of Chateaubriand and Alphonse Daudet. For me, La Fontaine's rat is still annoyingly proclaiming his parity with the elephant; Daudet's flocks of sheep and goats are still trampling through dust clouds to return to the farmyard from their summer grazing in the Alps, the peacocks screaming from the walls, with chickens, guinea hens, ducks, and turkeys careering around the yard in the welcoming din; and in Leconte de Lisle's ponderous and mesmerizing alexandrines I can still taste the "supreme and baleful 'volupté'" I revelled in, at age twelve, as I chanted his "Midi" and imagined my heart dipped seven times in divine oblivion:

Viens! Le Soleil te parle en paroles sublimes;
Dans sa flamme implacable absorbe-toi sans fin;
Et retourne à pas lents vers les citees infimes,
Le coeur trempé sept fois dans le Néant divin."

(Come! The Sun speaks to you in sublime words;
    absorb yourself forever in
its implacable flame; And return with slow steps
    toward the miniscule cities,
your heart dipped seven times in divine oblivion.)

I had grown up in a house of stories told and read aloud, of poems recited as naturally as breathing. Our parents were both writers. Reading had been for me, early on, an experience of "volupté," a perfect absorption such as Leconte de Lisle's "Midi" described. But those were poems and stories in English. And English was my parents' language. They wrote in it; they wrote whole books in it; all their friends—as far as I could make out—wrote books in it. English was a terrain already occupied. The year of the garden in

Magagnosc, I found languages I thought "my own." The first poems I memorized for myself were in French and Latin; the first verse forms I intuited, and imitated, for myself were in French and Latin. So I date my life as a reader, in one sense, to my twelfth year, when I began not only to take "dictée" from Mme. Péron's clear, expressive reading aloud, but to memorize: when I entered langauge consciously; when I had the illusion of living in languages, neither maternal nor paternal, but ancestral in a much vaguer sense, and therefore possessable.

To read is to take possession. But it is also to give oneself completely, if temporarily, to the keeping of another mind, and to enter another world. If the spell holds, it is a sensuous world, alive with texture, odor, and rhythm. It is voluptuous. At the age of twelve, one experiences imaginative absorption unreservedly, even as one glimpses the farther reaches of another "volupté" promised as yet obscurely by adult life in its unfolding. To read fully as an adult must be—I believe—to relive something of that wondrous childhood incipience tempered with the adult's chastened backward vision.

For me, the trail from the decrepit and promising garden led to years of sounding myself out in languages other than English. The road back to English was the road of growing up, the true falling away of childhood. That is another and a private story. But two scenes especially mark it for me. One occurred when I was eighteen, living for the first time on my own, attending art school in Rome, and visiting my family in the house they had rented for a year in Grenoble. Awkwardly no longer "jeune fille," and not yet young woman, out of sorts and out of place, I stayed up late at night while my parents and brother slept. By the weak lightbulb in the small, stone-flagged kitchen, I started reading poems I had picked up from my father's table: Roethke's *The Lost Son and*

Other Poems. Here were not Latinate stanzas, but a perilous groping, the small, dark lives of plant cuttings, bulbs, and slugs feeling their way out across the page:

> One nub of growth
> Nudges a sand-crumb loose,
> Pokes through a musty sheath
> Its pale tendrilous horn.
> (*from* "Cuttings")

and:

> When sprouts break out,
> Slippery as fish,
> I quail, lean to beginnings, sheath-wet.
> (*from* "Cuttings, later")

I knew this poetry was dangerous, because it leaned too intimately into my own, late-adolescent sprouting; I also knew it had lodged itself in my psyche for life.

The second scene took place some years later, when I had graduated from college and had spent a year living in Paris, vaguely painting and translating, surreptitiously writing poems. From France I had migrated to Crete for four months where I lived in an empty flat for forty dollars a month and pursued my exercises in oblivion. By October I was in Venice. Elder friends let me stay in their apartment during their absence, and I found myself invited, one sere weekend in late November, to a Palladian country house in the Veneto. I remember the house rising, in its rectangular majesty, from the flat, muddy fields, the whole scene swathed in mists and gusts of rain. Inside, the house was damply, dimly magnificent, with high ceilings, and little furniture. It rained all weekend. In the hours when my host was absorbed in his study, and my hostess had disappeared on duties of her own, I wandered like a ghost from room to room. On a shelf in one of the sitting rooms, I found, amongst an international miscellany of books, a small edition of selected poems of Thomas Hardy. It seemed, in that room, in that landscape, perfectly incongruous. It opened to "Neutral Tones:"

> We stood by a pond that winter day,
> And the sun was white, as though chidden of God,
> And a few leaves lay on the starving sod;
> —They had fallen from an ash, and were gray.

It was a poem my father loved, a poem his teacher had loved. Years of suppressed apprehensions broke upon me. I shuddered at the sturdy, homely particularities of this verse and its held-back breath, not French, not Italian, not Greek, not Latin. By the time the roadkill smile had died on the woman's lips in Hardy's poem—"The smile on your mouth was the deadest thing/Alive enough to have strength to die"—and the color had drained from its four stanzas, leaving "a pond edged with grayish leaves," I found myself weeping. I knew, with a definite and half heartsick knowledge, that this hard language was mine, and that I should have to live in it.

So I went home. "Home," that is, to North America. But more than that, "home" to English, which has always been a hospitable, hodgepodge tongue, and which has room in it, I have found, for parents and children, for the scent of eucalyptus, Leconte de Lisle's sun trance, and Latin verbs, as well as for Hardy's earthbound, mortal, cryptically Latinate poems.

Larry Watson

The Adult Section

Although literature is full of initiation stories, those moments when characters realize they're stepping from childhood's innocence and ignorance to adult experience and knowledge, in most lives those instances of passage—and they are multiple—are marked by calendars and the rules and regulations of governments and institutions. They tell us we can (or must) move from grade school to junior high. That we can be licensed as drivers. Confirmed as church members. Certified as graduates. That we must pay increased ticket prices at the theater or the ballgame. That we must register for the military draft. That we can vote. Marry without parental consent. And in the small midwestern city where I lived as a child, the local library made one of the first official declarations of our growing up. When we turned thirteen we were allowed to climb out of the basement children's library, to ascend the stairs and to check books out of the adult section.

How I had looked forward to that day! The books downstairs were for kids, for babies, for those who needed colorful covers to attract their attention and pictures in the text to hold it. Words were enough for me—words, words, and more words, and I took pride in the fact that I understood their meanings better than almost anyone my age.

But though the calendar told me I was of age, I obviously wasn't ready for the privilege because once I was free on that upper floor I did not immediately comb the shelves for erotica (or what would have passed for such in that predominantly Lutheran, morally conservative town—a comb with very wide teeth would have done the job). Instead I went looking for biographies, mostly of sports figures, and I specialized even further: mostly baseball players and mostly Yankees.

I had read all the sports stories in the children's section—all those novels ending with grand slam home runs or ninety-yard touchdown runs—and though I loved them, I knew they were fiction and improbable at that. I wanted true stories, the lives of real men whose accomplishments weren't concocted for plot but could be documented in the record books.

Of course what I got from those biographies and autobiographies were narratives as unreal, as contrived, as any in the Chip Hilton novels for boys. I was reading, you see, in the late 1950s and early 1960s, before the era of tell-all confessions, back when both the famous and the nonfamous usually made a strenuous effort in print or in life to conceal whatever shameful acts they might have to their names.

Consequently, in the accounts of the lives of the sports stars I read there were no confessions of adultery or philandery, no trouble with the police, no battles with drug or alcohol addiction. No one received treatment for venereal disease or turned in an inferior performance as a result of a hangover. No one grew up abused or grew into an abuser.

I had no idea I was being misled. Why would I? I was in the adult section, and though at that age I might have begun having doubts about the infallible wisdom of grown-ups, I still trusted them to tell the truth and nowhere more than in the pages of books. If it was set in type, printed, and bound, it was so. And I certainly did not feel deprived—the books I was reading were not only engaging but inspiring. They verified the lessons I had been given elsewhere: the secrets to athletic success were not secrets at all. Hard work, discipline, clean living, and good sportsmanship could get you there.

I should probably be able to mark another rite of passage in my life—the moment when I realized that true stories aren't necessarily true, that stories for "grown-ups" can be distorted, falsified, or prettified as easily as those for children. And bitterness could perhaps have accompanied that newly acquired knowledge.

But I don't recollect any such moment of discovery. I have, however, over time modified my belief in the truth. More accurately, I have expanded it. I no longer think of it as singular. And telling a true story can be a selective activity, a process of picking and choosing from a smorgasbord of available truths. And I have difficulty believing that I—or anyone—was served badly by plates—by pages—loaded with examples of courage, humility, hard work, gratitude, and grace.

Of course now I seldom read nonfiction and almost never a biography or autobiography of a sports figure. I prefer the truths of fiction. But I follow sports, and I reserve my most fervent admiration for those athletes whose significant accomplishments on the field or court seem to be matched by the rectitude and dignity of their personal lives.

Do I still belong in the basement?

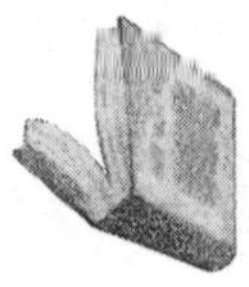

MEG WOLITZER

Traveling in Space

SOME WRITERS describe their work as character-driven. I guess I'd have to describe my imperative for reading and, eventually, for writing, as also having been character-driven. The characters, however, were all real people. Each of them, in some peculiar way, conspired to make me want to be a writer. The whole enterprise began in first grade with a teacher named Miss Gerbe, who invited me up to her desk for half an hour each day, so that I could dictate stories to her, which she would dutifully write down in her large, neat, teacherly handwriting. The stories were often, peculiarly, about young boys and their fathers traveling into space: ("Quick, Dad, get in the gravity chamber!") this was the mid-1960s, and everybody loved the space program. I think I made my characters male because the expansiveness of space and all its possibilities seemed to represent the province of power, which I longed to enter but didn't know how to. The only real power I had was over Miss Gerbe, who every day for half an hour became my personal creativity-slave and amanuensis.

The next person who helped shape me along literary lines was the children's librarian in our town, Ms. Fluckiger. (Between "Gerbe" and "Fluckiger," these names seem dreamed up by a writer armed with a telephone book, but they are innocent of creative intervention.) Ms. Fluckiger sat serenely at her desk in the middle of the children's room of the Syosset Public Library, and she knew her domain completely, having somehow read everything on the shelves, from the magnificence of *Charlotte's Web* to the insipid titles such as *Cherry Ames: Cruise Nurse.* She always knew what I might be in the mood to read, and she would beckon with her finger and take me into, say, the "L" section, where she would crouch down like a wood-sprite and pluck out the perfect selection. Books were treated reverently by her, and I learned to continue that reverence on my own.

I began to read and write all the time; my father-son space odysseys were eventually abandoned in favor of stories about Vietnamese orphans or teenaged girls who find out they were adopted. I wrote my own approximation of the books I loved to read. What I wrote was terrible and inadvertently hilarious, but was always encouraged by the adults around me. All overachievers find themselves doing things to please adults—going that extra distance to research the indigenous crops of Peru during Latin America week at school—but for me, the start of writing involved equal measures of overachieving and longing. I wanted to please these adults who respected writing, but I also began to understand that writing could provide me with an unparalleled, vast, adventurous pleasure—my own inert, meek version, I suppose, of traveling in space.

Afterword

The Center for the Book in the Library of Congress is pleased to be associated with Milkweed Editions in the publication of *The Most Wonderful Books: Writers on Discovering the Pleasures of Reading*. The question of why one reads is at the heart of the Center for the Book's mission: to stimulate public interest in books, reading, and libraries.

Established by Librarian of Congress Daniel J. Boorstin in 1977, the center is a small, catalytic, and project-driven office that promotes reading through a network of thirty-two affiliated state centers and partnerships with more than fifty civic and educational organizations. Its program of symposia, reading promotion and media projects, publications, traveling exhibitions, and special events is supported primarily by contributions from corporations and people who believe in the power of the printed word. Many of the projects sponsored by state centers for the book promote the literary heritage of a state or region, bringing authors and readers closer together.

"Building a Nation of Readers" is the theme of the Center for the Book's national reading promotion campaign from 1997 until the year 2000. For information about the campaign and the center's activities, write the Center for the Book, Library of Congress, Washington, D.C. 20540-4920. Our home page address is: http://lcweb.loc.gov/loc/cfbook/.

John Y. Cole
The Center for the Book
Library of Congress

About the Editors

MICHAEL DORRIS was the award-winning author of numerous books, most recently *Cloud Chamber* (Scribner, 1997), the young adult novels *Sees Behind Trees* and *Guests* (Hyperion, 1996 and 1994), the essay collection *Paper Trail* (HarperCollins, 1994), and the book-length essay *Rooms in the House of Stone* (Milkweed Editions, 1993). With his wife, Louise Erdrich, he wrote *The Crown of Columbus* (HarperCollins, 1991). Other works include *Working Men: Stories* (Warner Books, 1993), *Morning Girl* (Hyperion, 1992), *The Broken Cord* (Harper & Row, 1989), and *A Yellow Raft in Blue Water* (Henry Holt, 1987). As an anthropologist, Michael Dorris did fieldwork in Alaska, New Zealand, Montana, and South Dakota, winning the 1992 Center for Anthropology and Journalism Award for Excellence. Dorris held a M.Phil. in anthropology from Yale and served as adjunct professor and Montgomery Fellow in Native American Studies at Dartmouth College, a program he founded in 1972. Michael Dorris died unexpectedly in April 1997, shortly before publication of this book.

EMILIE BUCHWALD, in her prepublishing days, has been a poet, fiction writer, author of two award-winning novels for children (*Gildaen* and *Floramel and Esteban*), and a teacher of literature and writing (M.A., Columbia; Ph.D., University of Minnesota). She edited the journal *Milkweed Chronicle* for the seven years of its existence and is the cofounder and publisher of Milkweed Editions, a literary nonprofit press. Although Buchwald is the editor or coeditor of over one hundred books, she continues to believe that the next book she reads will be the best one yet.

About the Contributors

SHERMAN ALEXIE is a Spokane/Coeur d'Alene Indian and the author of ten books of poetry and prose, including *Indian Killer* (Atlantic Monthly Press) and *The Summer of Black Widows* (Hanging Loose Press). He wrote the screenplay for and co-produced, along with ShadowCatcher Entertainment, a feature film, *This Is What It Means to Say Phoenix, Arizona,* that will be released theatrically in 1998.

NICHOLSON BAKER was born in 1957 and attended The Eastman School of Music and Haverford College. He is the author of four novels—*The Mezzanine* (1988), *Room Temperature* (1990), *Vox* (1992), and *The Fermata* (1994)—and two works of nonfiction: *U and I* (1991) and *The Size of Thoughts* (1996). His writing has appeared in *The New Yorker, Atlantic Monthly, New York Review of Books, Esquire, The Best American Short Stories,* and *The Best American Essays.* He lives in Berkeley, California with his wife and two children.

MARION DANE BAUER is the author of nineteen books for young people. She has won numerous awards, including a Jane Addams Peace Association Award for her novel *Rain of Fire* and an American Library Association Newbery Honor Award for another novel, *On My Honor.* Her books have been translated into a dozen different languages. Her most recent publications are easy readers, *Alison's Wings* and *Alison's Puppy,* a picture book, *When I Go Camping with Grandma,* and a trilogy on writing, *What's Your Story: A Young Person's Guide to Writing Fiction, A Writer's Story:*

From Life to Fiction, and *Our Stories: A Fiction Workshop for Young Authors.*

CHARLES BAXTER was born in Minneapolis and received his B.A. degree from Macalester College. He is the author of three books of stories, *Harmony of the World,* published by Vintage, *Through the Safety Net* (Viking Penguin) and *A Relative Stranger,* published in hardback by W. W. Norton and in paperback by Penguin. He is also the author of two novels, *First Light* (Viking Penguin) and *Shadow Play* (Norton Penguin), a collection of stories, *Believers,* and a book of essays, *Burning Down the House* (Graywolf).

His work has appeared in *The New Yorker, Atlantic, Harper's, Paris Review, Grand Street, Boulevard,* and many other magazines, and it has been widely anthologized. He has received grants or awards from the Lila Wallace-Reader's Digest Foundation, the Guggenheim Foundation, and the National Endowment for the Arts. *Shadow Play* received the Harvard Review Award as best novel of the year. He lives in Ann Arbor, Michigan with his wife and son.

ETHAN CANIN is the author of *Emperor of the Air* (short stories), *Blue River* (novel), and *The Palace Thief* (novellas). He is also a physician and lives in California with his wife and daughter.

ALAN CHEUSE is a fiction writer and essayist, the author of three novels, among them *The Light Possessed* and *The Grandmothers' Club,* several collections of short stories, and a memoir, *Fall Out of Heaven.* He serves as book commentator for National Public Radio's evening news-magazine "All Things Considered" and producer and host of the Center for the Book/NPR short story magazine for radio "The Sound of Writing." His latest book is *Talking Horse: Bernard Malamud on Life and Work,* edited with Nicholas Delbanco.

Cheuse is a member of the writing faculty at George Mason University.

JENNIFER C CORNELL's collection of short fiction, *Departures,* won the 1994 Drue Heinz Prize for Literature and was published by the University of Pittsburgh Press in 1995. Her stories have appeared in the *Massachusetts Review, New England Review,* and *TriQuarterly,* among others. She teaches in the English Department at Oregon State University in Corvallis, where she is working on a second collection and completing a nonfiction book on the representation of Northern Ireland in British television drama.

An award-winning feature writer, essayist and book critic whose reviews appear widely, RUTH COUGHLIN was book editor of the *Detroit News* for nine years, and sat on the board of directors of the National Book Critics Circle for three. She is the author of a memoir, *Grieving: A Love Story* (Random House, 1993; HarperCollins, 1994), which has also been published in Austria, Germany, and Korea. She lives in Grosse Pointe, Michigan.

CHARLIE D'AMBROSIO was born and raised in Seattle, where he continues to live. He is the author of *The Point,* a collection of stories. His work recently received a grant from the National Endowment for the Arts.

DIANE DONOVAN, former literary editor of the *Chicago Tribune,* is now a member of the paper's editorial board. A native of Houston, Texas, she graduated from Spring Hill College in Mobile, Alabama in 1970, and has graduate degrees from the University of Missouri and the University of Chicago.

She has taught journalism and English courses at the University of Oregon, the University of Illinois at Chicago, and Northwestern University. She lives in Illinois with her husband and two sons.

KATHLEEN EAGLE is the author of over thirty novels and novellas, including critically acclaimed *Sunrise Song* (Avon, 1996). Her latest novel is *The Night Remembers* (Avon, 1997). She lives in Minnesota with her husband and their three children.

BOB EDWARDS is the host of the National Public Radio's "Morning Edition" and the author of *Fridays with Red* (Pocket Books).

GRETEL EHRLICH was born in Santa Barbara, California in 1946 and educated at Bennington College and UCLA Film School. She moved to Wyoming in 1976 where she lived and worked on sheep and cattle ranches for seventeen years. Her books include: *The Solace of Open Spaces,* essays (Viking Penguin, 1985); *Drinking Dry Clouds,* short stories (Capra Press, 1996); *Heart Mountain,* novel (Viking Penguin, 1987); *Islands, The Universe, Home,* essays (Viking Penguin, 1991); *Arctic Heart,* poems (Capra Press, 1992); and *A Match to the Heart,* memoir (Pantheon, 1991). *Questions of Heaven,* a travel memoir is due out from Beacon Press in 1996.

Her work has appeared in *Harper's, Atlantic, New York Times, Time, Life, Antaeus, Outside, Architectural Digest, Islands,* and *Traveler Conde Nast* among others. She has written the text for the Shioban Davies Dance Company in London, and is at work on the libretto for an opera. In 1981 she was the recipient of an NEA Creative Writing Fellowship; a Whiting Foundation Award in 1987; and a Guggenheim Fellowship in 1988. The American Academy of Arts and Letters honored her with the Harold B. Vurcell Award for distinguished prose in 1986. She is now at work on a novel and a book of nonfiction, and divides her time between the central coast of California and Wyoming.

BARBARA JUSTER ESBENSEN was the author of nineteen books, including seven collections of poetry for children. Her award-winning nature books and retellings of Native American legends have been honored by the NSTA and the NCSS/CBC as outstanding trade books in science and social studies, and in 1994, she received the NCTE Award for Excellence in Poetry For Children—a lifetime achievement award. Her book, *Dance with Me* was honored with the 1996 Lee Bennett Hopkins Poetry Award. Esbensen's recently revised 1975 book for adults, *A Celebration of Bees: Helping Children Write Poetry,* reissued in 1996, gives parents and teachers strategies for encouraging children to use their image-making powers. Barbara Esbensen died in the fall of 1996.

MICHAEL FELDMAN, who hosts the radio show "Whad'ya Know with Michael Feldman" over Public Radio International, has written three books, *Whad'ya Know?, Whad'ya Knowledge,* and *Thanks for the Memos.* His essays have appeared in the *New York Times* and *The Progressive.* He lives in Madison, Wisconsin with his wife and two daughters.

MAX GARLAND grew up in western Kentucky, where he worked as a rural letter-carrier for many years. His poetry and fiction have appeared in *Poetry, New England Review, Georgia Review,* and other journals. Awards include a National Endowment for the Arts Poetry Fellowship, the Tara Short Fiction Award, a James Michener Fellowship for Fiction, and inclusion in the 1995 *The Best American Short Stories.* His book of poems, *The Postal Confessions* (University of Massachusetts Press), is the winner of the 1994 Juniper

Prize for Poetry. He currently lives and teaches in Eau Claire, Wisconsin.

DAVID GATES's novel *Jernigan* came out in 1991; his second novel, *Preston Falls,* will be published by Knopf in 1998. His short fiction has appeared in *The Best American Short Stories* and *The O. Henry Prize Stories.* In addition to his regular pieces on books and popular music in *Newsweek,* he's written nonfiction for *Esquire, GQ, New York Times Book Review, Rolling Stone,* and the *Journal of Country Music.* He teaches in the M.F.A. writing program at The New School for Social Research.

DORIS GRUMBACH has written seven novels and four memoirs, the most recent of which is *Life in a Day* (Beacon Press, 1996). She taught English in high school, college, and university for thirty-one years, reviewed books in newspapers and magazines for fifty years, and on radio (NPR) for five. In the seventies she was literary editor of the *New Republic.*

THOM GUNN was born and raised in England. He has lived in San Francisco, or near it, for the last forty years. His recent books include *The Man with Night Sweats* and *Collected Poems.*

RACHEL HADAS is the author of eleven books of poetry, essays, and translations, most recently *The Double Legacy* (Faber & Faber, 1996) and *The Empty Bed* (Wesleyan University Press, 1995). She teaches at the Newark campus of Rutgers University and has also taught at Columbia and Princeton Universities. Among her awards are a Guggenheim Fellowship in poetry and an American Academy-Institute of Arts and Letters Award in Literature.

JUANITA HAVILL is the author of many picture books and novels for young readers, including *Jamaica's Blue Marker* (Houghton Mifflin Company), the fourth and most recent book about a character named Jamaica. *Sato and the Elephants* (Lothrop, Lee & Shepard Books) was an ALA Notable Book in the Field of Social Studies in 1994 and has been translated into five South African languages.

Havill is a member of the Authors Guild and the Society of Children's Book Writers and Illustrators. In addition to writing, she teaches writing courses and lectures on topics related to children's literature. She lives with her husband and two children in the desert north of Phoenix, Arizona.

URSULA HEGI has published five books of fiction: *Salt Dancers* (Simon & Schuster, 1995), *Stones from the River* (Poseidon Press/Simon & Schuster, 1994), *Floating in My Mother's Palm* (Poseidon Press/Simon & Schuster, 1990), *Intrusions* (Viking, 1981), and *Unearned Pleasures and Other Stories* (University of Idaho Press, 1988). She is the recipient of about thirty grants and awards, including an NEA Fellowship, a PEN/Faulkner Nomination, and five awards from the PEN Syndicated Fiction Awards. She has been on the board of the National Book Critics Circle, and has written over one hundred reviews for the *New York Times Book Review, Los Angeles Times, Boston Globe, Newsday, Washington Post,* and others. *Tearing the Silence: On Being German in America,* a book of nonfiction, is forthcoming.

BILL HOLM reads his books in Minneota, Minnesota, where he was born in 1943. For half the year he reads term papers, too, at Southwest State University in Marshall. For the other half he tries to read in train compartments, on ferry boats, in the aisle seat of airplanes, or (particularly in empty stretches of the Great Plains), at the wheel of his old car. In the meantime, he has written a half-dozen books of poetry and essays himself, most recently: *The Heart Can Be Filled Anywhere on Earth* (Milkweed Editions, 1996). One of the essays in that book, "Blind is the Bookless Man," describes the libraries of immigrant Icelanders that nourished him as a boy.

Ellen Howard is the award-winning author of thirteen books for children. She has also written short stories for young people and adults, among them "Running," published in the ground-breaking anthology of stories on gay and lesbian concerns for young adults, *Am I Blue? Coming Out of the Silence.* She was born in 1943 in North Carolina, was reared and spent most of her life in Oregon, and currently lives in Greeley, Colorado, with her husband, Charles Howard, Jr. They have four grown daughters and six grandchildren.

Susan Kenney was born in New Jersey, and spent her childhood in Pennsylvania, Ohio, and New York state. She graduated from Northwestern University, and holds a Ph.D. in English and American Literature from Cornell University. She is the author of three Roz Howard Mysteries, *Garden of Malice, Graves in Academe,* and *One Fell Sloop.* Her short story "Facing Front" was chosen for first place in the 1982 *Prize Stories: The O. Henry Awards,* and her novel *In Another Country* won the Quality Paperback Book Club New Voices Award in 1985. Her essays and short stories have appeared in *Epoch, Hudson Review, McCall's, Ladies Home Journal, Redbook,* and *Family Circle,* as well as in several anthologies. She has written numerous reviews for the *New York Times Book Review,* as well as the *Boston Globe, Newsday,* and *Down East* magazine. In 1993 she was appointed Dana Professor of Creative Writing at Colby College, where she teaches classes in the writing of fiction. She is presently at work on another novel.

PERRI KLASS is a pediatrician at Dorchester House, a neighborhood health center in Boston; Assistant Professor of Pediatrics at Boston University School of Medicine; and the Medical Director of the Reach Out and Read program, which works to make books and reading aloud part of pediatric well-child care. She is the author of the novels *Other Women's Children* and *Recombinations,* the essay collections *A Not Entirely Benign Procedure: Four Years as a Medical Student,* and *Baby Doctor: A Pediatrician's Training,* and a collection of short stories, *I Am Having an Adventure.* Her fiction has won five O. Henry Awards.

WAYNE KOESTENBAUM is the author of two books of poetry, *Ode to Anna Moffo and Other Poems* (Persea, 1990) and *Rhapsodies of a Repeat Offender* (Persea, 1994) as well as two works of prose, *The Queen's Throat: Opera, Homosexuality and the Mystery of Desire* (Vintage, 1993) and *Jackie Under My Skin: Interpreting an Icon* (FSG, 1995). He is also the author of a critical study, *Double Talk: The Erotics of Male Literary Collaboration* (Routledge, 1989). *The Queen's Throat* was nominated for a National Book Critics Circle Award, and the author has also won a Whiting Writers Award.

TED KOOSER makes his living as a vice president of a life insurance company. He reads, writes, and paints on an acreage near Garland, Nebraska, and he has been an active participant in the Great Plains literary community for over thirty years. His imprint, Windflower Press, has published a number of books including *As Far As I Can See: Contemporary Writers of the Middle Plains.* His most recent collection of poems is *Weather Central* from the University of Pittsburgh Press.

CAROLINE LEAVITT is an award-winning short story writer, essayist, and author of six novels, *Meeting Rozzy Halfway, Lifelines, Jealousies, Family, Into Thin Air,* and *Living Other Lives.* A recipient of a New York Foundation of the Arts Grant and a National Magazine Award nominee, she is currently at work on another novel. She lives in a 120-year-old restored rowhouse in Hoboken, New Jersey with her husband, baby son, a cranky cat, and a sardonic tortoise.

ELINOR LIPMAN is the author of the novels *Isabel's Bed, The Way Men Act,* and *Then She Found Me,* and a collection of stories, *Into Love and Out Again.* A new novel, *The Inn at Lake Devine,* will be published in 1998.

SUSAN LOWELL is the author of *Ganado Red: A Novella and Stories,* which won the Milkweed Editions National Fiction Prize in 1988. Her books for children include *The Boy with Paper Wings, The Tortoise and the Jackrabbit, I Am Lavina Cumming* (winner of a regional book award from the Mountains and Plains Booksellers Association), and *The Three Little Javelinas,* a Reading Rainbow book. She lives in Arizona with her husband and two daughters.

GREGORY MAGUIRE is the author of *Wicked: The Life and Times of the Wicked Witch of the West,* as well as more than a dozen books for children and young adults. His most recent titles include *Missing Sisters* and *Oasis,* and the first two installments of the Hamlet Chronicles, *Seven Spiders Spinning* and *Six Haunted Hairdos.* Maguire has lived in Cambridge and Boston, as well as in London and Dublin; currently he makes his home in Concord, Massachusetts.

J. D. MCCLATCHY is the author of four collections of poems, the latest of which is *Ten Commandments* (Knopf, 1998). His essays are collected in *White Paper* (1989), and he has edited many other books as well, most recently *The Vintage Book of Contemporary World Poetry*. He has written four opera libretti, and is editor of the *Yale Review*. He lives in Connecticut.

ALYCE MILLER's collection, *The Nature of Longing,* won the 1993 Flannery O'Connor Award for Short Fiction, and was republished in paperback by W. W. Norton. Her novel, *Stopping for Green Lights,* has been accepted by Anchor Doubleday. Miller's work has most recently appeared in *American Short Fiction, Southwest Review, Harvard Review, Glimmer Train, Michigan Quarterly Review,* and *Kenyon Review.* She lives in Bloomington, Indiana, and teaches in the creative writing program at Indiana University.

SUSAN MITCHELL's most recent book of poems, *Rapture* (HarperCollins), won the first Kingsley Tufts Award and was a National Book Award finalist. She has received grants from the Guggenheim and Lannan Foundations, and also from the NEA. She is working on a collection of essays and a new book of poems to be published by HarperCollins. A professor at Florida Atlantic University, she lives in Boca Raton.

LORRIE MOORE lives and teaches in Madison, Wisconsin. She is the author of four books of fiction, the most recent of which is the novel *Who Will Run the Frog Hospital?* Her stories and reviews have appeared in *The New Yorker, Paris Review, Yale Review, New York Times Book Review,* and in *The Best American Short Stories.*

DAVID MURA is the author of *Where the Body Meets Memory: An Odyssey of Race, Sexuality, & Identity; Turning Japanese: Memoirs of a Sansei;* and *A Male Grief: Notes on Pornography & Addiction.* His two books of poetry are *The*

Color of Desire and *After We Lost Our Way.* He has received the Carl Sandburg Literary Award, a PEN Josephine Miles Book Award, along with the Lila Wallace-Reader's Digest Writers' Award and fellowships from the NEA and the Bush Foundation. He has written and collaborated on several performance pieces, including *Secret Colors* with Alexs Pate and, most recently, *After Hours* with pianist Jon Jang and actor Kelvin Han Yee. Mura's essays have appeared in *Mother Jones, New York Times, New England Review, Conjunctions,* and the *Graywolf Annual V: Multi-Cultural Literacy.*

CORNELIA NIXON was born in Boston, grew up mainly in Northern California, and now teaches at Indiana University. She is the author of a novel in stories, *Now You See It,* and a book on D. H. Lawrence. Her stories have won prizes, including a first prize O. Henry Award in 1995.

HOWARD NORMAN is the author of *The Northern Lights* and *The Bird Artist,* both finalists for the National Book Award. His new novel, *The Museum Guard,* will be out next year.

KATHLEEN NORRIS is the author of two works of nonfiction, *The Cloister Walk* and *Dakota: A Spiritual Geography.* Her most recent book of poems is *Little Girls in Church.* She lives in South Dakota.

NAOMI SHIHAB NYE grew up in St. Louis, Jerusalem, and San Antonio. Her books of poems currently available are *Red Suitcase* and *Words Under the Words: Selected Poems.* Her collection of essays is *Never in a Hurry.* Her picture book *Sitti's Secrets,* illustrated by Nancy Carpenter, was named a *School Library Journal* Best Book for 1994 and also received the Jane Addams Children's Book Award. *Benito's Dream*

Bottle, illustrated by Yu Cha Pak, was published in 1995. Nye edited *The Same Sky,* an award-winning anthology of international poetry and *The Tree is Older Than You Are,* a bilingual collection from Mexico named a Best Book of 1995 by the American Library Association. She is featured on two PBS poetry specials: "The Language of Life with Bill Moyers" and "The United States of Poetry." She coedited *I Feel a Little Jumpy Around You,* an anthology for teenagers, with Paul Janeczko (Simon & Schuster, 1996). She has worked widely as a visiting writer for the past twenty-three years.

Born and raised in New Hampshire, ROBERT OLMSTEAD is the author of *America by Land, Soft Water,* and *A Trail of Heart's Blood Wherever We Go,* as well as a collection of short stories, *River Dogs* and recently a memoir, *Stay Here with Me.* His work has appeared in *Story, Granta, Cutbank, Black Warrior Review, Ploughshares, Graywolf, Epoch, American Literature, Spin,* and *Sports Afield.* He has received fellowships from the Guggenheim Foundation, the National Endowment for the Arts, and the Pennsylvania Council for the Arts. He still loves to read.

KATHERINE PATERSON is the author of twelve novels for children and young people including *Bridge to Terabithia* and *Jacob Have I Loved,* Newbery winners in 1978 and 1981 and *The Great Gilly Hopkins,* a Newbery Honor Book. *The Great Gilly Hopkins* and *The Master Puppeteer* were National Book Award winners in 1979 and 1977. Her novel *Lyddie,* set in Vermont and Massachusetts in the 1940s, was the 1994 United States representative for writing on the Honor List of the International Board of Books for Young People. Her latest novel, published in 1996, is *Jip, His Story.* It was an ALA Notable Book, a Best Book for Young Adults, a School Library Journal best Book of the Year, and received the Scott O'Dell Award for Historical Fiction.

Paterson was born in China. She is a graduate of King College, Bristol, Tennessee, and holds masters degrees from both the Presbyterian School of Christian Education, Richmond, Virginia, and Union Theological Seminary, New York City. She lived and worked for four years in Japan. The Patersons live in Barre where Dr. Paterson recently retired as pastor of the First Presbyterian Church. They are parents of four grown children. They have two granddaughters and a grandson.

ROBERT PINSKY is the Poet Laureate of the United States. His two most recent books are *The Inferno of Dante: A New Verse Translation* (awarded the 1995 Los Angeles Times Book Award in Poetry) and *The Figured Wheel: New and Collected Poems 1966–1996*.

MARK RUDMAN's recent books include *The Nowhere Steps* (Sheep Meadow, 1990); *Diverse Voices: Essays on Poets and Poetry* (Story Line Press, 1993); a long poem, *Rider,* which received the National Book Critics Circle Award in Poetry for 1994; *Realm of the Unknowing: Meditations on Art, Suicide, and Other Transformations;* and *The Millennium Hotel* (1996) (the latter three from Wesleyan). He has done many translations, from Euripides' *Daughters of Troy* (University of Pennsylvania Press, 1998) to Horace, to Bobrowski, to Char, to Pasternak's *My Sister-Life* (Northwestern). He is a Guggenheim Fellow for 1996/97, during which time he has completed a new book of poems, *Provoked in Venice.* He is assistant adjunct professor at NYU and Columbia's School of the Arts.

MARJORIE SANDOR is the author of *A Night of Music,* stories (The Ecco Press, 1989). Recent fiction has appeared in the *Georgia Review,* and nonfiction in the *New York Times.*

Her stories have appeared in literary magazines including *Antaeus, Shenandoah, Yale Review,* and others, and have been anthologized in *The Best American Short Stories 1985* and *1988, Pushcart Prize XIII,* and *America and I.* She currently teaches fiction writing and literature at Oregon State University in Corvallis, and is at work on a novel.

GREG SARRIS's books include *Mabel McKay: Weaving the Dream* and *Grand Avenue,* a novel in stories, which he adapted for a three-hour television miniseries and co-executive produced with Robert Redford. The miniseries premiered on HBO. Currently he is at work on a novel, due in late fall, 1997 from Hyperion.

GEORGE SHANNON is the author of many books for children including *Lizard's Song* (1981), *Climbing Kansas Mountains* (1993), *Heart to Heart* (1995) and the folklore series *Stories to Solve.* He has also written the young adult novel *Unlived Affections* (1989), an ALA Best Book of the Year, and the critical study *Arnold Lobel* (1989). He lives on Bainbridge Island in Puget Sound.

BAPSI SIDHWA has published four novels: *An American Brat, Cracking India, The Bride, The Crow Eaters,* and several short stories and essays. She has been translated into French, Russian, Urdu and German.

Sidhwa, who was on the advisory committee to Prime Minister Benazir Bhutto on Women's Development, has taught in the graduate program at Columbia University in 1989 and prior to that at Rice and the University of Houston. She is Distinguished Writer in Residence and Professor of English at Mount Holyoke College in Massachusetts, and is currently working on the screenplay of her novel *Cracking India.*

MONA SIMPSON is the author of *Anywhere But Here, The Lost Father,* and *A Regular Guy.* She teaches at Bard College, where she holds the Sadie Samuelson Levy Chair of Languages and Literature. She is working on *Virginity,* a collection of short stories, and a novel called *My Hollywood.*

DEBRA SPARK is the author of the novel *Coconuts for the Saint* (Faber & Faber, 1995; Avon, 1996) and the editor of *Twenty Under Thirty: Best Stories by America's New Young Writers* (Scribner's, 1986, 1996).

SCOTT SPENCER is the author of six novels, including *Men In Black, Endless Love,* and *Waking the Dead.* His new novel, *The Rich Man's Table,* will be published in 1998, God willing.

FAITH SULLIVAN began writing novels in 1975 when her youngest child started kindergarten. Her first novel, *Repent, Lanny Merkel,* was published in 1981 (McGraw Hill) and was followed by *Watchdog* (McGraw Hill, 1982), *Mrs. Demming and the Mythical Beast* (MacMillian, 1985), and *The Cape Ann* (Crown, 1988). *The Empress of One* (Milkweed, 1996) is her fifth novel and is, like *The Cape Ann,* set in a small town in Minnesota. Sullivan has also published numerous articles, essays, book reviews, and humorous pieces.

JANE RESH THOMAS is the author of eleven published novels and picture books for children, with four more works in production. Her next books will be *Celebration!,* a picture book, and a biography, *Behind the Mask: The Life of Queen Elizabeth I* (Clarion). From her home in Minneapolis, Minnesota, she also teaches, lectures, edits, and writes a regular column about children's literature for the *Star Tribune;* her reviews often appear in Cleveland's *Plain Dealer* as well.

ROSANNA WARREN is the author, most recently, of *Suppliant Women,* a verse translation of Euripides' play (with Stephen Scully); and of *Stained Glass,* a collection of poems. She teaches English and Comparative Literature at Boston University.

LARRY WATSON is the author of *Montana 1948, Justice,* and *White Crosses*. He teaches writing and literature at the University of Wisconsin/Stevens Point.

MEG WOLITZER is a novelist whose work includes *Sleepwalking* and *This Is Your Life,* among others. A 1994 recipient of a Fiction Grant from the NEA, Meg Wolitzer lives in New York City with her husband and two sons. Her fifth novel, *Surrender, Dorothy,* will be published next year.

The Most Wonderful Books has been set in Galliard type by Stanton Publication Services, Inc. The interior design is by Will Powers
Printed on acid-free Liberty paper
by Quebecor Printing

More anthologies from Milkweed Editions:

Changing the Bully Who Rules the World: Reading and Thinking about Ethics
Edited by Carol Bly

Clay and Star: Contemporary Bulgarian Poets
Edited by Lisa Sapinkopf and George Belev

Drive, They Said: Poems about Americans and Their Cars
Edited by Kurt Brown

Looking for Home: Women Writing about Exile
Edited by Deborah Keenan and Roseann Lloyd

Minnesota Writes: Poetry
Edited by Jim Moore and Cary Waterman

Mixed Voices: Contemporary Poems about Music
Edited by Emilie Buchwald and Ruth Roston

Mouth to Mouth: Poems by Twelve Contemporary Mexican Women
Edited by Forrest Gander

Night Out:
Poems about Hotels, Motels, Restaurants, and Bars
Edited by Kurt Brown and Laure-Anne Bosselaar

Passages North Anthology
Edited by Elinor Benedict

The Poet Dreaming in the Artist's House:
Contemporary Poems about the Visual Arts
Edited by Emilie Buchwald
and Ruth Roston

Sacred Ground:
Writings about Home
Edited by Barbara Bonner

Testimony:
Writers of the West Speak On Behalf of Utah Wilderness
Compiled by Stephen Trimble
and Terry Tempest Williams

This Sporting Life:
Contemporary Poems about Sports and Games
Edited by Emilie Buchwald
and Ruth Roston

Transforming a Rape Culture
Edited by Emilie Buchwald, Pamela Fletcher,
and Martha Roth

White Flash/Black Rain:
Women of Japan Relive the Bomb
Edited and translated by Lequita Vance-Watkins
and Aratani Mariko